SPY NET-WORK
in
MAHABHARATA

SPY NET-WORK
in
MAHABHARATA

Ramendra Narayan Sanyal

SHIPRA

Rs. 495; US$ 25

ISBN: 978-81-7541-467-9

First Published in India in 2010

SPY NET-WORK IN MAHABHARATA

Published by:

SHIPRA PUBLICATIONS

H.O.: LG-18-19, Pankaj Central Market, Patparganj,
I.P. Ext., Delhi 110092, Ph. 91-11-22235152, 22236152
Br. Off.: 115, Munish Plaza, 20, Ansari Road, Daryaganj,
New Delhi 110002; Ph. 91-11-65946453, 9810522367

Email: info@shiprapublications.com
Website: www.shiprapublications.com

To the sacred memory of our parents
Late Jnanendra Narayan Sanyal and Kamalini Devi who
were deeply inspired by the lofty teachings
of the Ramayana and the Mahabharata.

Preface

Most of the period in my service career was spent in Intelligence Bureau (I.B.), Government of India. One of the main functions of I.B. is to collect intelligence on divisive and separatist forces, which are active in the country. Naturally during war and social unrest this department becomes specially active. In the I.B. we generally collect information through secret agents recruited from within the enemy, through infiltration into enemy ranks, interception of messages exchanged between enemy formations, interrogation of arrested and captured enemy personnel, aerial photography etc. For intelligence collection we use both open and secret methods. Friendly members of the public very often come forward with information about the presence of enemy agents or personnel in their locality. Information about the enemy is also collected from the enemy's enemy and from the discontented elements in the enemy ranks. During the war these methods are specially activated.

Information collected by I.B. is collated with information obtained from other intelligence organizations to get a total view of the enemy's intentions and preparations. All these materials are then processed by an expert committee and produced before the Government to help decide its plan of action.

In the Mahabharata days also these basic principles of intelligence collection were followed. Present day sophistication however, was absent which is quite understandable. From my experience in I.B., I came to realize that during the war of our great epic 'Mahabharata', secret agents on both the warring sides had to play a big role.

After retirement from service, I started collecting information on methods and techniques adopted by the secret agents in those days. For this I read various books on the Mahabharata including its complete translations from the original in Bengali. I also consulted various websites. In course of my search I collected a plethora of information on the activities of secret agents. From the burning *jatugriha/lakshagriha* (house made of lac) mother Kunti and the five Pandavas were saved because of the prior information provided by secret agents of Vidura, a well-wisher of the Pandavas, on the dubious plan of the enemy Kauravas and its intelligent use by the Pandavas. In the Mahabharata, many similar activities of the secret agents on both sides find mention. In many cases, collection of intelligence by the secret agents and messengers has, however, not been clearly mentioned in the epic. This is certainly quite natural in a great epic like the Mahabharata. The poet here narrated the incidents, the theme of which was victory of *dharma* (justice) over *adharma* (injustice); he was not composing any spy story. From a deeper analysis of the events, the role of secret agents, however, becomes clear.

The information of Pandavas' one-year (incognito) stay at Viratnagara was not known to the secret agents of Duryodhana. Behind this failure of Duryodhana's secret agents was apparently the hand of Vidura. This seems to be a successful application of counter-espionage. Vidura, by cleverly infiltrating his own agents among the agents of Duryodhana was successful in keeping him in the dark about the happenings at Viratnagara. There cannot be any other plausible explanation about the successful one-year incognito stay at Viratnagara of such very well known persons like the Pandavas and their wife Draupadi.

In the Mahabharata, there are many very useful commands and instructions from sage Narada, grandfather Bhishma and other wise statesmen about the useful role of the secret agents, collection of intelligence, country's security, king's duties and responsibilities and various other aspects of statecraft. Evidently there existed during the era of the Mahabharata, a well developed system of state administration. One observation about the secret agents deserves special mention. Secret agents, it was maintained, are seekers of truth and they never take resort to untruth. Secret agents while reporting on matters concerning the state's security shall never hide facts. They shall always factually and truthfully present the facts to their higher authorities. There shall be no exaggeration or twisting of the facts to please the authority. The king or the ruler must also possess the mental equanimity to receive, without any qualms, all such unpleasant but true reports. Dharamaraj Yudhishthira had this virtue. He gracefully accepted all unpleasant reports and praised the honest work of the secret agents. During his wise administration, people were happy, and peace and prosperity prevailed throughout the kingdom. Even the rebel princes, as also the robbers and criminals, surrendered to him of their own accord. The greatest teaching of the Mahabharata is that good of the country and the people emanates from honest and righteous kings and rulers.

From the analysis of the events in the Mahabharata it appears that one of the main contributing factors for the victory of the Pandavas in the war was their ability to collect timely and accurate prior information about the intentions of the enemy and the eventual destruction of the enemy's principal warriors following Krishna's strategy. For want of war strategists like Krishna, on the Kaurava side it has not been possible for them to build any worth-while spy network to get information about the enemy. This vacuum could have been filled by Bhishma; but this was not to be, as he was against Duryodhana and a well-wisher of his enemy Pandavas. Though he happened to be the commander-in-chief of the Kaurava army, he did not hesitate to disclose to Yudhisthira how he could be killed in the battle-field to facilitate the victory of the Pandavas. For all such betrayals and short-comings, the Kauravas were vanquished despite of their being in possession of much greater man-power and resources. In fighting the war they seemed to be banking mainly on physical prowess.

In the Mahabharata, Krishna proved himself to be not only a brilliant war strategist, but also a very competent intelligence operator. In fact he proved himself to be superior to others in this respect. In the conduct of war his experience was tremendous. He knew that to win a war, prior information about enemy's strength, resources, strategies, intentions etc. is a must. He had close personal relationship with many kings and their senior courtiers and army commanders. From them he collected a plethora of information on different subjects. He himself built up an excellent spy network independent of the Pandavas and operated it himself. This helped in corroborating information collected from different sources. During discussions of his peace proposals with the Kauravas at Hastinapura, Krishna very tactfully managed to intensify internal dissensions among the Kaurava leaders. He also utilized his visits in exchanging information with Vidura. The information collected from Vidura proved very useful to the Pandavas in determining their war strategies. In the rival war camps, established at Kuruskhetra, a group of hunters used to supply meat. Many of them worked as double agents. Krishna very intelligently utilized them to collect information about the enemy while spreading disinformation in the enemy ranks through them. All this has not been clearly mentioned in the epic; but a deeper analysis of the events at that time seems to suggest that things happened in that fashion. We are overwhelmed with surprise at Krishna's farsightedness and flair for intelligence collection.

In describing the events in my book I have mainly depended on two books–*Kaliprasanna Singha* and Rajsekher Basu's *Mahabhatata in Bengali*. Comments, analyses and observations are all mine.

During the writing of the book my wife Smt. Krishna Sanyal, daughter Smt. Sanjukta Maitra and daughter-in-law Smt. Debalina Sanyal extended to me all help and cooperation. I convey my thanks to them. Sri Sourin Banerjee, former News Editor of the now defunct Hindustan Standard and a friend of mine, took the trouble of correcting the proof; but he passed away before completing the work. May his soul rest in peace. Dr. Samarendu Das, Ex-Professor, Ananda Mohan College, Kolkata took the pains of going through the entire draft, and suggested various changes. I express my deep gratitude to him for the hard work he unhesitatingly took upon himself to help me.

The subject-matter of the book is unique. In very few books the spy network in the Mahabharata has been discussed the way I have done, which I hope will be found interesting by the reading public. A glossary has been oppended for non-english terms used in the text.

The book is based on my earlier book in Bengali entitled *Mahabharate Goenda* with many additions and alterations.

Ramendra Narayan Sanyal

Contents

The Events Chronology

Introduction

The book is a critical appraisal of the events in the Mahabharata as also of the acts and policies of the principal characters like Krishna, grandfather Bhishma, King Dhritarashtra, Yudhishthira, Duryodhana and others with special emphasis on the role of secret agents. The kings and the wise men of those days were fully conversant with the importance of timely information to thwart the evil designs of the enemies. Secret agents were described as the eyes and ears of the kings.

On secret agents, their training, deployment, king's duties and responsibilities, statecraft and various other related subjects, we get many useful details from Kanika the Royal Counsellor on Ethics and Politics, Sage Narada, grandfather Bhishma, Prime Minister Vidura and equally other wise men. The principles laid down by them are relevant even today.

The long one-year incognito stay of the Pandavas in Viratnagara was completely unknown to the agents of Duryodhana. This seems to be due to the successful infiltration of Vidura's men in the ranks of secret agents of Duryodhana as also on account of the various precautions undertaken by the Pandavas on the advice of priest Dhoumya. Duryodhana's agents were completely misguided and they remained in the dark about the presence of the Pandavas at Viratnagar. This is another piece of brilliant execution of a difficult intelligence operation in extremely trying circumstances.

The emissaries and the secret agents of both the sides, who were specially activated during the period of war preparations, collected valuable information on war tactics and strategies of the rivals. Here also the Pandavas managed to hoodwink the Kauravas on many occasions. Arjuna with active connivance of Krishna got him on to his side in lieu of his *Narayani Sena,* which joined the Kauravas. Duryodhana failed to realize that Krishna with his divine power was much more powerful than his entire army. Krishna himself under the cover of his peace mission at Hastinapura managed to collect vital information from Vidura about the war preparations of the Kauravas, besides creating serious dissensions among the Kaurava leaders. All this proved immensely helpful to the Pandavas in deciding their own tactics and strategies. Duryodhana's successful ploy in disguise, to win over Salya, the powerful king of Madra, proved infructuous when he agreed, on request from Yudhishthira, to misguide and weaken Karna as his charioteer during the battle. Duyodhana's failure to get prior information of Salya's secret agreement of help to Yudhishthira proved extremely costly to him. It is an irony of fate that the same Salya who helped the Pandavas so much ultimately got killed in the battle by Yudhisthira himself. This, perhaps, is the inevitable fate of every traitor.

During the devastating 18-day war, collection of intelligence took different twists and turns. Here also the Pandavas had an upper hand over the Kauravas.

Krishna armed with the required information about King Jarasandha of Magadha, his arch enemy, managed to enter his capital by a circuitous path through the hills, and got him killed at the hands of Bhima. It was a daring operation very cleverly implemented.

Krishna's resort to the policy of everything is fair in war, using all tactics and *maya* power (power to create illusion) without any equanimity and Pandava warriors' particularly Arjuna's valour, along with adequate collection of information and its objective assessment, ultimately brought about the Pandavas' victory in the war against the Kauravas despite the latter having a larger army. Intelligence collection by the Kauravas was not only inadequate but assessment of the collected information was also faulty and half-hearted. A deeper study of the events in the Mahabharata reveals the existence of a well-organised spy network.

The book written in a simple and lucid language, seeks to narrate all the major events in the Mahabharata in a new perspective, which hopefully will be found interesting by the reading public.

MAHABHARATA AND THE SPY NET-WORK

1.

The Great War of the Mahabharata was fought at *Kurukshetra* approximately during 900–800 B.C. In this terrible fratricidal war which continued for 18 days between the Kauravas and the Pandavas over the capture of the royal throne, was joined on either side by all the kings and warriors of India with their armies. A total of 18 *akshowhinis (*divisions*)* were involved in the war. The Kauravas mobilized eleven *akshowhinis* and the Pandavas seven. The two armies almost entirely perished in the war. The devastating nature of the fighting became evident at the end when only ten prominent persons worth-mentioning remained alive – three on the Kaurava side namely– Ashvatthama, son of Dronacharya, royal weapons teacher; Kripacharya, royal priest and Kritavarma, king of Bhoj, and seven on the Pandava side namely – Yudhisthira, Bhima, Arjuna, Nakula and Sahadeva, the five sons of Pandu; Sattaki, the *Jadava* hero, and Sri Krishna.

It is easily conceivable that in a great war like this, preparations on both sides were on a tremendous scale. There was no stone unturned to obtain information about enemy's preparedness, resources, alliances and other required details. For this besides dispatching their trained agents to different directions, senior Kaurava and Pandava princes like Duryodhana and Arjuna personally visited the capitals of some of the kingdoms to persuade the kings to join their side in the war. Royal messengers were also sent for the purpose. There was virtually a tug of war between Duryodhana and Arjuna to win over the all powerful Krishna to their side.

In the matter of collection of intelligence, the Kauravas were far behind the Pandavas. Their assessment of the collected information was also faulty. Sometimes clues were not properly followed. As a result they remained dark in some cases about enemy's intentions and whereabouts. It was apparent that the Kauravas had no adequate supervision and control over their own agents. This was not the case with the Pandavas who under the guidance of Krishna, acted judiciously, utilized their agents intelligently and took timely action to achieve their objectives. They, on Krishana's advice, did not hesitate to take recourse to even blatant falsehood to achieve their objectives which, they considered, were just. The Kaurava prince Duryodhana's hatred of the Pandavas was extremely deep. This blind hatred made him determined to vanquish them by hook or by crook He was as a result unable to assess the ground reality objectively. For this, evil counsel of maternal uncle Shakuni and friend Karna was also responsible. Even the course of action chalked by them was not intelligently executed.

Yet, after the banishment of the Pandavas to the forest the entire resources of the kingdom came under the absolute control of Duryodhana. He had a strong well-trained army under him. His spy network was spread all over the kingdom. Besides, the Kauravas had on their side the wise and valiant grandfather Bhishma, royal priest Kripacharya and Dronacharya, both great warriors, Karna and many other warriors of great valour. Duryodhana himself was an expert in mace-fighting. His hundred brothers were all gallant warriors. Such a huge army of Hastinapura empire was destroyed (with all its senior-most commanders) in a mere 18-days' war, that too, by a comparably much weaker army of the Pandavas, and this indeed was sad.

In a war, the question of justice or injustice is rather secondary. However, there are some basic and accepted principles, violation of which is condemnable. In this regard, the Pandavas were more blameworthy. It is said that for the purpose of establishing *Dharmarajya* and to protect the good and punish the bad, the Pandavas on Krishna's advice resorted to various unfair means. The question arises whether *dharmarajya* was established or not in the country after the war. Following the death of countless kings and warriors the country virtually became devoid of able administrators and this led to its steady downfall. It took a long time to recover the lost ground. After victory in the war Yudhisthira ascended the throne of Hastinapura and reigned for 33 years. Of this period, for 15 years he performed royal duties exclusively on the advice of the eldest uncle Dhritarashtra. It is doubtful whether he could pay proper attention to the royal duties as he remained deeply shaken with sorrow on the death of his own sons and relatives, and innumerable other kings and warriors.

After abdication of the throne by Yudhisthira, Parikshita, Abhimanuya's son born of Uttaraa, became the king of Hastinapura. He could not achieve anything spectacular for the good of the people. He was fond of hunting. One day while chasing a deer in the forest he came across a hermit sitting in deep meditation. King Parkshita asked the hermit for the direction in which the deer had fled. As the hermit was then observing vow of silence, he remained mum without uttering a word. Parikshita then became enraged and to punish the hermit for his 'impertinence' he wrapped a dead snake around his neck with one end of the bow. This childish act is certainly unbecoming on the part of a king. Later Parikshita died of snake-bite on the curse of the hermit's son. This is just an example of the moral quality of the kings, the country got after the war.

Queen Gandhari, wife of Dhritarashtra, overwhelmed with grief, having lost all her hundred sons, accused Krishana saying that he alone could have stopped the war, but did not. She then uttered a serious curse that Krishna's *Jadava and Brishni* clan would be destroyed in the same way as the *Kurus*, and the same distress would befall the *Jadava* and *Brishni* womenfolk as the *Kuru* womenfolk. Krishna humbly accepted the curse and said that the curse coming from the virtuous Gandhari would come true. Indeed the curse came true. As a result of internal feuds the *Jadava* and *Brishi* clan was completely destroyed and their womenfolk fell in similar distress as the *Kuru* womenfolk. Krishna himself fell prey to a hunter's arrow.

In the Mahabharata, the Kauravas were depicted as wicked, and the Pandavas as virtuous. In the first dice-game Yudhisthira lost to the Kauravas everything including his empire, his four brothers and even their wife Draupadi. Draupadi was dragged to the open court where attempt was made even to disrobe her in the presence of the king Dhritarashtra (though blind, he could understand the on-going ugly happenings), Bhishma and other principal courtiers. When none came to the rescue of Draupadi, Dharma, the God of Truth saved her from shame with his supernatural power by continuously lengthening her wearing apparel. When all attempts by Dushashana, Duryodhana's brother, failed to disrobe Draupadi, she begged of the king to release herself and her five husbands viz, Yudhisthira, Bhima, Arjuna, Nakula and Sahadeva, from slavery which accrued to them following defeat in the dice-game. On the prayer being granted, the Pandavas left the royal court; but were soon called back by the king on Duryodhana's insistence to play for the second time. Having lost this time also the Pandavas, as described by the poet, left for the forest as per conditions agreed upon. During the first game Draupadi was subjected to many invectives by the Kauravas, particularly Duryodhana and Karna.

This story of the disrobing of Draupadi in broad daylight in the open royal court in the presence of the king and all his prominent courtiers seems absolutely absurd and impossible. The Mahabharata's poet apparently introduced this story to besmirch the image of the Kauravas and to depict the Pandavas as epitome of innocence and virtue. The subsequent developments in the Mahabharata centred round this story of disrobing of Draupadi. Circumstances indicate that the dice-game was held only once and the story of disrobing of Draupadi is an interpolation. After losing the game, the Pandavas in compliance of the conditions mutually agreed upon, went to the forest in exile for 13 years (including one-year incognito stay).

Yet, as described in the Mahabharata, Duryodhana was in possession of many virtues. He did not hesitate to pay due recognition to Karna's strength and valour though he knew him to be *sutaputra* while the Pandavas hated him. He even made him the king of *Angarajya.* Duryodhana did not forsake grandfather Bhishma, Vidura and other Kaurava leaders or initiate any action against them though he knew them to have sympathy with the Pandavas.

Yudhisthira, the eldest of the Pandavas was the symbol of virtue. Despite some very serious failings, the Pandavas, under his leadership, did perform many good deeds. On losing the dice-game he unhesitatingly left for forest with brothers and wife in compliance of the conditions of the play. Under his wise guidance the Pandavas could successfully complete their one-year incognito stay in Viratnagar. Yudhisthira tried his best to avoid the war and by way of settlement with the Kauravas wanted only five villages for the five brothers leaving the entire empire to them. Yudhisthira was not a great warrior; but even then he could kill Salya, the valiant king of Madra. While in exile in forest he released Duryodhana and other Kaurava leaders from the custody of the Gandharvas – an act of great magnanimity shown to the Kauravas who did not hesitate to send them to the forest through treachery. For adoption of unfair means in the war on Krishna's advice he suffered from intense remorse. On the death of relatives and other kings and warriors in the war his mental agony persisted till death. After the war he treated Dhritarashtra and other surviving Kaurava leaders with due respect. In the later part of his rule, Dhritarashtra was virtually the king of Hastinapura and he showed no hesitation to work under his guidance. All this underlines his greatness.

The events in the Mahabharata, as described by the poet, have occurred in conjunction, both with worldly and divine powers. The poet's intention is to emphasize that success in life cannot be achieved by means of only worldly powers, divine help is also necessary. It has been explained that divine help is bestowed only on those who are enterprising. Enterprise is thus the primary factor for success.

2.

In the Mahabharata, particular emphasis has been laid, among other measures, on the need to collect information about the enemy to ensure stability of the state. In this regard many sages and wise men enunciated principles of great value which are relevant even today. In this regard we first come across royal counsel on ethics and politics, Kanika's do's and don'ts for the kings in times of crisis. King Dhritarashtra was very weak and biased towards his own sons. He became worried at the continuous quarrels between them and those of his late brother Pandu. He was also jealous of the superior skill of the Pandavas, in archery and other arts of warfare, over his own children, bringing them wide applause from the public. He realized his sons were lagging behind the Pandavas in all respects, and that something had to be done urgently to retrieve the ground. He was not sure about his course of action. Pandavas were like his own sons and they achieved everything by merit and perseverance. There was no question of any action against them. Bewildered Dhritarashtra called Kanika for advice.

On hearing the king, Kanika said, "*Maharaj*, patience is the main virtue of a king. The king shall always bear everything patiently so that his anger, dissatisfaction or might remains concealed from others. On this the enemy will remain in a dilemma about his course of action, and they will not show any interest in collecting information about the king's financial and military resources. The king, on the other hand, by holding his patience shall silently engage himself to collect information about enemy's vices and virtues in order to use the same against them at the opportune moment. The king shall carefully conceal his own weaknesses, his alliances and plans of expansion of the empire. He shall similarly keep his policy secret of *sama (*conciliation), *dana* (generosity), *bheda* (dissension) and *danda* (punishment) prescribed for the enemy. *Maharaj*, the enemy must be destroyed by all means because even the weak enemy, by attaining strength, at a later stage can cause harm to the king. Sometimes it is advisable to behave with indifference and as a blind person to hoodwink the enemy. In this way the king by keeping his real intentions concealed, shall make friends with the enemy only to destroy him at the appropriate moment. Attempts should be made to obtain the enemy's weaknesses by winning over by bribering, the disgruntled elements in his court. After the purpose is served these dishonest traitors should be destroyed. Here no mercy, whatsoever, should be shown. *Maharaj*, attempts should be made to subdue the weak by threat, the brave by courtesy, the greedy by bribery and the equals by force. The king should remember that by destroying his principal aids it would be easier to destroy the main enemy. Even if the son, friend, brother, father or the preceptor work like enemy, they must be destroyed. For destruction of the enemy all means including poisoning are justified. In case the enemy is found to be equally strong and intelligent, the king shall make every effort to increase his own strength by mobilizing additional resources. Otherwise success will be impossible. *Maharaj*, the king shall never proceed against the enemy simply out of anger without proper assessment of the whole situation. The fear of the enemy should first be allayed by sweet words, religious instructions, and good behaviour. Even after that, if there is no sign of improvement in his attitude, no mercy should be shown to him, whatsoever. Unreliable persons must not be believed. At the same time excessive faith, even on known reliable persons, would be inadvisable. Because reliable persons may also succumb to the temptations and harm the king. The king should always collect information through well-trained secret agents engaged in consultation with trustworthy ministers. Sometimes information can also be collected by using the services of criminal elements as also of the holy and saintly persons.

The criminals can easily associate with their counterparts in the enemy kingdom and obtain information of various nature with their help. Similarly saintly persons, who are well respected everywhere, can move around freely in the enemy kingdom and come in contact with people of high position, affording them opportunity to gather the required information. All such information can be used against the enemy. *Maharaj*, all consultations must always be conducted in complete secrecy. For this, places like garden, temple, eating house, place of pilgrimage, forest etc. may be selected. Consultations conducted in such places will remain unknown to the enemy agents. *Maharaj*, you may decide your course of action with regard to the Pandavas on the basis of the principles explained by me."

3.

In Mahabharata the principles on royal duties, security, secret agents and other related matters enunciated by *Devarshi* Narada are highly valuable and universal in import. The Pandavas built a new capital with the help of *Danava* architect Moy after destroying the forest at Khandabadaha and named it Indraprastha following division of the old Hastinapura empire. At Indraprastha, *Devarshi* Narada appeared before King Yudhishthira and gave him his blessings. In course of discussions Narada explained to Yudhishthira certain principles following which he could make himself a successful king.

Narada said, "*Maharaj*, you should always perform royal duties following the footsteps of your glorious ancestors. Worldly matters must not overtake your religious pursuits. You should always hold in high esteem all holy persons observing religious austerities. All courtiers and friends should be well looked after. Royal revenue and other levies should be regularly collected from the people to augment the treasury. *Maharaj*, kingdom's stability and integrity is the primary responsibility of the king. For this you should build forts at strategic places and maintain a well-trained standing army. Special attention should be paid to ensure that your ministers and advisors remain always loyal to you. Any dereliction in duty on their part must not be tolerated under any circumstances. Always remain alert about envoys/messengers with evil intentions from foreign kingdoms. They may engage themselves in collecting strategic information about your kingdom and use the same to harm you. *Maharaj*, information both about friends and foes should be collected by engaging trusted agents. Remember, today's friend may turn into a foe tomorrow. Always appoint trustworthy persons of good lineage as ministers. Remember, successful accomplishment of a deed entirely depends on healthy consultations. For this consultations should be conducted with only wise and trusted ministers so that all decisions remain completely secret. Never hold consultations alone or with many. Consultations with oneself are of no use, while consultations with many may disclose all secrets. Places like garden, temple, pilgrimage centre, forest etc. should be selected for consultations with trusted persons to keep them secret.

"*Maharaj*, remain very careful with regard to the appointment of secret agents. Their reliability should be judged before appointment. Trusted and specially trained agents should be engaged to identify enemy agents and frustrate their inimical designs. *Maharaj*, all royal appointments should be made after carefully judging the importance of the job and qualifications of the candidates. Right persons should get the right jobs. Every good work should be rewarded.

"*Maharaj*, when the enemy king is engaged in luxury and addiction, then you should attack his kingdom after assessing your own strength and take adequate measures to protect your own capital. In order to weaken the enemy you should secretly bribe his army commanders. Always ensure that persons engaged in royal duties, in your kingdom or in occupied areas, do not get involved in unnecessary bickering among themselves. This may cause disaster.

"*Maharaj*, always remain vigilant to ensure that none is punished on false evidence. This will give a bad name to the king and the people will lose confidence in him. Never appoint on royal duties the greedy, the inimical persons, the persons with criminal background and those whose family and conduct are unknown. Corrective action should be taken without delay whenever any adverse report is received. All bad people must be punished and the good ones protected. No secrets should be disclosed to the women as they are prone to disclose all secrets to others."

At the end, Narada advised Yudhishthira to scrupulously avoid fourteen vices to which kings are generally susceptible. These are atheism, falsehood, anger, procrastination, abandon-ment of wise people, laziness, fickle-mindedness, constant pursuit of wealth, consultation with unworthy people, inaction in matters already decided, indifference in keeping secrets, non-execution of good work, irrational rejection, and arrogance.

After respectfully listening to the instructions of Narada, Yudhisthira paid obeisance to him and said, "*Devarshi,* I shall try to carry out my royal duties always keeping in mind your valuable instructions. I shall never deviate from the path of virtue. But I must confess I am not equal to my great and virtuous ancestors."

On comparison of the instructions of Kanika to Dhritarashtra with those of Narada to Yudhishthira on royal duties, it will be seen that the latter are much superior in content. Kanika's instructions were aimed at protecting the interests of the jealousy-stricken Kauravas in the context of superiority of the

Pandavas. Practically Kanika advised Dhritarashtra to take appropriate decision treating the Pandavas as enemy. He did not give any good advice to bring about reconciliation among the cousins. His advice was negative and destructive in nature. Kanika's instructions have rightly been denounced in the Mahabharata as evil-counsel. It may be mentioned that Dhritarashtra in pursuance of Kanika's instructions, sent the Pandavas to Varanavat along with mother Kunti virtually in exile in consultation with Duryodhana and other Kaurava well-wishers. Duryodhana and maternal uncle Shakuni hatched a conspiracy to burn the Pandavas alive at this Varanavat in a house *(Jatugriha)* constructed with lac which is highly inflameable, and with other combustible materials. The conspiracy, however, failed.

On the other hand, Narada's instructions were intended to remind Yudhishthira of *Rajdharma* in order to make him an ideal democratic king with dedication to serve the welfare of the people. The instructions which were positive and constructive, bore fruit ultimately.

It is, however, true that instructions of both Kanika and Narada, regarding secret agents, are extremely valuable and will prove useful to any king to ensure good administration, and stability and integrity of the kingdom. In extreme situation Kanika's instructions may also have to be resorted to by the king.

4.

Regarding secret agents many more details are also mentioned in the Mahabharata. The Pandavas during exile in forest were living at one time in a hermitage near *Badarikashrama* near the bank of the *Bhagirathi* river. One day a lotus of thousand petals driven by wind fell in front of Draupadi. Charmed at its beauty she asked the second Pandava Bhimasena to bring for her a bunch of the same flowers. Immediately Bhimasena left the hermitage and in course of search reached a plateau at the foot of the mountain *Gandhamadana.* After taking bath in the nearby lake he raised a roar in thundering voice, which was heard by Hanumana, the great devotee of Lord Rama who on being bestowed with the boon of immortality from Him, was living in the adjacent plantation grove. Bhimasena entered the grove and soon saw Hanumana lying across the path. Without knowing his identity he (Bhimasensa) asked Hanumana to make way for him. After some altercation, Hanumana asked Bhimasena to raise his tail and proceed. But the great hero Bhimasena despite all efforts, failed to raise the tail. He understood Hanumana was endowed with divine powers and respectfully requested him to disclose his real identity. Hanumana then disclosed his identity and narrated the story of Rama's banishment to forest, and abduction by Ravana and rescue of Sita during the earlier *Treta-Yuga*. It was then, Bhimsena and Hanumana came to know that they were brothers being the sons of God Pavana, On Bhimasena's request Hanumana explained for his knowledge, among other matters, the characteristic features of different *jugas*, duties of the *Kshatriyas* and the principles of state administration.

Hanumana, a person of profound knowledge said, "Brother, the main duties of the *Kshatriyas* are to protect the people and the country. The king should always run the state administration in consultation with the wise, learned, and experienced persons. Punishment to the bad is one of the principal duties of the king. If the king is licentious, his downfall is inevitable. The king will always collect information through secret agents about enemy's strength, and location and fortifications of his forts. The agents should also be engaged to collect information on social, economic and political situation, public opinion, condition of the forts, people's morale and their successes and failures etc. in his own country. This will help the king to take timely corrective action in case any deviation is brought to his notice. Always remember that success depends on collection of correct information, own power of judgement, honesty, proper consultations and one's own capability. Success becomes easier if the principles of reconciliation, generosity, dissension, punishment and indifference are judiciously applied either singly or collectively. Consultations are the principal part of the king's duties. These consultations should always be conducted with the virtuous. Under no circumstances should consultations be conducted with women, the immature, the very old, the fickle-minded persons, and the insane. It is advisable to engage religious persons for religious purpose, eunuchs for the women and the cruel persons for heinous works. Always decide your course of action by engaging trusted agents whenever a new situation arises. Brother, remember that the king can earn respect of the people mainly by protecting the good and suppressing the bad."

Thereafter, Bhimasena took the path shown by Hanumana and collected the divine lotus from a river after defeating the Gandharvas who were guarding the place.

5.

In the Mahabharata, grandfather Bhishma's instructions about king's duties, security, secret agents and other matters are multifaceted and more exhaustive, worthy of emulation even today. Yudhisthira was overwhelmed with grief following death of innumerable relatives in the war. His brothers and even Krishna failed to alleviate his agony. Krishna then brought Yudhisthira and others to dying Bhishma who was lying on the bed of arrows in Kurukshetra battle-field.

Bhishma, with father's boons of non-destruction in the battlefield and death at will, did not breath his last as he wanted to die after sun's movement to the Tropic of Cancer. Krishna told Bhishma, "O' Great Soul, we have failed to alleviate Yudhisthira's terrible distress on the death of relatives in the war. You may now kindly explain the nuances of truth and virtue in order to bring peace to his mind. You are the only person who can do this job."

Bhishma expressing satisfaction at his words said, "O, Lord of the Universe, what shall I narrate? You are the repository of all knowledge. With piercing arrows, my mind is in distress, body badly exhausted and brain defiled. Because of the weakness my speech is impaired. How shall I obey your command?" On this Krishna, by bestowing a boon, removed all discomforts from the body of Bhishma, who then came to possess all the divine attributes. Bereft of other low-level qualities, he gained divine vision with which he could observe everything in true perspective. Armed with these divine powers from Krishna, Bhishma spoke to Yudhisthira on religion, material possession, human desire, sacrificial rites, duties in hermitage, king's duties, administration, secret agents and various other matters. Many of these instructions of Bhishma are universal in character.

On royal duties Bhishma said, "My son, always keep in mind, only the enterprising kings can achieve success. While performing royal duties always depend on your own efforts. Do not depend only on divine grace. You need not be perturbed when you encounter any obstruction. Then you are to make extra efforts to achieve the objective. Always perform duties with devotion to truth in a simple manner. Own weaknesses should, however, be kept concealed from the enemy. Always remain careful to detect lapses of the enemy. Secrecy must be maintained at all costs.. There is nothing wrong if falsehood is resorted to in the matter. In the scriptures four kinds of fort are mentioned. Of them *naradurga* i.e. the people's forts are the strongest and impregnable. Always, therefore, try to seek cooperation of the people by ensuring their welfare. Such a king will receive spontaneous cooperation of the people in any danger of the kingdom. The king should follow a middle path in all his actions. He should not be too harsh or too mild. The king should adopt various direct or indirect means in deciding his course of action, after carefully assessing the strength of the enemy. The king should always maintain patience. With the servants and the subordinate employees, the king should maintain reasonable distance. Too much intimacy with them should be scrupulously avoided. Otherwise they may take its advantage and even harm the king."

Continuing, Bhishma said, "My son, remember, king's life is like a rat in a snake's hole. He is in constant danger. The king, therefore, while depending on his own efforts, will have to remain ever vigilant to protect his kingdom. The kingdom is composed of seven components. These are – king himself, courtiers, friends, treasury, kingdom, fort and army. Whoever – whether a friend or a preceptor – will go against anyone of the above, must be destroyed. The king will never repose too much confidence in anyone. Everybody's work should be looked upon with some suspicion, because any time anyone can go against the king. Success comes to the king when he finds enemy's weakness, brings under his control enemy commanders by bribery, holds consultations with wise persons, shows eagerness to know the unknown, engages himself for the good of the people, and maintains complete secrecy about the work of the spies and strategic consultations. You can not conquer the enemy without first conquering yourself. Only the morally strong king with the cooperation of the loyal subjects, can conquer the enemy. Therefore, get rid of the vices, if any, from within yourself."

On secret agents Bhishma said, "My son, the secret agents must be physically fit in all respects as they are required to work under adverse circumstances. They must be capable of withstanding hunger, thirst, fatigue and other privations. Only intelligent persons should be appointed as agents. Information has to be collected about secret activities of the courtiers, princes, feudal kings, and the town and village people, as the king must be aware of the evil designs of all classes of people. Care should be taken to ensure that the secret agents do not know each other's identity. Only impartial persons should be engaged to supervise the performance of secret agents. The king must remain vigilant about the activities of enemy agents. For this, careful watch should be maintained by the king through his trusted agents, located in places like eating houses, wrestling arenas, money-lender's establishments, beggars' colonies, assemblies of learned people, courtyards, royal courts, religious places etc. which are thronged by the people. One very important work of the king is to identify the enemy agents and to eventually win them over through bribery. Sometimes the deaf and dumb, the blind and similar other disabled people, with suitable training, may be utilized for the collection of intelligence as their movements will not arouse any suspicion. At the same time vigilance has to be maintained on similar people who may be working as enemy agents."

Regarding principles of military campaign, Bhishma said, "My son, the king should start military campaign against the enemy who is weak, friendless or mad with power and vanity. Here also the enemy should not be taken lightly. A powerful army should be mobilized for the offensive. A weak king must not openly start any military offensive against a comparatively strong king. He should better try to harass and weaken such an enemy with methods like selective armed action, arson, poisoning, causing dissensions within his commanders and allies. During war time when enemy agents are generally very active, consultations to be kept secret, should be held in open space, religious places etc. The king must not hesitate to take firm action against his own men suspected to be engaged in anti-state activities. Those doing good work must be rewarded."

Regarding principles of punishment, Bhishma said, "My son, always remember, only through judicious application of punishment are the bad subdued and the good protected. Out of fear of punishment different classes of people also perform their allotted duties. The king's fame stems from sincere religious practices, successful fulfillment of tasks without showing any arrogance, sweet talks, performance of heroic deeds without indulging in self-praise and similar other good works. The king must avoid deviations like friendship with dishonest people, hostility with friends, engagement of untrustworthy persons as secret agents, disclosure of state secrets to untrustworthy people, self-advertisement, acceptance of help from wicked people, advertisement of strength before success, abandonment of friends, punishment of honest people, disrespect to the defeated enemy, unnecessary expression of anger and mild action against the wrong-doer.

Regarding appointment of ministers, Bhishma said, "My son, king's friends are of four kinds. They are *samartha*, *bhajamana*, *sahaja*, and *krittim*. Besides them, the king has friends who are virtuous. These virtuous persons only help the virtuous king. The king should keep all his irreligious decisions secret from his virtuous friends. Remember, the king can not always achieve victory in war only by following righteous path; on occasions he has to take recourse to fraud and untruth to achieve his objective."

Continuing, Bhishma said, "Of the above-mentioned four kinds of friends, the *bhajamana* and the *sahaja* friends are the best. About the rest of the friends the king should remain always suspicious. They must not be fully believed. King's preceptors and virtuous friends who are simple in character, intelligent, skilful and indifferent to both honour and dishonour and who are agreeable to live in his palace, may be believed without hesitation. There is absolutely no danger in disclosing even the closest secrets to them. Only those who are able, reserved in speech, virtuous, bear no malice to anyone and self-restrained are to be appointed as prime minister. And those who are of good lineage, compassionate, bear no pride, and are well-versed in their duties and responsibilities, should be appointed as ministers.

"My son, it is always advisable to be careful about the blood relations. It is seen that they are naturally jealous of one another. At the same time it is a matter of sorrow to have no relations. Do not, therefore, repose complete confidence in them; but behave with them as if they are trustworthy. It is not difficult to bring them around with generosity, simplicity and softness. Remember, dissensions within are more dangerous than the enemy abroad.

"My son, generally the king should not abandon many for the sake of one. If, however, that one person is in possession of extraordinary qualities, the king should not hesitate to seek his counsel forsaking the many. The king should hold consultations with only loyal persons. The characteristics of a loyal person are that he does not harbour any inimical design against the king on being scolded or even after dismissal from service. Remember, welfare of the kingdom depends on the good counsel imparted by the ministers to the king. The designated ministers should collect information not only about the enemy and the suspected local people but also about the king's deviant activities, if any. These activities should then be respectfully brought to the notice of the king for suitable remedial action. Consultations and secret agents have an extremely vital role in ensuring kingdom's security and stability. An expert committee of three or four experienced courtiers may be constituted to advise the king on all important security and other related issues. King's courtiers and advisors must be very careful about their body language while holding consultations in an open place as any loud voice or unusual movements of their hands and feet may attract the attention of enemy agents."

While explaining king's behaviour towards the defeated enemy, Bhishma said, "My son, due honour should always be shown to the defeated enemy who earlier did good to him. The king should not remain indifferent and contented after behaving unpleasantly with anyone. He must try to assuage the offended person's feelings at the earliest opportunity. Otherwise, he may try to do harm to the king at the moment of his own choosing. Remember, with sweet words even a foe can be turned into a friend."

After describing the whole gamut of king's duties, security, intelligence collection and many other subjects like divine ordain etc., Bhishma told Yudhisthira not to entertain any grief for those who had died in the war. He explained that their death had been caused due to the influence of *Kaal* as a result of their own past actions. They did not die because of his fault or Duryodhana's.

With Bhishma completing his marathon speech, sun moved to the Tropic of Cancer, his chosen time for final departure from this world. As he breathed his last, the great Bhishma's soul was blessed with showers of flower from the heaven. Yudhisthira, his grief largely alleviated, then left the place with Krishna and others for the preparation of the last rites of Bhishma.

6.

The Pandavas on completion of 13-year exile in forest and one year incognito stay demanded return of their kingdom of Indraprastha. On the Kauravas' refusal, war between them seemed inevitable. King Dhritarashtra sent Sanjay, his charioteer to the Pandavas at Viratnagara with peace proposals to avoid the war. Sanjay on return after discussions, reported to Dhritarashtra that Pandavas were determined to go in for war if their kingdom was not returned or at least five villages were not given to them and that the entire *Kuru* clan would be completely destroyed in this fratricidal war. Blaming Dhritarashtra for the developments, Sanjay told him that he would be responsible for this catastrophe as his indulgence had turned Duryodhana arrogant and uncompromising.

Alarmed at the words of Sanjay, Dhritarashtra called his virtuous brother Vidura for advice. Vidura's instructions on *rajdharma,* security, secret agents and various other subjects are multi-faceted and have universal acceptance. These are relevant even today.

Vidura said "*Maharaj*, a wise person has certain special attributes. He keeps his intentions and consultations completely secret until success is achieved, proceeds to accomplish his objectives without fear and panic, maintains mental equanimity in times of danger, does not insult the weak, remains indifferent to enemy's weaknesses so as not to arouse any suspicion, does not antagonize the strong, and demonstrates his valour only at the appropriate time. On the other hand a foolish person bereft of any virtue, sacrifices his own interest and remains concerned about the welfare of others, plays falsehood with friends, considers enemies as friends, envies his genuine friends, believes those who are untrustworthy, and proceeds out of greed to achieve his objectives without considering his own strength."

Continuing Vidura said, "*Maharaj*, you should try to bring under your control your friends, enemies and the indifferent by carefully applying the principles of *sama, danda, bheda* etc. There should not be any forcible collection of taxes from the people. Never consult the affairs of the state with those who are unintelligent, dilatory and sycophant. Otherwise, state secrets might be disclosed. Before commencement of work, all aspects require to be carefully assessed. Please remember, the king sees everything through his secret agents.

"*Maharaj*, there are six reasons for which secrecy of all consultations might be disclosed. These are: (1) king's mental confusion (2) procrastination and sleepiness (3) ignorance about enemy agents (4) king's own attitude and body language (5) confidence on dishonest courtiers and (6) competence of enemy envoys/messengers. In this regard, the king must remain extremely careful. Success always depends on king's own enterprise."

In this way, Vidura after explaining various principles of statecraft and many other subjects, advised king Dhritarashtra to treat Pandavas as his own sons and return their kingdom to them. Otherwise, he warned that the entire *Kuru* clan would be destroyed at the hands of the heroic Pandavas. Dhritarashtra replied to Vidura that even though he was in full agreement with him, he was unable to do anything as he felt nervous whenever he thought of Duryodhana who had lost all sense of right and wrong.

Despite being blind partiality to his sons, Dhritarashtra as a king was endowed with profound knowledge on various subjects. At the last stage of his life, before departure to the forest, Dhritarashatra gave valuable instructions to Yudhisthira on many matters including politics, security, and importance of intelligence collection by secret agents. Dhritarashtra, referring to the eight components of the kingdom as explained by Vidura earlier, asked Yudhisthira to maintain constant vigilance to safeguard them.

Dhritarashtra said, "My son, in the discharge of your royal duties always follow the advice of the wise people. You should appoint ministers only those who are trustworthy, patient, and of good lineage. Enemy's intentions should be ascertained by engaging your trusted agents The place of your stay must be well-protected. Always hold consultations with wise people at secure places so that secrecy is assured. Through secret agents you should probe into faults and lapses of your subjects in order to detect their inimical designs. No guilty people should go unpunished. All serious offenders must be given death sentence.

"Son Yudhisthira, always ascertain enemy's weaknesses by engaging secret agents. Attempts should also be made to create dissensions amongst his friends and relatives. In this way enemy should be weakened and eventually destroyed. Enemy should be destroyed one by one."

At the end Dhritarashtra asked Yudhisthira to govern his subjects according to his instructions. He expressed the hope that Yudhisthira by following the virtuous path, would be happy in this world and enjoy heavenly bliss after death.

7.

It is evident that in the principles enunciated by sage Narada, Bhishma and others on royal duties, security, secret agents etc. there are many common points and that are quite natural; because the principles are time-tested and obtained from long experience. The effectiveness of the principles has been successfully established in the society prevailing in those days. In fact the principles being universal in significance, are relevant and useful even in the present days. Collection of intelligence and counter intelligence to ensure state's stability and integrity is largely based on the same principles today as in the days of Mahabharata. Only methods of collection of information have undergone changes thanks to the advancement of science and technology. All this indicates that in the Mahabharata days a very superior administrative system was in vogue and that this was possible only because of the high moral calibre of the kings or the rulers. Apparently the kings and the statesmen in those days deeply thought of the security threats to the state and other related problems and successfully managed to evolve with their knowledge and experience a system of administration where the people lived in peace and happiness. We are surprised when we see the most revered sage Narada, who had the rare distinction of being blessed by God Vishnu himself, speaks to Yudhisthira on a mundane subject like security and spies. This only underlines the importance of the subject.

In the changed democratic social system of the present day the primary responsibilities of the ruling class have remained the same and in the execution of these responsibilities adherence to the principles enunciated in the Mahabharata is imperative. The society marked by corruptions, violence and other anti-social activities is apparently due to the disregard of these established principles.

In various events of the Mahabharata, we find successful application of the principles of spying, security, safeguarding of secret consultation and other related matters. Examples of non-application and wrong application are also many. From the very beginning, relations between the Kaurava and the Pandava boys were bitter. The second Pandava brother, Bhimasena was physically extremely strong. Out of fun he used to oppress the Kaurava boys very often in course of play. Aggrieved at this, Duryodhana, the eldest brother among the hundred Kauravas, hatched a plan to kill Bhimasena by poisoning him. He accordingly got built a few beautiful houses on the bank of the Ganges where Bhimasena, a voracious eater, was entertained with sumptuous dishes of many varieties along with all the Kaurava and the Pandava brothers. Duryodhana showing a deep sense of amity and brotherly feelings, himself put *Kheer* which was mixed with poison, into the mouth of Bhimasena. Out of fun other brothers also put *kheer* into each other's mouth. After the feast, all the brothers got down into the Ganges for water-sports. Bhimasena, while engaged in sports, soon became unconscious due to the effect of poison. Duryodhana then bound Bhimasena with creeper and pushed him deep into the river. None of the brothers got any inkling of this as they in the mean time had returned to their camp house. According to the story, Bhimasena while getting drowned in the water, was bitten by a poisonous snake. As a result, the poison in the *kheer* lost its effect and Bhimasena got back his consciousness. Soon he found himself in the beautiful palace of *Nagaraj* who knowing his identity made Bhim comfortable with food and drinks. The *Nagaraj* gave him many presents. The biggest gift Bhimasena got from *Nagaraj* was *amrit*. He drank this nectar and physically became many times stronger.

After the water sports Yudhisthira and other Pandava brothers without finding Bhimasena thought he had already gone to the palace. Without waiting for him any longer they returned to the palace and there also they did not find him. On this the Pandava brothers with mother Kunti became very worried. When Bhimasena was not found anywhere, they thought he had been killed by cruel Duryodhana. Vidura on knowing the incident warned everybody not to disclose the matter to anyone else. He, referring to the prediction of sage Vyasa, assured mother Kunti that all her sons would be long-lived. After eight days when Bhimasena appeared at the palace safe and sound, all their worries subsided. The story of Bhimasena's disappearance, his sojourn in *Nagaloka* and attaining immense strength on drinking nectar, as narrated by him, caused them great surprise.

Two things became evident from the incident. First, none on the Pandava side had any hint regarding Duryodhana's plan to poison Bhimasena. This is no doubt a success of Duryodhana's meticulous planning and on the other hand a failure of the Pandavas. It is of course true that the Pandava boys were then very young in age. The eldest brother Yudhisthira himself was then only sixteen or seventeen years old. They were all simple in nature without any understanding of the strangeness of human psychology. They, therefore, could not conceive that Duryodhana, their own cousin brother, could hatch such a heinous crime as to kill Bhimasena by poisoning. We are, however, astonished to see how such a conspiracy could remain unknown to the Pandava well-wisher Vidura, a person of great experience and intellect. He was aware Duryodhana was harbouring a grudge against Bhimasena for his rough behaviour with the Kaurava brothers. On the occasion of the water sports in the Ganges, buildings were constructed for the temporary stay of the princes and for holding of the feast. A large quantity of food articles and other materials were brought there. Many cooks with their assistants had also to be mobilized to cook and serve the food. It was easy to conceive that behind all these elaborate arrangements some sort of conspiracy was involved. Unfortunately Vidura's agents remained completely in the dark. This was certainly a very serious failure on the part of Vidura.

Secondly, at the same time it has to be admitted that it was due to Vidura's foresight that none others in the palace could know anything about Bhimasena's long absence for eight days. This greatly benefited the Pandavas. All this was the result of successful non-disclosure of secret consultations. We have seen that all the wise men have laid special emphasis on the importance of maintaining secrecy. Bhimasena's absence gave a false belief to Duryodhana that he (Bhimasena) had actually died of poisoning. The Kauravas thus got immersed in self-satisfaction. When Bhimasena's presence was noticed, their surprise knew no bounds. Both the Kauravas and the Pandavas for different reasons preferred to remain silent about the incident on the day of the water sports. Duryodhana thought that the Pandavas could not know anything about his misdeed. They, thus remained in the dark about Bhimasena's attaining immense physical strength on drinking nectar given by the *Nagaraj.* The Pandavas were then bereft of any resources and supporters. They, thus on Vidura's advice, refrained from bringing any open charges in the matter lest this should further embitter their relations with the Kauravas and even endanger their lives. This was indeed a great act of Vidura's prudence. After this incident the Pandavas became extremely careful and remained vigilant about every move and action of the Kauravas. In the first round, the Kauravas were defeated. Their conspiracy failed miserably; while the Pandavas came out victorious.

8.

Gradually the situation became normal. The Kaurava and the Pandava boys resumed their normal activities together. The Pandava brothers, particularly Arjuna continued to show excellence in archery and other sports and earned praise from everybody. Yudhisthira was liked for his simplicity, knowledge and wisdom by all. The Kaurava boys lagged behind all of them. In the mean time, in deference to the wishes of the people and the suggestion of the grandfather Bhishma and other senior courtiers, Yudhisthira, the eldest of the cousins was installed as the Crown Prince. Duryodhana was himself a claimant to this position as he happened to be the eldest son of reigning king Dhritarashtra who had ascended the throne on the death of Pandu. Duryodhana's claim was disregarded as he was younger to Yudhisthira by one year. On this, Duryodhana became desperate at the instigation of Shakuni, Karna and his own brothers. In consultation with them he hit upon a conspiracy to burn the Pandava brothers alive. King Dhritarashtra was also himself worried at the growing popularity of the Pandavas and resentment among his own sons. He sought Kanika's advice, as mentioned earlier, regarding the steps to be taken to suppress the Pandavas.

One day Duryodhana accompanied by Shakuni, Karna and Duhashsana met Dhritarashtra and requested him to banish the Pandava brothers on some plea to Varanavat, a place near the holy city of Prayaga. Duryodhana's intention was to capture the entire Hastinapura empire during the absence of the Pandavas from the capital. At first Dhritarashtra did not like the suggestion on the ground that Bhishma and other elders as well as the public would not tolerate anything wrong against the Pandavas. For the success of his plan, Duryodhana then devised a novel method. He, with his brothers won over by bribery, a section of prominent citizens of Hastinapura who on their prompting started propagating that Varanavat was a beautiful place. Dhritarashtra secretly supported the move. On his advice some of the ministers also narrated many good aspects of Varanavat. This propaganda widely spread among the people. It reached the ears of the Pandavas who on Vidura's advice gladly agreed to go to Varanavat and stay there for sometime. Dhritarashtra realizing Pandavas' willingness to go to Varanavat, himself spoke highly of the place and approved of their stay there. Bhishma and other elders withdrew their earlier objection in the matter.

Vidura knew the Kauravas after their failure to kill Bhimasena by poisoning and was soon to hit upon another plan to harm the Pandavas. He thus smelt something sinister behind the move in sending the Pandavas to Varanavat. He thought it would be easier for him to foil the evil design of the Kauravas at Varanavat than at the capital Hastinapura where the latter had a stronger presence. At Varanavat, Duryodhana would have very few accomplices with whose assistance he might have planned to harm the Pandavas. With appropriate counter measures he was confident of dealing with them. He thus advised the Pandavas to move to Varanavat without raising any objection in order to keep the Kauravas off guard. Vidura at the same time got down to unearth details of Kauravas' plan at Varanavat.

Happy at the developments, Duryodhana now devoted himself to execute his plan. By paying bribe he won over a person by name Purochana and with his help he planned to burn the Pandavas alive. Explaining the plan he directed Purochana to get a beautiful house constructed at Varanavat with hemp, lac, clarified butter and other combustible materials for the stay of the Pandava brothers and mother Kunti and dump sufficient quantity of such materials around the house. He warned him to complete the construction in extreme secrecy. Purochana was advised to ensure every comfort to the Pandavas during their stay and set fire to the house after winning their complete confidence. Duryodhana explained that after the death of the Pandavas everybody would think that the Pandavas had died in accidental fire and that there was no foul play.

Purochana after ascertaining all necessary details left, on a fast-moving horse, for Varanavat. Vidura, in the mean time, got details through his secret agents about Duryodhana's evil design behind the banishment of the Pandavas. He, however, behaved as if he knew nothing. He also advised the Pandavas accordingly. His intention was to keep the Kauravas off guard. Here Vidura was completely successful. Duryodhana felt contented that the Pandavas had agreed to go to Varanavat willingly.

As decided, the Pandavas with mother Kunti after obtaining blessings from the elders left for Varanavat. The general people on learning about the banishment of the Pandavas openly demonstrated their anger. Yudhisthira consoled them by explaining that Varanavat was a healthy place where they were going for a change of climate. Vidura who accompanied the Pandavas up to certain distance once found Yudhisthira somewhat alone. He then verbally conveyed to him a message having double meaning, unheard by anybody else in a peculiar tribal language known only to him and Yudhisthira. The message said, "It is easy for fire to burn hemp into ashes; but it cannot harm a man staying in an underground hole. It is possible to kill a person with weapons other than those made of iron. He who is patient, keeps in mind the layout of the path and is capable of ascertaining the direction with the help of stars, can save his life."

Yudhisthira got the message that attempt would be made to burn them alive at Varanabata and how to save themselves. He simply told Vidura, 'Understood.' Vidura then returned to Hastinapura.

At Varanavat the local citizens warmly received mother Kunti and the Pandavas. Purochana who had already arrived at Varanavat, arranged their stay at a local palace. Mother Kunti and the Pandavas stayed there for ten days and then shifted, on Purochana's request, to the newly constructed *jatugriha*. In an effort to dispel all suspicion. Purochana named the new house as Shiva.

On entering the new house, Yudhisthira got the smell of clarified butter, lac etc. and told Bhimasena that Purochana on Duryodhana's instruction had constructed this house with combustible materials in order to burn them alive. On hearing this, Bhimasena suggested immediate shifting to a new place. Yudhisthita did not agree and explained that this would arouse suspicion in the mind of Purochana who, wicked as he was, would then by force burn them alive. He said in order to gain confidence of Purochana they should rather live here. He suggested, on the plea of hunting they would see the surrounding areas and find out the paths coming out of the house. All this, he cautioned, must be done in complete secrecy without any knowledge of Purochana.

In pursuance of the decision of Yudhisthira, mother Kunti and the Pandavas decided to live in the house constructed by Purochana. After a few days a person from Vidura, said to be an expert in digging earth, appeared before Yudhisthira secretly and told him that wicked Purochana had decided to set fire to this house on the night of the *chaturdashi*. In order to dispel any doubt about his true identity, he referred to the last word 'understood'. On being satisfied that the person had actually been sent by Vidura, Yudhisthira allowed him to stay in the house.

The *khanaka* dug a hole in the floor and through it constructed over several days a long tunnel beyond the boundary wall of the house. The mouth of the hole was concealed with a cover in order to keep the matter completely secret from others. The Pandavas started going out for hunting during day-time and in the night they slept in the tunnel with weapons for safety.

This went on for a year. Purochana presumed that the Pandavas had not get any hint about his design. He waited for the predetermined date for setting fire to the house. Yudhisthira decided to flee to safety through the tunnel after setting fire to the house before Purochana's strike. Mother Kunti one day invited a few local *Brahmins* for food. After their departure, one hunter woman with her five sons came to the house and they were lavishly entertained in the dinner by mother Kunti. They drank a large quantity of liquor and in an unconscious state remained in the house. In the dead of night when everybody fell asleep, the Pandavas with mother Kunti fled through the tunnel after setting fire to the house. Soon the house built with combustible materials was reduced to ashes. In the fire Purochana who was sleeping in the outhouse as also the hunter woman and her five sons perished. The local people did not know that the hunter woman with her sons were staying in the house and as such they thought mother Kunti with the five Pandavas had died. When six burnt skeletons were found in the house, they had no doubt about the death of mother Kunti and the Pandavas. The burnt skeleton found in the outhouse was believed to be that of Purochana. The *khanaka* while clearing the debris, destroyed the tunnel in such a way that none got any idea of its existence. His real identity remained unknown to all.

The Pandavas with mother Kunti after coming out of the house reached the bank of the Ganges after crossing certain distance on foot through the path earlier marked by them during hunting. One person with a machine-operated boat was waiting for them there. As directed by Vidura he disclosed his identity in a coded language. With all doubts removed, the Pandavas with mother Kunti crossed the river in his boat and came to safety to the other bank. Thus ended the great escape of the Pandavas from *jatugriha.*

In time, the news of burning of *jatugriha* reached Hastinapura. On the 'death' of the Pandavas with mother Kunti the Kauravas as also Dhritarashtra, though happy in mind, feigned to be extremely sorrowful. Grandfather Bhishma and other senior courtiers felt genuinely aggrieved. Vidura knew the Pandavas were alive; even then he expressed grief only for public consumption. The purpose was to hoodwink the Kauravas. He knew the truth would come out one day; but the Pandavas required time to further move away without being pursued by enemy agents. Hence, this false acting of Vidura. On Dhritarashtra's direction Duryodhana performed religious rites for the peace of the departed souls.

To even superficial observers, the plan of burning the Pandavas alive in a house built with combustible materials would seem impractical. There was absolutely no need to build such a house. The plan could have been executed in the palace where the Pandavas first moved in. If that was not possible, some other method could have been evolved for the purpose. The *jatugriha* plan was indeed the brain-child of some people with unhealthy mind. It took several days to build the house. A large number of skilled and unskilled workers had to be engaged for the purpose. Combustible materials of different kinds had to be collected. In all likelihood this would have evoked curiosity and suspicion among the local people. The planners seemed to be oblivious of this fact – a great omission indeed! Any house built with materials mixed with clarified butter, lac etc. must emit a pungent smell. Yudhisthira on entering the house got this smell and grew suspicious and Vidura's warning which was conveyed through the coded message was confirmed. The Kauravas' plan chalked out with so much hope to burn the Pandavas alive got exposed long before its execution – no doubt a grave security lapse.

The Kauravas also miserably failed to build up intelligence operations in executing their plan. They were completely indifferent to the activities of the Pandava well-wisher Vidura who was a powerful person in the court of Hastinapura kingdom with vast resources and manpower under his command. He was privy to all decisions and consultations held in the royal court. The Kauravas kept no information about the movements and activities of Vidura's agents. They were completely in the dark with regard to Vidura's successful unearthing of their plan against the Pandavas at Varanavat. Moreover, they did not mount any effective surveillance on the new house at Varanavat. Because of this the *khanaka* could enter the house unnoticed by anyone and met Yudhisthira with the message of Vidura from Hastinapura. The Pandavas stayed in the house for about a year. Purochana did not apply his mind to the possibility that the Pandavas, who were strong and armed, might devise some way to flee from the house. He and his men also failed to detect the presence of the boatman at the bank of the Ganges sent by Vidura from distant Hastinapura. It appears the Kauravas were doubly sure about the success of their plan to burn the Pandavas alive and as such they did not consider it necessary to devise any contingency measures in order to meet unforeseen developments. This is against the established principles of security. The Kauravas paid a heavy price for these lapses. They not only failed to execute their plan but also lost one of their key men, Purochana.

Even after the destruction of the house, the Kauravas did not act prudently. They believed the report of the citizens about the death of the Pandavas and mother Kunti without any verification whatsoever. If the six burnt skeletons found in the house had been examined by the experts, their real identity could have been easily established. The hunters were short in size while the Pandavas were tall. With expert examination it could have been easily established that the skeletons were not of the Pandavas and of mother Kunti. The burnt house was also not searched properly. If that was done, some remnants of the tunnel even after repairs by *khanaka* could have been detected. The footprints of the Pandavas along the path of retreat and on the river bank could also have been found.

There seemed to be no limit to the worthlessness of the Kauravas. On the other hand Vidura's counter measures right from the beginning of unearthing of the plan of the Kauravas, were meticulously planned. Yudhisthira, assisted by his valiant brothers and the *khanaka* executed them timely and intelligently ensuring their successful escape. In this daring intelligence operation Vidura was indeed the principal spy-master.

9.

The close and intimate relations of Vidura with the Pandavas, particularly Yudhisthira, give rise to certain questions. To get some idea we shall have to delve into the story of birth of three brothers viz. Dhritarashtra, Pandu and Vidura. Shantanu, the king of Hastinapura had a son named Devavrata, later known as Bhishma (meaning capable of performing the most arduous tasks) by wife Ganga. In due course Devavrata, then a young man of great valour, was installed as the Crown Prince. In the mean time Ganga for some differences with king Shantanu, had departed for her original abode, the river Ganges. Shantanu was forlorn and unhappy. One day in the course of his tours he saw Satyavati, the beautiful daughter of the local king of the fishermen and wanted to marry her. The fisherman king, however, laid the condition that his daughter's son would have to be made the king of Hastinapura after him. This condition was not acceptable to Shantanu.

He returned to the capital very sad. His health deteriorated with the passage of time. He could not pay attention to the royal duties. Devavrata heard everything, went to the fisherman king and accepted his condition for the marriage of his daughter. He also declared, in the presence of the accompanying courtiers and others that he would not accept the throne and would remain unmarried throughout his life, paving the way for his daughter's son to become the king. After this great vow Devavrata came to be known as Bhishma.

King Shantanu had two sons Chitrangada and Vichitravirya by Satyavati. Chitrangada while young lost his life at the hands of Gandharvas. On the death of Shantanu, Vichitravirya ascended the throne. Bhishma, who as the elder brother was running the affairs of the kingdom, brought three daughters of the king of Kashi viz. Amba, Ambika and Ambalika by force from the *Swayambarasabha* for marrying Vichitravirya. Of them, the eldest Amba refused to be married to Vichitravirya as she was already betrothed to king Shalya. The marriage of Vichitravirya with the other two princesses was solemnized with great pomp and grandeur. Vichitravirya died without having any issue. Mother Satyasvati was worried about the future heir to the throne. On her wishes Vyasa (her son before marriage from union with sage Parasara) fathered three sons viz. Dhritarashtra, Pandu and Vidura from the widows and maidservant of Vichitravirya.

Dhritarashtra was blind from birth and as such his first claim to the throne was bypassed. Pandu was made the king. Soon after ascending the throne he went on a military campaign, conquered many countries and brought huge tributes which he presented to his blind elder brother, Dhritarashtra. He thereafter went to the Himalayan forests with his queens Kunti and Madri and stayed there.

Pandu was impotent. The story of the curse of a sage that he would die if he had union with any woman, seems to be a later interpolation in order to hide the stigma. He went to the far away Himalayas, to live there permanently with the intention of begetting children from the queens by some other person. He thought the lonely Himalayas would be more suitable to accomplish the act without the knowledge of others. He begged Kunti to beget children for him by some Brahmin. As described in the Mahabharata, Kunti then told Pandu about the *mantra* she received from sage Durvasa for her services to him before marriage and claimed she could invoke any god to beget children by reciting this *mantra*. (She did not disclose the birth of Karna with Sun God before her marriage.) To Pandu, impotent as he was, it was godsend and he readily agreed to Kunti's proposal. Kunti then with the help of this *mantra* invoked Gods Yama, Pavana and Indra and got three sons – Yudhisthira, Bhima and Arjuna. She, also on Pandu's request taught the *mantra* to the junior queen Madri who with its help invoked the heavenly twins Ashwinikumaras and got twin sons – Nakula and Sahadeva.

Circumstances, however, seem to indicate that Vidura is actually the father of Yudhisthira. There are several factors which give credence to this conclusion. We have already got an idea of Vidura's close and intimate relation with Yudhisthira. Only a father is expected to make so much efforts under grave risk to save the lives of his son and his other brothers as in the Varanavat incident. It may be mentioned, Vidura from the very beginning was against Duryodhana who, he thought, would be a rival claimant to the throne in future. His main aim thus was to ensure Yudhisthira's accession to the throne at the proper time. When on Duryodhana's birth some evil omens were seen, Vidura along with some *Brahmins* suggested his immediate abandonment predicting that his remaining alive, would be the cause of destruction of the Kuru clan.

Dhritarashtra, however, did not agree and Duryodhana's life was saved. We know, Vidura's assessment was correct and the Hastinapura throne became the main bone of contention ultimately between Yudhisthira and Duryodhana.

Pandu announced at the time of departure for the Himalayas that he was going out on a hunting expedition. No king ever took their queens while on hunting. When queens Kunti and Madri accompanied him, it was evident that the purpose of moving to the Himalayas was different. As already mentioned, he planned to have children in complete secrecy. Vidura as *Mahamantri*, it can be reasonably assumed, used to visit this locality periodically to look after the welfare of the royal family. During such visits Vidura developed a close personal relationship with Kunti whose conjugal life was unhappy as Pandu was impotent. The result was the birth of Yudhisthira. Pandu, however, knew him to be the son of the God Yama (Dharma) on the strength of Kunti's *mantra* received from sage Durvasa.

Vidura communicated the secret message to Yudhisthira about the conspiracy of Duryodhana at Varanavat in a peculiar tribal language known to both of them (according to the Mahabharata it was *Mlechcha bhasa* – non-aryan language). This language was not spoken in Hastinapura area. It seems to be the language of local people of the region where Pandu with his royal family was living. Yudhisthira learnt this language in course of conversation with them. It was not difficult for Vidura to pick up the language during his visits to the region. Vidura rightly concluded that communication of the secret message in this language, which was known only to him and Yudhisthira, would remain undisclosed to others. This is also an indirect proof of Vidura's periodic visits to this Himalayan region.

There were deep similarities of character between Vidura and Yudhisthira. Both were embodiment of virtue, truth, justice and wisdom. Dhritarashtra loved his virtuous brother Vidura and summoned him for advice whenever he was in difficulty. In course of such advice, Vidura always pleaded justice for Yudhisthira and his brothers and implored Dhritarashtra to treat the Pandavas like his own sons. Even though he agreed with Vidura, Dhritarashtra pleaded his inability to do anything in the face of Duryodhana's intransigence.

After the death of Vidura in the forest, sage Vyasa told Dhritarashtra that Dharma (Yama) was born on the curse of sage Mandavya as Vidura. He disclosed, 'On the command of Brahma, I fathered Vidura, your brother for Vichitravirya. Vidura is highly esteemed for his devotion to truth, control of senses, adherence to non-violence and charity. Yudhisthira has also been born from Dharma. He who is Dharma, is Vidura and he who is Vidura, is Yudhisthira. By dint of spiritual power Yudhisthira has entered into the body of Vidura.'

This fact of Vidura entering the body of Yudhisthira at the time of his death in the forest has been mentioned in details in the Mahabharata. Vidura accompanied Dhritarashtra, Gandhari, Kunti and Sanjaya to the forest in their old age for penance, *Vaanprastha*. One day Yudhisthira came to the hermitage of Dhritarashtra in the forest to enquire about their welfare. At the hermitage he did not find Vidura. On enquiry from Dhritarashtra he learnt that Vidura was wandering in the nearby forest. He immediately went to the forest and saw Vidura some distance away naked and in emaciated condition. He loudly called Vidura saying he had come to see him. Vidura then leaning against a tree gave a penetrating look at Yudhisthira as he stood in front of him and on the strength of yogic power entered into the body of Yudhisthira organ by organ. Immediately thereafter the lifeless body of Vidura dropped down on the ground.

In ancient days, the father before his death bequeathed to his son not only his material possessions but also his spiritual acquisitions. There was even a special ritual for this purpose. In the *Koushitaki Upanishada*, we find a mention of this ritual. In front of sacrificial fire in a decorated house the father, while reciting the prescribed *mantra,* would touch all the *indriya* of the son one by one and offer his own to him. The son would then accept them. In this way, all the senses i.e. the acquisitions of the father would be transmitted to the son. Vidura similarly transmitted all his spiritual acquisitions to Yudhisthira though there was no elaborate formal ritual as mentioned in the Upanishad – a solemn duty only preserved for the father to his son before death. With regard to Vidura fathering Yudhisthira by Kunti, certain questions may justifiably be raised. Why has not this fact been mentioned in the Mahabharata clearly and unambiguously? The author of the Mahabharata has always been very liberal in depicting sexual exploits of man and woman – high and low. The silence on Vidura's clandestine love affairs with Kunti apparently seems to be a deviation from the normal practice. A deeper analysis of the events of the Mahabharata would, however, show that there was a plausible reason behind this silence. The poet in the Mahabharata has placed before us a wonderful canvas of events centering round the war for the throne of Hastinapura, kingdom of *Kshatriya* dynasty. Only a *Kshatriya* is entitled to ascend to this throne. If Yudhisthira was known to be the son of Vidura, he would earn the stigma of *sutaputra* (Vidura was a *sutaputra* being the son of the maid-servant) thus losing all claim to the throne. Vidura, it may be mentioned, was never considered eligible for the throne. Yudhisthira as the son of Dharma played a key role in the Mahabharata from the beginning to the end. We cannot conceive of any other role for Yudhisthira. As *sutaputra* he would have a minor role, if at all, in the great epic. In fact, we would have then got an entirely different Mahabharata – a proposition beyond our imagination.

Another factor also seems to weigh upon the poet to keep the secret relation between Vidura and Kunti unknown to others. This is the question of stigma that would have been attached to the glorious royal family of

Hastinapura. Engaging an outsider as the wife to beget children was quite acceptable those days. But this was to be done with the consent of the husband, if living, or the family elders. In the case of Yudhisthira it was entirely different. He was born out of illicit union between Vidura and Kunti. Pandu who was living, remained in the dark. He was given to understand that Yudhisthira was born through union with Dharma.

There is yet another reason behind the secrecy of Vidura's relation with Kunti. Vidura from the very beginning tried his best to install Yudhisthira on the throne of Hastinapura – an honour he himself was deprived of as he was a *sutaputra*. He did not want the same misfortune to befall his son Yudhisthira. It seems very likely that on Vidura's advice Kunti concealed Yudhisthira's true identity from Pandu. Everybody knew Yudhisthira as Dharmaputra and the legal son of Pandu. This ultimately paved the way to Yudhisthira's accession to the throne of Hastinapura kingdom.

Evidence – direct, indirect, spiritual and circumstantial – as explained, seems to strongly suggest that Yudhisthira was actually the son of Vidura. This being the fact, behind-the-scene operation of Vidura underlines his deep political foresight besides his competence as a shrewd intelligence operator in successfully keeping his plans, programmes and consultations hidden from the enemies. We shall see similar behind-the- scene operations of Vidura in later incidents also.

10.

Coming to the main story, we find the Pandavas with mother Kunti on reaching the other bank of the Ganges entered the deep forest. Here also they remained tail-conscious like trained spies and kept a vigilant eye all around against possible attack of Duryodhana's agents who might be pursuing them.

Some distance away, Bhima killed a demon named Hidimba when he attacked them. Soon Hirimba's sister Hidimbi appeared before them and sought to marry Bhima. Satisfied with her sincerity, mother Kunti gave approval to the marriage. A son by name Ghatotkacha was born to Bhima from this wedlock. The demon women gave birth immediately after conception and the new-born child also grows up instantly. Ghatotkacha turned out to be as strong as his father and left the place promising all help to the Pandavas.

Thereafter, the Pandavas in the disguise of ascetics began to move through different places. On the way grandfather sage Vyasa advised them to remain in disguise warning that their danger was not yet over. In course of movement they reached a place named Ekchakranagara and put up in the house of a local *Brahmin*. From the *Brahmin* they heard many stories of atrocities committed by a demon by the name of Bakarakshasa. Bhima killed Bakarakshasa, and after placing his dead body at the entrance of the village secretly returned to the *Brahmin*'s house. On the direction of the Pandavas, the *Brahmin* propagated among the people that a great soul possessing mystic power out of kindness had killed Bakarakshaka to save them from his tyranny. The people easily believed this story.

In this way, true identity of Bhima and other Pandava brothers remained unknown to others. It is evident that strict adherence to the principle of maintaining secrecy brought dividend to the Pandavas. This was easier as there was no enemy surveillance on their movements since the Varanavat incident. The death of the terrible Bakarakshasa at the hands of a 'unknown' person created a stir amongst the local people. Any intelligent agent of Duryodhana could have easily found out the mystery of the death. The presence of the Pandavas would have also been found out. The Pandavas survived a great danger because of Duryodhana's failure to be vigilant.

At Ekchakranagara, the Pandavas came to know of the *swayambarasabha* of Draupadi, princess of Panchal kingdom. Grandfather sage Vyasa again appeared before them and disclosed that Draupadi would have five husbands. He advised them to proceed to Viratnagara, capital of Panchal kingdom, to win over Draupadi as their wife. The Pandavas accordingly moved to Viratnagara and stayed as guests in the guise of *brahmacharis* in a potter's house. They began to earn their livelihood by begging.

The Pandavas attended the *swayambarasabha* and took their seat in the enclosure reserved for the *Brahmins*. They saw Duryodhana, Karna and Shakuni in the assembly of suitor kings and princes in a separate row. None could recognize them. Krishna, with elder brother, Balarama was also present in the gathering some distance away. They had only come to witness the ceremony. The Pandavas did not notice them. Krishna, however, recognized the Pandavas and told this only to Balarama. None else got any hint about the presence of the Pandavas in the *swayambarasabha.*

Panchalraj Yajnasena had a strong desire to marry his beautiful Draupadi to the most renowned archer Arjuna, son of king Pandu. With this end in view he got prepared a very strong bow with suitable arrows. His idea was that none other than Arjuna would be able to string and lift the bow. A special target fish was ordered to be placed in the air behind a revolving machine. Panchalraj declared that he would marry his daughter to the person who could pierce the eye of fish with arrow after putting the string to the specially prepared bow.

At the appointed time Dhristadyumna appeared at the *swayambarasabha* along with Draupadi and after announcing the conditions, invited the assembled kings and princes one by one to hit the target with the bow and the arrows kept nearby. Many of the kings and the princes including Duryodhana failed even to string the bow. Some of them thought it prudent not to make any attempt. When Karna advanced towards the bow, Draupadi announced she would not marry a *sutaputra*. Karna then returned to his placed without touching the bow. It was then announced that anyone present in the sabha who could hit the target with the bow and the arrows, would get the hands of Draupadi.

Arjuna then came forward, easily strung the bow and hit the fish's eye five times in the revolving machine. Arjuna's success brought him wide applause from the members of the royal family and other well-wishers. When Draupadi garlanded Arjuna accepting him as her husband, the assembled kings and princes pounced upon the *Brahmins*. In the ensuing battle Bhima and Arjuna defeated them. Karna without recognizing Arjuna praised his archery highly. He, however, had a suspicion about Arjuna's true identity. The battle stopped at the intervention of Krishna. The Pandavas along with Draupadi then returned to their place.

Mother Kunti without seeing Draupadi, asked the Pandavas to divide among them whatever they had brought. Mother's word being inviolable Yudhisthira understood Draupadi would become the wife of all the five Pandava brothers. In the mean time Krishna and Balarama arrived there and congratulated the Pandavas on their successful escape from the *jatugriha* and also for their victory at the *swayambarasabha*. Krishna advised them to remain incognito. The Panchalraj was initially against the marriage of his daughter to the five *Brahmins*. Later when the true identity of the Pandavas was known, he, at the intervention of sage Vyasa, agreed to the marriage.

11.

We find serious lapses on the part of Duryodhana, Karna and Shakuni that they did not notice their presence though they had known the Pandavas more intimately and closely for a much longer period than Krishna. Krishna on entering the *swayambarasabha* immediately recognized the Pandavas in the guise of *Brahmins*. In fact, in the Mahabharata here we find Krishna for the first time in physical form. We understand Duryodhana was engrossed in the thought of Draupadi and had no inclination to look around. But what about Karna and Shakuni? They were said to be very cunning and intelligent. They must have certainly cast their eyes on the assembly. It is baffling how they could miss the presence of the Pandavas though their disguise as *Brahmins* was also not so elaborate as to completely hide their normal physical features. Krishna had no difficulty at all in recognizing the Pàndavas in this disguise. It appears Duryodhana, Karna and Shakuni were so sanguine about the death of the Pandavas at Varanavat that it was beyond their imagination that they could be present in the *swayambarasabha*. Had they been detected before the starting of the ceremony, Arjuna would have got no opportunity to participate in the archery contest. The Pandavas would have also landed in another problem as they were carrying weapons inside their apparel. Though it would have not helped Duryodhana in any way as he failed even to lift the bow, he was to have the satisfaction that at least for the time being, Arjuna, his arch enemy, could not obtain Draupadi.

After the marriage of Draupadi with the Pandavas, Duryodhana who by then had returned to Hastinapura got full identity of the *Brahmins* from his agents who attended the *swayambarasabha*. He knew that the *Brahmin* who had successfully hit the target and defeated Karna, was no other than the third Pandava Arjuna and the *Brahmin* who defeated Madraraj Shalya was the second Pandava Bhima. The agents also informed about the details of marriage of Draupadi with the Pandavas. Duryodhana and all others at Hastinapura understood that the Pandavas did not die in the fire at *jatugriha* Their surprise knew no bounds. This indicates utter failure of Duryodhana's agents to collect timely information about the movements and whereabouts of the Pandavas. Indeed it was a very costly failure for Duryodhana. Had he got the information in advance, he could have planned suitable counter measures to checkmate the Pandavas. Is there also any Vidura's behind-the- scene role in this victory of the Pandavas? The Mahabharata is silent in the matter. We shall discuss the subject later with other details.

12.

The steps taken by the Pandavas, on the other hand, are in sharp contrast with those of Duryodhana and his well-wishers. The Pandavas, we have seen, did not slacken their vigilance even for a moment since they left Varanavat. They kept their identity a secret till they were completely out of danger; they did not give up their disguise as *Brahmins*. During the battle at the *swayamvarasabha*, Arjuna intelligently dispelled Karna's doubt about his identity by telling him that he was a *Brahmin*.

Krishna's role was also correct. Though he could recognize the Pandavas, he preferred to remain silent about their identity. Even after return of the Pandavas to the potter's house along with Draupadi, Krishna rightly advised them to continue to remain in disguise. He thought danger was not yet over for the Pandavas as the Panchalraj was still not reconciled to the marriage of Draupadi to the five unknown *Brahmins* and the hostile kings and the princes had not yet departed. When the Panchalraj came to know of the real identity of the *Brahmins* and the circumstances of their remaining in disguise, he readily agreed to the marriage. In the meantime, the suitor kings and princes had all returned to their respective capitals. Then only the Pandavas were free from danger as they were no longer without friends and allies. The might of Panchalraj was now behind them. With heroes like the Pandavas on his side the Panchalraj also felt relieved of the fear from his enemies.

In addition, the Pandavas had another very important gain. This was the friendship of Krishna. From now on Krishna became the Pandavas' most reliable friend, philosopher and guide. In the alliance of the Pandavas and the Panchal clan with active guidance from Krishna, a formidable military and political power-center was born. Later this power-center became stronger with the joining of other allies and played a vital role in the subsequent developments.

At Hastinapura, Dhritarashtra on hearing the news that the Pandavas were alive and had got Draupadi as their wife, felt very much dejected. He, however, suppressed his feelings and told Vidura he was very happy at the news. He even gave the words that he loved the Pandavas more than his own sons and predicted that one day his wicked sons would perish at the hands of the Pandavas. Duryodhana heard everything and told Dhritarashtra that it was not the time to praise the enemy but to devise means to suppress them.

The weak-minded Dhritarashtra immediately agreed with him and told him that he was praising the Pandavas before Vidura only to keep him in the dark about his real intentions against them. Duryodhana then put forward his various alternate plans against the Pandavas before Dhritarashtra. These were–

1. to create dissension between the three sons of Kunti viz. Yudhisthira, Bhima and Arjuna and the two sons of Madri viz. Nakula and Sahadeva by engaging reliable *Brahmins*,
2. to win over the Panchalraj, his son Dhrishtadyumna and his courtiers by paying them handsome amount of money in order to induce them to forsake the Pandavas or to influence the Pandavas to stay on in the Panchal kingdom so as not to allow them to enter Hastinapura,
3. to create division between the three sons of Kunti by engaging reliable people,
4. to poison the mind of Draupadi by pointing out the sin committed by her in accepting five persons as husband,
5. to kill Bhima, the strongest among the brothers, by engaging an assassin in disguise in order to weaken the Pandavas,
6. to destroy the Pandavas immediately on their return to Hastinapura,
7. to destroy the Pandavas later at a convenient time even if they would remain subservient to the Kauravas,

8. to allure the Pandavas with the help of a beautiful woman in order to create an adverse opinion in the mind of Draupadi against them; and
9. to bring the Pandavas to Hastinapura by deputing Karna and to kill them by some means.

Duryodhana requested Dhritarashtra to accept anyone of the means considered most appropriate. Karna was also requested to give his views in the matter. Karna then said, Duryodhana, "We should not forget we tried various means in the past to destroy the Pandavas; but all our efforts went in vain. I am certain that it would be impossible to destroy the Pandavas by trickery. The Pandavas were then living at Hastinapura helpless and without any resources. Now they have gained strength with active assistance of Panchalraj and are staying in his kingdom in complete security. I am sure the Pandavas will not be swayed by any allurement. The Pandavas are devoted to one wife and as such it is very likely that their brotherly love is very deep. It is, therefore, not easy to drive a wedge among them. Moreover, Draupadi fully knowing Pandavas' miserable condition, has on her own volition married them. It is unthinkable that she will forsake them under any temptation. Specially, it is a great fortune for a woman to have more than one husband. Draupadi has achieved this most coveted thing virtually without any effort. It is unthinkable that she will ever develop any hatred against the Pandavas. The Panchalraj is reported to be a highly religious person without any greed. He will not forsake his own sons-in-law under any allurement. His sons are all virtuous and attached to the Pandavas. They also will not abandon them. In the circumstances it is almost certain the Pandavas cannot be destroyed by any means however special these might be."

Karna then turned to Dhritarashtra and said, "The Pandavas are still without any kingdom and militarily weak. The Panchalraj also is not very strong militarily. The powerful Yadava army under Krishna's leadership has not yet joined the Panchalraj and the Pandavas. This is the best time, I think, to attack the Panchals and the Pandavas. The enemy have to be struck when they are weak. The policy of reconciliation, financial inducement and division as explained in the scriptures, though applicable, would be of no avail in the present situation. This is the time for direct military expedition."

The intelligence operation prepared by Duryodhana to deal with the Pandavas was no doubt elaborate with every detail. It had, however, no relation with the objective situation. Duryodhana took no notice of the strong character of the Pandavas, Draupadi, Panchalraj and his sons. He had no patience to devote his mind to all these details engrossed as he was in his strong intent to destroy the Pandavas at the earliest. He did not even discuss such an important matter with his closest friends and well-wishers. He mainly wanted to accomplish his objective with allurement of money. He forgot that everything could not be achieved with money only. Here, we cannot but praise the practical common sense of Karna, who correctly pointed out the lacunae of Duryodhana's operational plans, and correctly suggested waging of war against the comparatively weak Panchals and the Pandavas. This is completely in accordance with the established war policy which maintains that the king would attack the enemy when he is weak. Of course in the present case any such military expedition against the Pandavas would go against all principles of morality and justice. Yudhisthira was the Crown Prince of Hastinapura kingdom. They had got legitimate claim to the kingdom. They did not do any thing wrong against the Kauravas. The Karauvas rather always tried to harm them and even made attempts to kill them by taking recourse to falsehood. The Pandavas by successfully foiling all their heinous conspiracies, obtained Draupadi by dint of their own strength. Now if the Kauravas did wage war against the Pandavas, it was not only to be naked violation of the moral code, but also an act of abject barbarism. This would also certainly cause widespread discontent among the people of Hastinapura kingdom who held the Pandavas in great love and esteem.

13.

Grandfather Bhishma on hearing everything straightway dismissed Karna's plea to go in for war against the Pandavas and instead suggested division of the Hastinapura kingdom between the Kauravas and the Pandavas in order to permanently put an end to the unending animosity between them. Vidura and other elders supported Bhishma. Dhritaraṣhtra with the approval of the elders thereafter sent Vidura to the Panchal capital and cordially brought back the Pandavas along with Draupadi to Hastinapura. The Pandavas were informed of the decision to divide the kingdom and directed them to build their own capital at a place named Khandavaprastha. The Pandavas thereafter accompanied by Krishna went to Khandavaprastha and built there, with the help of Danava architect Moydanava, an exquisitely beautiful capital with many well-designed mansions. This was actually a gift of Moydanava to the Pandavas for his gratitude to Arjuna for saving his life from the fire of Khandava forest. (On the request of God Agni, Arjuna destroyed the forest by fire, killing innumerable forest-dwellers in order to quench his hunger). On the suggestion of Krishna the capital was named Indraprastha. Yudhisthira became the king of the new kingdom. Krishna, grandfather Bhishma and other elders as also the Kauravas, among many others, were present in the religious ceremony performed with great fanfare on the occasion of the formal entry into the newly-built palace.

Soon Devarishi Narada appeared at Indraprastha and advised the Pandavas to mutually devise a system so that there was no dissension among them over Draupadi. The Pandavas accordingly made a rule that Draupadi would live with one brother at a stretch for a period of one year and that if any one of the other brothers came within his sight during this period, he would have to spend his life for twelve years in the forest practicing austerities. One day Arjuna had to come to the building where Yudhisthira and Draupadi were staying in order to collect weapons for the purpose of protecting the *Brahmins* who were being oppressed by the robbers. This being a violation of the agreed rule, Arjuna went to the forest.

During this period of exile, Arjuna married Manipura princess Chitrangada and Krishna's sister Subhadra. Though this was negation of stipulated austerities, these matrimonial alliances with Yadavas and Manipuris considerably strengthened Pandavas' military and political power. Arjuna returned to Hastinapura after twelve years along with Subhadra.

Sage Narada after some time again came to Indraprastha, as mentioned earlier advised Yudhisthira, on royal duties, security, secret agents etc. Yudhisthira by following Narada's advice soon established an administration in which the people were happy with all their wants and grievances removed. Yudhisthira was held in high esteem and treated by all as their own father. He became known as a person having no enemy. Yudhisthra's affectionate behaviour, Bhimasena's firm rule, Arjuna's successful suppression of the enemy, Nakul's righteous conduct and Sahadeva's natural modesty throughout the kingdom created an atmosphere of peace with all the worries and fears of the people completely removed. As a result of this benevolent role economic activities received tremendous boost. All dishonest employees now engaged themselves in the service of the people.

All rebellion in the conquered territories also ended, restoring law and order throughout the kingdom. It is evident that Yudhisthira and his brothers kept themselves abreast of the situation prevailing in different parts of the kingdom. For this they had to collect information – both good and bad – through various sources. Engagement of secret of agents was one of the principal methods. Yudhisthira in concert with his brothers particularly Bhimasena and Arjuna, took timely action on the basis of the collected information. On many occasions the people on their own came themselves forward to furnish information with their knowledge to the king or his representatives. The secret agents who were well-trained and possessed high morale hardly failed in their mission. Supervision on their work was thorough. All this was possible because of Yudhisthira's just and righteous conduct as the king.

14.

Happy at the prosperity of the kingdom, *Maharaj* Yudhisthira decided to perform *Rajasuyayajna* (sacrifice performed to celebrate king's supremacy over other kings.) On learning Yudhisthira's decision Krishna said, '*Maharaj*, you are adorned with all the qualities to perform *Rajasuyayajna*; but there are some obstacles, which require to be removed first. Yarashandha, the king of Magadha is now very powerful. Shishupala, the powerful king of Chedi, is the commander-in-chief of the vast Magadha army. With active support from a large number of kings, Yarashandha at present is virtually invincible. Realizing it would be impossible to subdue him I myself along with friends and relatives have fled to the hilly region of western India. *Maharaj*, Yarashandha is an ardent worshipper of Lord Mahadeva. He has decided to perform an extremely abominable Yajna to propitiate Him. For this purpose he has already kept under captivity 86 kings and with the capture of another 14 kings he would then sacrifice all the 100 kings in the proposed Yajna. He is a terror throughout his kingdom. It would not be proper for you to perform *Rajasuyayajna* without first destroying Yarashandha.

Describing Yarashandha's birth history Krishna said, "Magadharaj Vrihadratha married two twin daughters of the king of Kashi: but none bore him any son. One day, sage Chandrakoushika appeared at his capital and the king received him with many presents. On learning that the king was without any son, the sage out of kindness gave him a mango purified with hymns saying this fruit would fulfill his wishes. The queens partook the mango and in due course they gave birth to two human lumps each with one eye, one arm, one foot and half face and buttock. The queens were afraid at the sight of the two strange-looking human lumps and on their direction the female attendants threw the lumps outside. A *Rakshashi* named Yara was passing through that side and as she united the two lumps, a strong boy was formed. The boy immediately began to cry like rumble of clouds. On hearing the cry the king and the queens brought him inside the palace. As the boy came into existence on being united by Yara Rakshashi, the king gave his name Yarashandha. After some time, sage Chandrakoushika again came to the capital and predicted that the new-born prince would become very powerful and possess huge wealth. No other king would be as powerful. Any one opposing him would face sure death. He would not feel any pain even if struck by gods. The prince would have the rare fortune of having an audience with the Supreme God Mahadeva. Continuing Krishna said, 'All the predictions of sage Chandrakoushika came true. On ascending the throne, Yarashandha successfully established his supremacy over other kings. Mahadeva on being satisfied with his worship actually appeared before him. With Mahadeva's blessings he became more powerful.

Explaining his plan to kill Yarashandha, Krishna said, 'Yarashandha's two powerful followers Hangsa and Dimbaka are already dead. His son-in-law Kangsa had also been killed by me. This is the best time to destroy Yarashandha. He, however, cannot be killed in any frontal attack. We shall have to take recourse to disguise in entering his capital and induce him to a wrestling combat. I can claim to be a strategist while Bhimasena is physically strong. Both of us will be protected by heroic Arjuna Our combined strength will kill him easily. When we attack him alone, Yarashandha will certainly choose one of us for wrestling. I am certain he will invite Bhimasena who is the strongest among us. *Maharaj*, if you have confidence in me, you may please allow Bhimasena to accompany us".

With Yudhisthira's approval, Krishna, Bhimasena and Arjuna left Indraprastha in the guise of *Brahmin* youths and after passing through many areas, entered Magadha kingdom. Krishna, who knew the topography, was the guide. Avoiding the main entrance they took a different route to Giribraja, the capital city. *En route* they destroyed a hill top and entered the city. They also destroyed three big drums made of the skin of a demon placed near the entrance. The drums were designed to create a sound on being struck which continued for one month. With their destruction there was no warning sound. The entry of Krishna, Bhimasena and Arjuna thus remained unnoticed by others.

In the mean time Yarashandha's *Brahmin* priests felt the advent of some bad omens. On their instruction, Yarashandha performed some religious rituals for his protection.

In the city, Krishna forcibly collected garlands and other decorative materials from a flower vendor and put them on. He then entered the palace unopposed along with Bhimasena and Arjuna in the guise of *Brahmins* as those days *Brahmins* had free access everywhere. They, after passing through many alleys, ultimately appeared before Yarahandha at the hall for sacrificial rites. Yarahandha at that time was on fast performing some special religious rites. He welcomed them with articles of offering and wanted to know the purpose of their visit. Krishna by pointing to Bhimasena and Arjuna said they were observing silence because of religious restrictions and would not speak anything now. Yarashandha then left them at the hall and went inside. He returned after mid-night and performed his prescribed rites. Thereafter he observed, *Brahmin* youths put on garlands and other decorations only at the time of joining any religious assembly. "I am rather surprised to see you all dressed in red and wearing garlands with sandalwood marks. Moreover, there are bowstring– marks on your arms. Avoiding the main gate you have entered the capital through another route after destroying the Chaitya mountain. I also find no reason why you have refused my offerings. You do not seem to be *Brahmins*. I would ask you to disclose your real identity", he said.

Krishna said in reply, "King, *Brahmin*, *Kshatriya* and *Vaishya* (trading class) are all free to take up religious austerities. There is also no restriction for them to put on garlands and other religious decorations. We are *Kshatriya*; physical strength is our main stay. If you so wish, you may show your valour even today. The intelligent people enter the enemy's house secretly and the friend's openly. We have not accepted your offerings because we have entered enemy's house now."

Yarashandha then said, "I do not remember to have committed any hostile act against you. Why are you considering me as your enemy? I am devoted to my own religion. I have not done any harm to my subjects."

Krishna, thereafter, narrated various charges against Yarashandha and said, "You have kept in captivity many kings to sacrifice them in order to propitiate Lord Mahadeva. We shall in no case allow you to perform this sinful act. For this, we have entered your palace secretly to kill you. I am Krishna, son of Vasudeva and my companions are the sons of Pandu. If you do not agree to release the kings from captivity, your death is certain at our hands. You may select any one of us for wrestling'.

Krishna's earlier anticipation proved correct. Yarashandha selected Bhimasena for wrestling who was the strongest among the three. The fierce wrestling between Yarashandha and Bhimasena was held in the royal wrestling ground in the presence of a large gathering and it continued for thirteen days. On the fourteenth day Yarashandha who was on fast, became tired. On Krishna's signal Bhimasena tore him apart. His lifeless body lay motionless on the ground in two parts as at the time of his birth.

On Yarashandha's death all the kings in captivity were released. Yarashandha's son, Shahadeva was installed on the throne of Magadha kingdom. The new king and the other released kings accepted the invitation to attend the Rajasuyayajna at Indraprastha.

In the entire incident over the death of Yarashandha, we find a successful application of the various principles with regard to politics, security and intelligence operation. Behind this success lie Krishna's farsightedness, resourcefulness, indomitable courage and ability to take risk. Krishna planned to destroy Yarashandha mainly for two reasons:

First, he wanted to ensure peaceful performance of Yudhisthira's *Rajasuyayajna*. Krishna realized Yarashandha, powerful as he was, with a standing army of 23 *akshowhinis*, would not allow any other king to perform *Rajasuyayajna*. His destruction, therefore, had to be accomplished first. As it was impossible to defeat Yarashandha in any frontal attack, Krishna had to take recourse to deception. Of course this involved serious risk. He had to give an opportunity to the enemy to choose his own rival. Yarashandha could have easily chosen physically weaker Krishna or Arjuna for wrestling, result of which would have been disastrous. But Krishna was sanguine Yarashandha as a true *Kshatriya* would never choose a weaker rival for the fight. This, we know, came correct. At the same time it would have been quite justified for Yarashandha to reject Krishna's suggestion of wrestling and instead straightaway destroy, by any method of his own choosing, Krishna, Bhimasena and Arjuna who had secretly entered his palace to kill him.

Secondly, Krishna was determined to stop Yarashandha's extremely abominable plan of sacrificing the kings held in captivity on the plea of propitiating Lord Mahadeva. As Yarashandha was in no mood to relent from his plan, his destruction became inevitable.

There was another hidden but very important reason behind this plan against Yarashandha. We are aware that Krishna had to flee to the western region of the country out of fear of Yarashanhas. He never forgot this humiliation and was seeking an opportunity to take revenge. This opportunity arose when Yudhisthira decided to perform *Rajasuyayajna.* It was not possible to perform the *yajna* as long Yarashandha was alive. At the same time without the help of Bhimasena and Arjuna. it was impossible to kill him. Krishna, therefore, after explaining the situation, managed to obtain Yudhisthira's consent in allowing them to accompany him in the operation against Yarashandha. On the death of Yarashandha, as per the plan, Krishna's principal enemy was eliminated – a successful act of revenge which he was pining for long. His aim of obtaining the release of the captive kings was also fulfilled. Judged from this angle, Krishna's success was a marvellous achievement.

On the death of Yarashandha, the Pandavas became stronger with the support of the released kings and other allies. Krishna came closer to the Pandavas.

Krishna was an experienced war strategist. He knew the importance of operational intelligence. From the friendly kings and courtiers as also from the secret agents, he collected all the required information about Yarashandha and his kingdom. All such advance information contributed to the success of his plan against Yarashandha.

We come across some rather serious lapses in executing the plan. Krishna, Bhimasena and Arjuna did not seem to have taken adequate steps to keep their identity concealed on entry into the Magadha kingdom. It was imprudent on their part to forcibly collect garlands and other decorative materials from the flower vendor in the capital risking the exposure of their identity. We did not expect such an immature act on the part of Krishna. We wonder why they did not purchase the articles with money. We also find no reason why they did not enter the capital through the main gate. As *Brahmin* youths, their movements were unrestricted and as such they could easily pass through the main gate. The other route through the hilly area was obviously risky.

Yarashandha's lapses were many. His secret agents were in the dark about the entry of the three into the capital not to speak of Krishna's secret plan. The incident of forcible collection of flowers etc., by Krishna and others, was also unknown to his men engaged for the maintenance of law and order. In the guise of *Brahmins* they managed to appear before Yarashandha in the sacrificial hall inside the palace without being asked a single question on the way by the security personnel. This seems very unusual. It appears from his talks with Krishna that Yarashandha knew before hand about their entry into his capital by a different route avoiding the main gate. Though this surreptitious entry was obviously ill-motivated, no action was taken against them. We find no explanation for all these serious lapses. Did Yarashandha have the premonition of the impending danger to his life following the evil omens? Death being inevitable did he realize the futility of any security measures? His inaction or indifference was almost suicidal.

All said and done, there is no gainsaying the fact that Yarashandha was a great king. As a warrior he was second to none. Krishna himself, a great hero with supernatural powers, was afraid of meeting him in any frontal attack and preferred to take shelter in safety in a far-off land. Yarashandha built a large empire by conquering many territories. His standing army was the largest at that time. He was a highly religious person with ardent devotion for Lord Mahadeva. The story of his plan to sacrifice the captive kings to propitiate Mahadeva seems unbelievable. Lord Mahadeva is known to be the god of well-being and it seems absurd that Mahadeva would demand the sacrifice of so many kings for Himself. The poet of the Mahabharata apparently introduced this story of human sacrifice to prove Yarashandha's cruel nature thereby justifying Krishna's intervention to destroy him. Krishna, in fact, wanted to eliminate Yarashandha as he was his arch enemy and the principal architect of the rival power-centre.

Yarashandha was a simple-hearted warrior. He was true to his *kshastriyadharma.* As a kshatriya king, he could not refuse any invitation to war even in adverse circumstances. He could also not fight with anyone inferior to him in strength. He thus chose Bhimasena, the strongest of the three as his true rival in wrestling. He fought for thirteen long days while in fasting and died a very painful death – due to Krishna's treachery in his own capital in presence of his courtiers, army commanders and many others – his body being pierced through the middle by Bhimasena.

15.

Following the death of Yarashandha, preparations were afoot at Indraprastha for the *Rajasuyayajna.* At this time, Krishna appeared at Indraprastha from Dwaraka where he had departed after the operation at Giribraja. On invitation grandfather Bhishma, Drona, Kripa, Vidura, the Kaurava princes as also Shishupala and many other kings and *Brahmins* came to attend the *yajna.* On the day of *yajna,* Sahadeva with the approval of Bhishma, presented the best oblation to Krishna in recognition of his superior valour and strength. None else among the assembled wise men, kings and princes was considered eligible for this honour. At this, Shishupala, the arch enemy of Krishna with memories of the horrible death of Yarashandha still fresh in mind, took exception to this special honour and respect shown to Krishna, first rebuked Bhishma and Yudhisthira and then insulted Krishna with very ugly invectives. He even defiantly challenged Krishna for a fight. All attempts to pacify him went in vain. Krishna earlier had promised not to harm Shishupala who happened to be his cousin (aunt's son) till his completion of one hundred offences. With the latest invective his hundredth offence being completed, Krishna beheaded him with his *chakra.* None among the assembled dignitaries came forward to his help. With the removal of all obstacles, performance of the *yajna* passed off peacefully. Krishna then bid adieu to all and returned to Dwaraka.

It is evident from the above episode that Shishupala had completely lost all sense of judgement because of his ego and blind hatred for Krishna. He dared to challenge Krishna who was second to none in valour and strength and that too in a place where the brave Pandava brothers and their allies were present. He forgot the command in the scriptures regarding behaviour towards the strong. When he could have thought of dealing with Krishna by some tactful means, he foolishly preferred to go in for direct confrontation. He apparently learned nothing from the death of Yarahandha. In the death of Shishupala another anti-Krishna power centre came to an end. The Pandavas also gained immensely.

Duryodhana, while attending the *Rajasuyayajna*, was dumbfounded to see the wonderful artistic design of the assembly hall. Such artistic works he had not even seen at Hastinapura. While moving through the palace buildings made of crystals, causing optical illusion, he fell into water and got his clothes wet as he was passing through a dry plot of land. At another place a plot of dry land was thought to be submerged under water and he started walking through it after raising his clothes lest those get wet. Similarly, an open door was mistaken to be closed and he turned back without proceeding further. Bhimasena, Arjuna and Draupadi burst into laughter at the predicament of Duryodhana. Utterly harassed, Duryodhana returned to Hastinapura very sad. He then became engrossed in hatching a new conspiracy against the Pandavas.

Shakuni, on hearing everything assured Duryodhana that he would win over for him the entire kingdom of Yudhisthira with all its wealth and resources by defeating him in dice-game in which he had special expertise. He advised Duryodhana to invite Yudhisthira to Hastinapura for the dice-game. Duryodhana accordingly requested Dhritarashtra to send an invitation to Yudhisthira for the game. Initially Dhritarashtra was against such a game. Ultimately on Duryodhan's insistence, he agreed to send the invitation to Yudhisthira disregarding the advice of Vidura and other elders. Vidura was sent to Indraprastha with the invitation.

We are aware of the subsequent developments to which we have earlier referred in a different context.

16.

Duryodhana was utterly disappointed at the failure of his plan to capture the Indraprastha kingdom. He also became particularly worried at the thought that the Pandavas and specially Bhimasena would never forgive the Kauravas for the humiliation of Draupadi. The only course now open to him was to send the Pandavas to exile in the forest by defeating them in the dice-game again. On his insistence, Dhritarashtra, as we know, recalled the Pandavas to play the game for the second time. This time also Shakuni played the game on behalf of Duryodhana with the consent of Yudhisthira and won. The Pandavas along with Draupadi then went to the forest. At that time, evil omens were seen indicating a serious calamity for the Hastinapura kingdom. The dice-game made the war inevitable between the Kauravas and the Pandavas.

Vidura, Bhishma and other elders were all against the dice-game. Vidura's protestation was most vocal. He, however, could not get any advance information about Duryodhana's conspiracy behind the game. It seems he was only worried about the harmful consequences of the dice-game between the cousin brothers and warned Dhritarashtra, accordingly. He could not conceive that the dice-game would take such an ugly turn, and that it was only a clever ploy meticulously planned by Duryodhana to capture the Indraprashtha kingdom by sending the Pandavas to the forest. Vidura knew Duryodhana had returned from Indraprashtha very sad and dejected. Duryodhana's frequent secret parleys with Shakuni and Karna were also not unknown to him. It was only expected of a person of Vidura's knowledge and experience that he would initiate action to unearth the motive of Duryodhana, a known enemy of the Pandavas. Dhritarashtra, with whom he was in constant touch, was himself a party to this conspiracy. Yet, he could get no hint of the conspiracy. Had he known of the conspiracy beforehand he could have forewarned Yudhisthira against agreeing to Shakuni, a person of conspiratorial character and an expert in dice-game, playing on behalf of Duryodhana. This was a great success of the Kauravas in keeping their consultations completely secret. On the other hand, this was a serious intelligence failure on the part of Vidura for which we apparently find no explanation, whatsoever. Yet, we know how successfully Vidura had unearthed the bigger conspiracy to burn the Pandavas alive at Varanavat. The explanation of this rather unusual intelligence failure on Vidura's part, perhaps, lies elsewhere. In the story of the Mahabharata, as depicted by the poet, Yudhisthira's defeat in the dice-game and the exile of the Pandavas and Draupadi to the forest has been the most important incident. Despite many contradictions, the poet has very skilfully presented his wonderful story on this central theme of Yudhisthira's defeat in the dice-game. He has rightly brushed aside any other factor that may interfere with his grandiose scheme. Vidura's 'failure' to unearth the conspiracy is indeed a reflection of the poet's deliberate intention in conformity to his planned presentation of events in the Mahabharata.

Duryodhana has justified the seizure of Yudhisthira's kingdom through deceitful dice-game. According to him, it is incumbent on the part of a *Kshatriya* king to expand his empire by conquering foreign kingdoms. There is no question of any morality or immorality here. If the objective cannot be achieved by direct confrontation, deception must be taken recourse to. This is why, he maintains, he did not hesitate to adopt deceitful means against Yudhisthura. Krishna and the Pandavas, as we shall see later, also took resort to such deceits and falsehoods to achieve their objectives. In those days this characteristic of the *Kshatriyas* was an accepted fact. The relations between the Kauravas and the Pandavas reached a point of no return. Duryodhana's jealousy to see the wealth and resources and the might of Yudhisthira at Indraprashtha, was quite natural. Besides, his mind was poisoned at the humiliation and jeering he suffered at Indraprashtha. All this rather spontaneously roused his spirit of revenge. He found in the suggestion of Shakuni, adept in the various tricks of the dice-game, to play the game on his behalf, a ray of hope towards fulfillment of his long-cherished desire to vanquish the Pandavas. He felt relieved when Yudhisthira himself consented to play the game with Shakuni and agreed to the terms and conditions of the game as laid down by Duryodhana. In this, Duryodhana can no way be blamed. In the excitement of the game Yudhisthira lost everything and for this catastrophe he alone is responsible. Actually Yudhisthira had a desire to capture the Hastinapura empire by winning the dice-game. He, however, only loved to play the dice-game without having the necessary expertise. His defeat was thus only a foregone conclusion when a person like Shakuni happened to be his opponent.

Draupadi's humiliation at the hands of the Kauravas in the open royal court (if at all such an incident took place as depicted in the Mahabharata. The dice-game as explained earlier most probably took place only once) was grotesque and utterly condemnable. We are surprised to see the indifferent attitude of grandfather Bhishma, the doyen of the Kuru clan known for his sense of justice and fair-play, to Draupadi's humiliation in the open court – an act that tantamounts to his support to Duryodhana's despicable actions. He had earlier pledged to protect the Hastinapura empire under all circumstances, and it is an irony of fate that the dice-game and Draupadi's humiliation which took place in his very presence, ultimately brought down the same empire following a fratricidal war.

After the defeat in the dice-game, the Pandavas along with Draupadi went to the forest. Royal priest Dhyaumma and many *Brahmins* accompanied them. After covering a long distance, they established their first hermitage on the bank of the river Saraswati near the gulf of Kutch.

17.

On this side at Hastinapura, Dhritarashtra perturbed at the departure of the Pandavas to the forest, told Vidura, "You possess pure wisdom. You are aware of the finest elements of *dharma.* Moreover, you have no sense of distinction between the Kauravas and the Pandavas. Now tell me how justice can be done to both the sides."

Vidura said in reply, "*Maharaj*, your sons have defeated Yudhisthira in the dice-game through deceitful means. Now your best course would be to return him his kingdom. Otherwise, I warn, the entire Kuru clan would be destroyed at the hands of the Pandavas. I suggest let Duryodhana, Shakuni and Karna owe their allegiance to the Pandavas, and Duhshasana seek pardon from Draupadi and Bhimasena. You may pacify Yudhisthira and install him again in his kingdom."

Vidura's advice was not liked by Dhritarashtra. He said, 'Vidura, it appears you are telling me all these things only for the good of the Pandavas. How can I forsake my own sons? Your advice is insincere and deceitful. I don't require you any more. You may go anywhere you like'.

Chastised by Dhritarashtra, Vidura went to the hermitage of the Pandavas in the forest. Narrating the incident to Yudhisthira, Vidura said, 'Yudhisthira, I am giving you some advice, listen to me attentively. Remember, he who waits with an attitude of forgiveness even after suffering indignities at the hands of the enemy, is great. He alone can enjoy the entire world. He who enjoys worldly comforts equally with his friends, is certain to get all help from them in times of difficulty.' Vidura meant to say Yudhisthira should be mentally prepared to forgive the Kauravas after the period of exile was over and at the same time he should continue to maintain good relations with his friendly kings. Vidura thus intelligently put forward Yudhisthira's future course of action. He maintained Yudhisthira on return from exile should first try for a honourable settlement with the Kauravas and if that failed, he must be prepared for war with the help of his friends and allies.

In the meantime, Dhritarashtra became restless at the absence of Vidura at Hastinapura. He called back Vidura by sending a messenger and all ill-feelings between them ended.

Duryodhana was alarmed at the return of Vidura. On the suggestion of Karna he prepared a plan to destroy the Pandavas in the forest by direct armed action. It was thought that the Pandavas without any outside help in the forest were now militarily weak and this was the best time to attack them. Sage Vyasa came to know of Duryodhana's plan with the help of his spiritual powers and persuaded him to cancel his proposed expedition. He advised Dhritarashtra to keep his sons under strict discipline. Later, sage Maitreya met Dhritarashtra and advised him to amicably settle all differences. He warned Duryodhana against doing anything evil against the Pandavas who, he said, were devoted to truth and possessed immense power. Besides, all-powerful Krishna happened to be their patron. Under no circumstances, he warned, the Pandavas could be defeated. Duryodhana, however, was not impressed and he continued to conspire against the Pandavas.

Duryodhana's assessment about the power of the Pandavas was entirely wrong. They were not militarily weak even in the forest. Besides Krishna with his divine power, the might of the king of Panchal was behind them. The Pandava brothers themselves were all extremely proficient in the art of warfare. In the fight with clubs Bhimasena was unparalleled. In archery, Arjuna's competence was well-known. Nakul and Sahdeva, though young, were also great warriors. Among the brothers only Yudhisthira was somewhat comparatively weak in martial art. His strength, however, lay elsewhere. Duryodhana took no notice of these facts and imprudently decided to proceed against the Pandavas.

18.

On hearing the news of the Pandavas' exile, Krishna along with his friends arrived at the hermitage of the Pandavas in the Kamyaka forest on the banks of river Saraswati to enquire about their welfare. At this time Draupadi's brothers and relatives also arrived. They heard from Yudhisthira about the circumstances leading to their exile to the forest. On hearing everything Krishna told Yudhisthira, "*Dharmaraj*, you may be rest assured that Duryodhana, Karna, Shakuni and Duhshasana who had committed deadly sins, must untimely die.

We shall defeat your enemies and install you on the throne. According to *sanatanadharma* the followers of the wicked are also liable to be killed." While speaking Krishna flew into a flame of anger. It appeared he would destroy the entire universe. Alarmed at the sight of Krishna, Arjuna pacified him by singing his earlier great deeds. Krishna assuming his normal self said, 'Partha, (Arjuna's another name) you and I are one and undivided. He who hates you also hates me. You are *Nar* and I am *Narayana*. We have been born in this world as *Nara-Narayana*).'

Thereafter, Draupadi reciting the song of praise for Krishna said, "Keshava, (Krishna's another name) now I am realizing I am without husband and son; I know I have no friend, no brother, no father and not even you. Disregard shown by you all towards me and my humiliation in the open court and Karna's sarcasm in my predicament are burning my heart day and night." Draupadi overwhelmed with grief then starting sobbing with tears rolling down her cheeks.

Krishna was deeply moved at the terrible mental distress of Draupadi. Consoling her he said, "*Bhabini,* (charming lady) please know it that those who have humiliated you shall all die by Arjuna's arrows. I shall leave no stone unturned to fulfill your wishes. I am taking the true vow I shall install you as the empress."

Brother Dhrishtadyumna said, "Dear sister, I tell you in the battle field I shall kill Drona, Shikhandi, our brother will kill Bhishma, Bhima will destroy Duryodhana while Arjuna will eliminate Karna. We are capable of even defeating Indra, king of gods with the help of Krishna and Balarama (Krishna's elder brother – a great hero)."

Turning to Yudhisthira, Krishna said, "*Maharaj*, your sufferings have been caused because of my absence from Dwaraka. Even though I was not invited, I would have gone to Hastinapura and stopped the dice-game explaining its dangerous consequences to both the sides. But Shalba, son of Shishupala attacked our capital city to avenge his father's death. After repulsing his attack I had to proceed to Shouvanagara, capital of Shalbaraj to destroy it. This is why I was delayed and could not attend the dice-game."

Thereafter, Krishna discussed their future strategy with the Pandavas and the assembled kings and princes and assured the Pandavas of all help. On conclusion of the discussion Krishna and others left for their respective kingdoms leaving the Pandavas in the forest.

It was clear from the observations of Krishna and Dhristadyumna that war with the Kauravas was inevitable, and that the Pandavas would capture the entire Hastinapura empire on the defeat and death of the Kauravas and their allies. Could Duryodhana collect, through his secret agents, the details of this very important meeting of Krishna with the Pandavas, Dhristadyumna and others in the forest? It does not seem so. There is no mention of this fact in the Mahabharata story. During the stay of the Pandavas in the forest, many sages with spiritual powers of predicting the past, present, and the future, gave blessings to Yudhisthira of getting back his kingdom at the end of their present ordeal. In those days such predictions or blessings of virtuous sages did not go in vain. In the determination of future events such predictions and blessings were an important factor. Duryodhana was apparently indifferent to such matters. That the Pandavas were determined to take revenge on the Kauravas was also a known fact. It was easily conceivable that the Pandavas would try to increase their strength while in exile. That Krishna and the relatives and allies of the Pandavas would come to their help in such a difficult time, was a foregone conclusion. Duryodhana also did not seem to have given adequate attention to such matters, either. He seemed to be happy and contended only by sending the Pandavas to the forest. He apparently learned no lessons from the successful escape of the Pandavas from the *jatugriha* at Varanavat.

19.

After this, the Pandavas shifted to the Dvaita forest on the bank of the same Saraswati river. One day sage Markendeya appeared at their hermitage and on casting his look on the Pandavas burst into laughter. On being asked by Yudhisthira about the reason, the sage said, "Son, I did not laugh out of any happiness. Suddenly the story of exile of virtuous Ramchandra, son of Dasharatha came to my mind. Though profoundly wise and possessing power just like Indra, he suffered immensely by going to the forest on the wishes of his father. There is no doubt you also like Ramachandra would one day regain your kingdom with your own strength after undergoing suffering in the forest." The Pandavas were happy to hear his prediction.

One day the Pandavas and Draupadi were discussing about their exile among themselves. Draupadi asked Yudhisthira, "*Maharaj*, would you forgive those who are responsible for our present terrible sufferings in the forest? It is said there are no *Kshatriyas* who are without anger. But you seem to be different. The *Kshatriya* who does not show anger, is despised by everybody. The demon king Bali once asked his virtuous grandfather Prahlad - which is superior between forgiveness and force? Prahlad then explained, no good work is possible only by forgiveness or force. He who always forgives the offenders, is unable to establish his sway over others. The enemy taking advantage of his weakness, ultimately destroys him. Similarly the person who is always guided in his action by anger and force, brings his own downfall by creating enmity with everybody. Prahlad advised Bali to take recourse to forgiveness and force on due consideration to place, time and the person concerned. *Maharaj*, I think it is time for you to take recourse to force against your enemy. The Kauravas, who out of sheer greed, have deprived you of your kingdom, do not deserve any mercy and must not be forgiven."

Consoling Draupadi, Yudhisthira said, "My dear, all evils originate from anger. At the same time good comes to the person who can control his anger. Those capable of controlling their anger have been described as strong by the wise men. Forgiveness is the only distinction of a person known for his truth and virtue. How can I forsake forgiveness? I believe the Kauravas would ultimately return our kingdom on the efforts of Bhishma, Krishna and other elders who are all wedded to peace. Duryodhana is unsuitable for royal duties. He has no idea about the greatness of forgiveness. I am superior to the Kauravas in all respects. This is why forgiveness is rooted in me. I shall never forsake forgiveness."

Expressing surprise at the words of Yudhisthira, Draupadi said, '*Maharaj*, so far you have performed all your duties according to *dharma.* Except *dharma,* you have forsaken everything including even your wife and brothers. I have heard *Dharma* does not forsake the king who performs his duties according to the tenets of *dharma.* Now I find *Dharma* is not protecting you. It is beyond our imagination how you, being the embodiment of all virtues including simplicity and truth, could lose your sense of judgement during the dice-game. To see your misfortune and wicked Duryodhana's wealth I am constrained to believe that God is not impartial. For this partisan behaviour I lay all blame on God."

Yudhisthira said in reply, "My dear, I perform religious rites as prescribed in the scriptures without expecting any return. It is not unknown to you that many sages and saints have attained better glory than even the gods by performing their duties in accordance with the tenets of *dharma.* You should not blame *Dharma* or God simply because I have not yet got anything in return. Shun your atheism. Do not ever show any disregard to the Almighty God."

Draupadi on hearing Yudhisthira mellowed down somewhat. She said, "*Maharaj*, I am not despising *Dharma* or God. Being overwhelmed with grief I am only expressing my mental anguish. I have something more to say. I would urge you to kindly give up your inertia during our present difficulty and resume manly activity. Kindly do not waste your time by simply depending on divine powers."

On hearing the arguments and counter arguments between Yudhisthira and Draupadi, Bhimasena became furious. Addressing Yudhisthira he angrily said, "*Maharaj*, wicked Duryodhana has deprived us of our kingdom by deceitful dice-game. We are now living in forest in extreme distress. By accepting your allegiance we are causing pain to our friends and allies and happiness to our enemy. In the name of *dharma* you have remained indifferent to the worldly affairs losing your manliness. The *dharma* which gives pain to oneself and his friends and allies is not *dharma* at all. It is mentioned in the scriptures that every person should pursue *dharma,* wealth and salvation equally. Only by using force wealth can be acquired. I would request you to take steps to destroy the Kauravas with the help of myself and Arjuna. It is possible to create dissensions among the enemy by bribery. We are aware that the gods defeated the more powerful demons by adopting various stratagems. Kindly apply those methods against your enemy. *Maharaj*, all sections of the people of the kingdom love and respect you and they are eagerly waiting for your return. With the help of Krishna, your heroic brothers and the friends and allies it would not be at all difficult to regain our kingdom."

Yudhisthira said in reply, "Brother, I can't blame you though your words are very harsh. I know I alone am responsible for our present distress. I was aware of Shakuni's deceit in the dice-game. But out of anger I lost my patience and continued to play. In the process I lost everything. With the loss of patience a person loses all his good qualities including manliness. This also happened to me. When the dice-game started for the second time, neither Arjuna nor you raised any objection. Now we have come to the forest for twelve years on the solemn promise given to the Kauravas on losing the game. On completion of this period, we are also promise-bound to live incognito for one year. Now it would not be proper to break this promise given in the open court. During the dice-game you, out of anger, were about to destroy my arms; but Arjuna prevented you. Why did you not show your anger before the promise was given? If that happened, I would have perhaps withdrawn from the game. I remained silent at the humiliation of Draupadi. This sorrow has deeply wounded my heart. I am also not finding any strength in my body. Even then I would say we should now wait with patience. I have no doubt we shall see good days again.'

Yudhisthira's words had no impact on Bhimasena. He said, "*Maharaj*, human life is very short. Perhaps during this period of thirteen years, we all shall lose our life. In our misfortune you are simply chanting some instructions of the preceptors without understanding their meaning. How have you been born in the *Kshatriya* clan as a kind-hearted person like a *Brahmin*? You have told us about our one year incognito stay. This is like covering the Himalayas with grass. How would a well-known hero like Arjuna remain incognito for one long year? How and where would our exquisitely beautiful Draupadi live keeping her identity undisclosed? Since boyhood I am well-known among our people. Where would I hide myself either. Your achievements and greatness are universally accepted. How and where would you remain in hiding? I am certain spies of Duryodhana would find us out during our incognito stay and in that case we shall have to go to exile in the forest again. Thus there would be no end to our suffering. The best course for you would be to treat thirteen years as thirteen months and then wage a war for the restoration of the lost kingdom."

At the suggestion of Bhimasena, Yudhisthira thought over his duty for some time. He then said, "My mighty brother, what you have said is no doubt justified. But the work which is performed only by bravery, is sinful. Only that work which is performed after due consultations and considering all aspects, ultimately becomes fruitful. Then divine grace would also be forthcoming. You are embarking on a daring adventure swayed by sheer restlessness without any regard to the actual situation. The Kauravas and their allies are all proficient in the art of warfare. Many of our former allies have joined the Kaurava side. The Kauravas have successfully secured the allegiance of many warriors by showing them proper respect. These kings and warriors will not hesitate to give their lives for the sake of the Kauravas. There is no doubt, despite their impartial attitude grandfather Bhishma, Drona and Kripa will desperately fight for the Kauravas to repay their indebtedness to them for their livelihood. Being armed with divine weapons they are even invincible for the gods. Karna is a hot-tempered person. His body is covered with impenetrable armour. It is not easy to face him. On the other hand, we are virtually helpless and without any resources. In the circumstances it appears impossible for us to defeat the Kauravas."

Bhimasena remained silent on hearing Yudhisthira's reasonable arguments. At this time sage Vyasa appeared there and told Yudhisthira, "My son, I could read your mind by dint of my divine powers. I have found out a way by which Bhishma and others could be prevented from doing any harm to you." After saying this sage Vyasa called Yudhisthira aside and imparted him the all-powerful *pratiswriti* mantra and stated that Arjuna with the help of this mantra will be able to obtain many divine weapons after securing the grace of Lord Mahadeva and Indra, king of the gods. Arjuna accordingly, after learning the mantra from Yudhisthira, left for the Himalayas armed with various weapons.

In the assertions of Draupadi, Yudhisthira and Bhimasena we come across many moral principles with regard to forgiveness, protection of truth, *dharma,* war, practical wisdom, role of secret agents etc. There are some truths in everybody's assertion. Regarding forgiveness, Draupadi's explanation seems to be realistic. Though forgiveness is no doubt a great virtue, its indiscriminate application is definitely counter productive. Success can be achieved mainly by one's own efforts and for this one need not depend only on divine grace – there is also a lot of truth in this statement of Draupadi. The Pandavas' exile to the forest on losing everything following deceitful dice-game cannot be justified in the name of *dharma* as maintained by Bhimasena. There was also truth in his fear that Duryodhana's spies would hunt out the Pandavas during their incognito stay with their consequent re-exile and unending suffering. Bhimasena's suggestion to immediately wage a war against the Kauravas was, however, untenable on account of ground reality.

A closer scrutiny of the arguments of Yudhisthira indicates his profound wisdom with regard to both spiritual and worldly affairs. Frankly admitting his own fault in the dice-game, he stubbornly stuck to the principles of *dharma*, and maintained that every honest effort patiently performed for a right cause ultimately bears fruit with divine grace. He maintained that it would be palpably immoral and repugnant to the principles of *dharma* to go against the solemn promise of living in exile for thirteen years. He was at the same time not oblivious of the practical situation. Even in exile he kept due notice of the strength of the Kauravas and the attitude of Vishwa and others. His knowledge on war strategy bears stamp of an experienced general. His comparative analysis of the strength of the two sides was intended to emphasize the fact that any all-out war with the Kauravas at this stage would be disastrous and that the Pandavas should first try to increase their own strength, and collect information about the preparedness of the Kauravas. Draupadi and Bhimasena seemed to be fully satisfied with Yudhisthira's stand-point and refrained from further arguments. The advice of sage Vyasa to send Arjuna to acquire divine weapons from Lord Mahadeva and Indra, lent further credence to Yudhisthira's assessment of the situation.

It may be mentioned that many Indian sages did possess deep worldly knowledge along with divine powers. We have already referred to sage Narada's advice to Yudhisthira on such mundane affairs like king's duties, security and role of secret agents. Sages like Ramakrishna Paramahansa and Swami Vivekananda, of recent times, also possessed worldly knowledge of high order on different subjects. Divine powers are actually the root of all knowledge and Yudhisthira who was an embodiment of truth and virtue, was no exception. Yudhisthira knew there was substance in Bhimasena's fear about their whereabouts during incognito stay being found out by Duryodhana's spies. We shall see later how the Pandavas in disguise successfully completed their one-year long incognito stay in the palace of king Virata. This was entirely due to the meticulously planned intelligence operation of Yudhisthira. Here his knowledge of worldly affairs was evident again.

The arrival of sage Vyasa at the hermitage of the Pandavas and his advice to send Arjuna to acquire divine weapons, was a very important incident. Duryodhana's agents could not get immediate information about this vital development. There was also no attempts by his agents to follow Arjuna to the Himalayas. Information in this regard reached Hastinapura much later when he had already arrived at Indra's kingdom. This is indeed a serious intelligence failure on the part of Duryodhana. On the other hand, the Pandavas scrupulously followed the principles of security by keeping their consultations completely secret.

20.

In the mean time, Arjuna on instructions from Yudhisthira arrived at the Himalayas and met Indra in the guise of a hermit. Being satisfied with talks with Arjuna, Indra disclosing his identity asked him to pray for a boon. On showing his eagerness to learn the use of all weapons, Indra asked him to first satisfy Lord Mahadeva by undergoing religious austerities. On Indra's departure, Arjuna engaged himself in deep austerities when one day a demon by name Muka, in the guise of a boar, was about to attack him, he immediately struck the boar with an arrow. Just at the same time Lord Mahadeva in the guise of a hunter also pierced the boar with an arrow. On the question as to who first struck the boar an altercation ensued between them. This ultimately led to a duel. Being satisfied with Arjuna in the fight, Lord Mahadeva disclosing his identity asked Arjuna to pray for a boon. On Arjuna's prayer, Lord Mahadeva gave him *pashupat* weapon by name *brahmashira* and taught him the method of its application and retrieval. He told Arjuna, none in the world, not even gods, could stand against this weapon. After this Lord Mahadeva removed all his pain from the body by touching him and advised him to go to Indra in his kingdom.

After the departure of Lord Mahadeva, Indra and queen Indrani accompanied by Yama, Varuna and Kuvera appeared before Arjuna. On Indra's wishes, Arjuna got divine weapons like *danda* (iron staff) from Yama, *pash* (noose) from Varuna and *antardhyana* (stealth weapon) from Kuvera. Indra informed Arjuna he would give him his own divine weapons after he (Arjuna) completed some great deeds in the *swargarajya* (heavens). After this, Arjuna arrived at Indrapuri, accompanied by Indra and Indrani, by Indra's chariot and stayed there for five years. During this period he learned the use of many weapons besides dance and music under the guidance of Chitrasena, king of the Gandharvas. One night *apsara* (heaven's prostitute) Urvashi came to Arjuna's residence to have union with him. On being refused she cursed Arjuna that he would turn into a eunuch dancer losing all honour among the women. On hearing everything Indra asked him not to worry saying the curse would later come to his benefit.

One day, sage Lomasha visited Indrapuri and was surprised to see Arjuna sitting by the side of Indra. Understanding his mind Indra told him Arjuna was his son born of Kunti. Arjuna, he said, had come here for acquiring weapons for some special purpose and would soon return to earth on completion of his task of destroying the demons by the name *Nivathkavacha.* Indra requested sage Lomasha to give this information to king Yudhisthira now staying at Kamyaka forest.

Sage Vyasa was aware of the activities of the Pandavas. On learning from him that Arjuna was now in *swargarajya* to acquire divine weapons from Indra, Dhritarashtra became worried. Disclosing this information to his charioteer Sanjaya he expressed the fear that Duryodhana would soon lose his kingdom as he found nobody on the Kaurava side capable of facing Arjuna in the battlefield as he was now armed with the divine weapons. Agreeing with Dhritarashtra, Sanjaya said, "*Maharaj*, I have heard Arjuna has also got divine weapons from Lord Mahadeva. The Pandavas, it appears, are now invincible even for the gods. The destruction of your sons at the hands of the Pandavas, who are raging in anger of fire, is almost a certainty."

Meanwhile, though delayed Duryodhana's agents informed Hastinapura about the details of the discussions of Krishna, Dhristadyumna and other kings and princes with Yudhisthira in the forest. On hearing Krishna's vow and Dhristadyumna's prowess, Dhritarashtra burst into loud lamentation. He expressed deep regret for disregarding Vidura's warning against the dice-game.

One day when sage Vrihadashwa appeared at the hermitage of the Pandavas, Yudhisthira enquired of him if any other king had suffered like him in the forest. On this sage Vrihadashwa stated King Nala had undergone similar sufferings and then narrated the whole story of Nala and his wife Damayanti. The story reveals how skilfully Damayanti like a shrewd intelligence operator, rescued her missing husband, King Nala, bringing an end to their sufferings.

21.

Nala was the king of Nishadha. In appearance, deeds and heroism he was second to none. His knowledge in dice-game as also his experience about horses was profound. Damayanti – the daughter of king Bhima of Vidarva – was exquisitely beautiful. Even gods were enamoured of her beauty. Many people used to praise Damayanti before Nala and Nala before Damayanti. As a result, Nala and Damayanti developed a deep sense of attachment to each other without even seeing the other. One day Nala captured a beautiful swan with golden wings in the royal garden. Afraid for his life the swan begged

Nala not to harm him promising to perform some work dear to him. He assured Nala he would praise him before Damayanti so that she were to remain ever attached to him. As promised the swan on being released met Damayanti and lavishly praised Nala before her. He later said, "Princess, you are jewel of a woman. Similarly Nala is the best of men. Union of the best man and the best woman is always desirable." After obtaining Damayanti's consent, the swan returned to Nala and reported everything.

In the mean time, the king announced *swayamvarasabha* for his daughter Damayanti and sent invitation to different kings. On getting this information from Narada, gods Indra, Agni, Varuna and Yam all Gods assuming human form left together for the *swayamvarasabha* and *en route* met Nala who on invitation was also proceeding to the *sabha* as a suitor of Damayanti. Such was the irony of fate that Nala appeared before Damayanti on request of the gods as their messenger. On seeing unknown Nala, Damayanti said, "O! greatest of the men, who are you? What is the purpose of your coming here? I am unable to control my emotion." Concealing his identity Nala said, "O lucky woman, I am the messenger of the gods. Indra, Agni, Varuna and Yama who are eager to have you as their wife. My request, you may accept one of them as your husband. With the help of the gods I have entered your apartment unseen by anybody." Damayanti understood that this messenger of gods was Nala himself. Paying obeisance to the gods within herself she with tears in her eyes said, "*Maharaj*, I shall accept none else other than you as my husband." Nala said in reply, "Bound by promise I have come here as the gods' messenger. Now how can I accept your offer?' Damayanti said, "I am telling you a faultless way. You may please attend the *swayamvarasabha* along with Indra and other gods. On recognizing you I shall put on the garland around your neck."

At the *swayamvarasabha*, Damayanti saw among the assembled kings and princes five dignitaries of the same appearance. Everybody looked like Nala. Having failed to recognize Nala, Damayanti paid obeisance to the gods saying, "I have chosen Nishadha king Nala as my husband. Pray, I do not become sinful by marrying another person. Kindly bless me so that I can recognize Nala." Indra and other gods had assumed the appearance of Nala in order to create confusion in the mind of Damayanti. Satisfied at the pitiable prayer of Damayanti, the gods took up their respective signs seeing which she recognized Nala and garlanded him.

At the marriage of Damayanti with an ordinary king in disregard to the gods, god Kali became furious. Indra and other gods tried to pacify him explaining Damayanti's marriage with Nala had been solemnized with their approval and blessings. Kali's anger, however, did not subside. He declared he would bring about separation between Nala and Damayanti after depriving Nala of his kingdom. Kali accordingly entered into the body of Nala and destroyed his sense of judgement. On the conspiracy of Kali, Nala played dice-game with his younger brother Puskara and lost. In accordance with the agreed conditions, Nala's kingdom with all resources went into the possession of Puskara and Nala with wife Damayanti wearing only their apparel went in exile to the forest.

In the forest also Kali pursued Nala and caused him immense sufferings. Nala's only wearing apparel was also taken away through a trick. Nala somehow allayed his shame with half wearing apparel of Damayanti and started wandering in the forest leaving her alone. Damayanti while moving about in the forest in search of Nala passed through many dangers and ultimately managed to reach the capital of king Shubahu of Chedi following a group of merchants.

In the mean time, Nala while wandering in the forest saved a serpent from the forest fire. The serpent coming out of the fire stung him in the forehead and immediately his earlier appearance completely changed. Assuring Nala the serpent said, "I have stung you so that none could know your true identity. The evil power which is inside your body will now suffer intense agony being stricken by my poison. Now you may go to king Rhituparna of Ayodhya and introduce yourself as a charioteer giving your name as Bahuka. The king on knowing your good qualities would soon become your close favourite. You would soon get back your wife and the kingdom." Accordingly Nala came to Ayodhya and introduced himself to the king as a person with wide experience about horses. The king appointed him as the principal officer of the royal stable. Thus started Nala's incognito stay in the kingdom of king Rhituparna. He remained always sad without having any information about Damayanti.

King Bhima of Vidharva on hearing rumours about reversal of fortunes of Nala and Damayanti, deputed many *Brahmin* agents to different places to get information about them. One *Brahmin* agent Sudeva by name, in course of search, found out Damayanti in the palace of king Chedi and brought her with the consent of the queen-mother to her father's place. The king on hearing all details from Damayanti sent out *Brahmin* agents to different directions to find out Nala. Simultaneously Damayanti without informing anybody also deputed a separate group of *Brahmin* agents to the capitals of different kingdoms to search out Nala. Before their departure she instructed them to repeatedly pronounce the following in the royal courts: "O! dice-player, your lady-love is devoted only to you. Where have you gone after tearing away half of her wearing apparel leaving her alone in the forest? She is weeping for you wearing only half the apparel. Please give your reply to her queries with a delightful mind. It is the duty of every husband to protect his wife. Despite being a virtuous person why are you behaving differently?" Damayanti asked the agents to carefully remember name, place of stay, profession etc. of the person giving any reply and inform her on return. She warned the agents to ensure that her own identity and whereabouts were not to be disclosed under any circumstances.

After a long time, one *Brahmin* agent by the name of Parnad on return told Damayanti, "I have pronounced your words in the court of king Rhituparna at Ayodhya; no reply came from the king or any of his courtiers. When I was coming out, one royal official by name Bahuka called me aside. He is ugly-looking and dwarfish and happens to be the King's charioteer. He possesses special expertise in horse-riding and cooking. He heaved a deep sigh with tears in his eyes and enquired of my welfare. Thereafter he said, a chaste woman protects herself by dint of her own power even in danger and does not get angry even when forsaken by the husband. King Nala without wearing any apparel is passing his days in extreme distress."

On getting this information Damayanti realized Bahuka was none other than king Nala, her husband. She did not tell anything to her father. In consultation with her mother she deputed Sudeva to the king of Chedi with the message that king Bhima had again called a *swayamvarasabha* for her daughter Damayanti as he was doubtful whether her husband Nala was still alive. If the king of Chedi was eager to get Damayanti as his wife, he should immediately attend the *swayamvarasabha.*

On being invited, as the time was short, king Rhituparna reached Vidharva by the fastest possible horse-driven chariot with Bahuka in the guise of Nala as the charioteer. The king was an expert astrologer and dice-player. On the way he learned all the intricate nuances of horse-riding from Bahuka and in exchange gifted him his knowledge in dice-play. Surprisingly the poison, as also the Kali, immediately came out of Nala's body and he became free from all afflictions. His appearance, however, remained disfigured as before.

When the chariot reached Vidharva making sound like the roar of clouds, Damayanti understood Nala had come along with king Rhituparna as the sound of Nala's chariot was well-known to her. King Bhima respectfully received King Rhituparna and enquired of him the purpose of his arrival. Damayanti or the queen did not tell him anything about *swayamvarasabha.* King Rhituparna was surprised at the silence of king Vidarva regarding the *swayamvarasabha.* He also did not notice any preparation in the capital for the ceremony. Sensing some mystery behind the whole matter, he simply said he had come to meet them. King Rhituparna was accommodated in the royal guest house. Nala on the other hand went to the building earmarked for the horse-riders and rested there.

Overwhelmed with grief at the sight of disfigured and ugly looking Bahuka from the palace window, Damayanti sent a lady emissary, Keshini by name, to enquire about him. On being asked about the purpose of his coming here, Bahuka said he as the charioteer of king Rhitupana of Ayodhya had brought him here for the *swayamvarasabha* of princess Damayanti. On instructions Keshini requested Bahuka to repeat for the information of the princess what he had told the *Brahmin* about Damayanti at Ayodhya, and Bahuka replied giving the earlier details. In the king's party there was a third person Barshneya by name who was previously Nala's charioteer. Bahuka said he was now working as an additional charioteer of king Rhituparna. He was not aware of the whereabouts of Nala.

On hearing the details, Damayanti was further convinced that Bahuka and Nala are one and the same person. Even then she again deputed Keshini to keep a close watch on the activities of Bahuka in the kitchen. Keshini was dumbfounded to see the happenings in the kitchen. She hurried back to Damayanti and reported as follows: "I have never seen or heard anything like this before. Water, fire and many other objects are behaving like obedient servants of charioteer Bahuka. I saw the closed doors being opened and expanded automatically on his arrival. On his casting a glance the empty pitchers were filled with water. As he meditated on the Sun the firewood was ignited of its own. He remained unburnt even by touching the fire. Rubbed flowers did not get deformed, but started spreading more fragrance."

Damayanti's efforts to establish the identity of Bahuka did not end here. She brought cooked meat from Bahuka by sending a maid and by tasting it she was convinced it was cooked by Nala. This time she sent with Keshini her two children – Indrasenaa (daughter) and Indrasena (son) – to Bahuka. On seeing them Bahuka lost all patience and began to weep profusely. He told Keshini he could not suppress his tears to see the girl and the boy as they resembled his own children. He forbade Keshini not to come to him again as he was alone here as the guest of the king.

Being satisfied in all respects about Bahuka's identity, Damayanti told her mother that Bahuka was none other than Nala, their beloved son-in-law. King Vidharva on getting this information from the queen, immediately brought Bahuka to the royal palace where he narrated all details in the forest saying his separation from Damayanti and their sufferings were entirely due to the evil influence of Kali. At that moment on the blessings of Nagaraj Karkoteya, king Nala got back his former beautiful appearance. Thereafter Nala and Damayanti were united again. King Rhituparna was happy at the turn of events and after blessing the couple left for his own kingdom. King Nala after a few days came to his own capital accompanied by Damayanti, defeated his brother in dice-game and regained the kingdom.

22.

Describing this wonderful story of Nala and Damayanti, sage Vrihadashwa assured Yudhisthira he would also one day regain his kingdom like king Nala. He imparted his knowledge in dice-game to Yudhisthira so that he did not get defeated in the game again. We shall see later this knowledge also stood him in good stead during the Pandavas' incognito stay in the court of king Virata.

In the story of Nala and Damayanti, we come across a number of examples regarding successful collection of intelligence through secret agents. Behind this success *Brahmin* agents had a big role to play. That some times women could also be used for intelligence collection was also evident. Vidarvaraj, we have seen, found out his daughter Damayanti from the palace of Chediraj with the help of *Brahmin* emissaries. He also deputed *Brahmin* emissaries to search out Nala. Damayanti similarly depended on the *Brahmin* emissaries. Our surprise, however, lies elsewhere. Here she decided everything alone; Vidarvaraj knew nothing of her activities. Such was the depth of her self-confidence. The answers to the questions posed by the *Brahmin* emissaries in the different royal courts on her instructions were known, as we are aware, only to Nala. This was no doubt the only means to identify Nala in the midst of others. When the answer came from Bahuka, king Rhituparna's ugly-looking charioteer and head of his stable, Damayanti rightly suspected him to be Nala. This was a marvellous act of intelligence operation sometimes eluding even the most seasoned intelligence operators. Her decision to bring Bahuka within one night along with king Rhituparna to her father's capital to test his knowledge of horse-driving on the plea of her *swayamvara,* was unbelievably daring though justified on practical grounds. Damayanti's union with Nala was possible when at Vidarva under her direct supervision Nala's (in Bahuka's guise) true identity could finally be established with proof of his supernatural powers.

The entire intelligence operation – a very difficult one indeed – was meticulously planned and executed. Damayanti was always at the centre-stage and alone. No problem arose anywhere. It moved on with clock-like precision giving the stamp of professional competence. Our head bows down in regard to this gracious woman with the proverbial love and devotion to her husband yet possessing profound worldly wisdom. The Nala-Damayanti story underlines the eternal conflict between nature and fate. Despite being bestowed with all the gifts of nature, they could not avoid the vicissitudes of fate. Of course their adherence to *dharma* ultimately brought about the defeat of the evil forces paving the way to their reunion and regaining of the lost kingdom. In fact, the Mahabharata war was fought to establish this basic theme of triumph of good over evil. On hearing the story of Nala and Damayanti from sage Vrihadashwa, the Pandavas felt somewhat relieved at the thought that they would regain their lost kingdom after victory over the Kauravas.

23.

At Dvaita forest, sage Lomasha appeared before the Pandavas and told them that Arjuna had obtained divine weapons from Lord Mahadeva and Devaraj Indra, learned dance and music from Gandharvaraj Chitrasena at Indra's court and would soon return and join them. The Pandavas who were worried about not getting any information about Arjuna for long, were happy and relieved. Thereafter they moved to Vadarikashrama, and while staying there Bhimasena, in course of search for lotus flowers for Draupadi, accidentally met his brother Hanuman of the Ramayana fame in the forest and received from him many valuable instructions regarding politics, security, secret agents etc. about which we have discussed earlier.

The Pandavas again shifted to a new place in the Himalayas. Here a *rakshasa* by the name of Jatasura was staying with the Pandavas introducing himself as a devout *Brahmin* well-versed in religious scriptures. Everybody in the hermitage was happy with his talks and behaviour. One day during the absence of Bhimasena, Jatasura by dint of his magical powers assumed a huge body and forcibly tried to abduct Draupadi, Yudhisthira, Nakula and Sahdeva by placing them on his shoulder. Chastising Jatasura for betraying their trust, Yudhisthira by divine powers increased his body weight completely impairing his movement. In the mean time, Bhimasena returned to the hermitage and on seeing him Jatasura declared that he would drink his blood to avenge the death of the *rakshasas* Baka and Hirimba at his hands. In the fierce duel Jatasura was killed by Bhimasena.

Did Jatasura try to abduct Yudhisthira and others only to avenge the death of his kinsmen? It does not seem so. Of course it is true that Duryodhana would have been the happiest person had the Jatasura's attempt been successful. It is equally true that Jatasura was pining for revenge against Bhimasena. The prevailing circumstances, however, seem to indicate that Jatasura was infiltrated by Duryodhana into the hermitage of the Pandavas. Jatasura knew magical powers with the help of which he could assume any disguise any time. Moreover the Pandavas were the common enemy of both Jatasura and Duryodhana. It is only expected that Duryodhana would seek revenge-seeking Jatasura's help to harm the Pandavas. Here also Jatasura joined the Pandavas as a pious *Brahmin* without creating anybody's suspicion. It is possible that Jatasura had received necessary advice from Duryodhana's men in the operation as also with regard to the form of disguise. The Mahabharata's poet is silent about these details possibly to avoid any unnecessary digression in the narration of the events in the great epic.

Jatasura's attempt to harm the Pandavas miserably failed as he was unable to correctly assess their strength. Yudhisthira possessed superior divine powers which completely overwhelmed Jatasura's ordinary magical powers. With the help of divine powers he easily stopped Jatasura's movement to give enough time to Bhimasena to return. He foolishly invited Bhimasena having superior physical strength for a duel without taking any notice of the fate of the other *rakshasas* at his hands earlier. The result as expected was his inevitable death. If the Kauravas had a hand in this incident (as it is strongly suspected to be so), the bankruptcy of their plan was again evident. Their possible acquiescence to this unequal duel between Bhimasena and Jatasura was palpably untenable. The result was the failure of the entire plan. Some errors of the Pandavas are also noticed. They had no prior information about the infiltration of such a dangerous *rakshasa* like Jatasura into their camp. Obviously there was no adequate check on the new entrants. They accepted the statement of Jatasura in the guise of a *Brahmin* without any verification whatsoever. They should have been more vigilant as they were not unaware of the pursuing agents of Duryodhana to harm them.

After staying for five long years in the court of Devaraj Indra, Arjuna with various divine weapons returned to their hermitage at *gandhamadana* mountain in the Himalayas. He narrated his encounter with Lord Mahadeva in the Himalayas and other experiences in *swargarajya* to his brothers and said, "Devaraj Indra assured me that there is nobody who can defeat me as I am now endowed with all the divine weapons. In the battle field Vishwa, Drona, Karna, Shakuni and other Kaurava warriors will not be able to show even one-sixteenth part of my strength. Devaraj has been pleased to give me his impregnable armour, gold garland, *devadatta* conch, divine apparel and cover of the body. He with his own hands placed the divine crown on my head. I spent my days in complete comfort in the *swargarajya.*" On hearing Arjuna, Yudhisthira observed that the defeat of the Kauravas was now imminent. He expressed his desire to see the divine weapons. The following morning, as Arjuna was about to explain the application of the weapons to his brothers, sage Narada appeared there and forbade him warning any unnecessary application of the divine weapons which could cause irreparable damage. He said that everybody would be able to witness their application in the battlefield. On Narada's advice, Arjuna closed the weapons.

The Pandavas thereafter returned to Kamyaka forest. One day Krishna appeared there and on learning Arjuna's acquisition of divine weapons, expressed great satisfaction. Later praising Yudhisthira he said, "*Maharaj*, in your life you have never deviated from *dharma*. For the sake of *dharma* you have given up everything including your kingdom and wealth. The patience you have shown, by remaining silent, during the disrobing of Draupadi in the royal court, was only possible for you. If you think your vow has been fulfilled, we may immediately proceed to destroy the Kauravas and recapture your kingdom." Politely refusing Krishna's suggestion, Yudhisthira said, "We have almost completed thirteen years in exile. We still have to stay incognito for another year in accordance with the promise given to the Kauravas. On completion of this period we shall again meet you and seek your help and guidance to decide our future course of action. Pray we remain always under your protection." Yudhisthira refused to go in for war against the Kauravas at the present moment mainly on moral ground. He, at the same time, was concerned about the ground reality. He wanted to buildup first a strong army capable of meeting the formidable Kaurava army. This would be possible only after their completion of the entire period of exile when a clear picture would emerge about their support among the kings and the princes. Yudhisthira's strategy ultimately paid dividend.

One day *maharshi* (great sage) Markandeya appeared at the hermitage of the Pandavas and narrated on request, the characteristics of kings and sages, consequences of one's action, distinctive features of different ages etc. Later in answer to a question of Yudhisthira he said, "*Maharaj*, always remain compassionate and govern your subjects with truthfulness, impartiality and mildness. Do not forget to observe the religious rites. Never deviate from the path of *dharma*. Redress by offering gifts to all unjust actions mistakenly committed. Scrupulously avoid self-praise. Always perform your duties with humility. Do not get overwhelmed by the present misfortune. I bless you – you live happily after conquering the entire world." Yudhisthira assured sage Markandeya that he would always try to perform his duties according to his instructions. It is needless to mention that sage Markandeya's instructions are all axiomatic truths pursuance of which brought success to Yudhisthira.

24.

At Hastinapura the Kauravas continued their parleys to hit upon new conspiracies against the Pandavas. Shakuni, the villain of the piece, told Duryodhana, "O greatest of the Kauravas, you are very fortunate. By dint of your own wisdom you have captured Pandavas' kingdom and wealth. Innumerable kings and princes are now waiting in eagerness to help you.

"I have heard the Pandavas are now living in a wretched condition on the bank of a lake in Dwaita forest. You may go there pompously to derive satisfaction at their sorrowful plight. The Pandavas will be immersed in a sea of sorrow to see your prosperity. Draupadi will blame her own fate to see the Kaurava wives wearing beautiful apparel and ornaments. My son, remember, to see the enemy in distress is more pleasing than even seeing one's own children." Karna readily supported Shakini's suggestion.

Duryodhana, though delighted, expressed doubt whether king Dhritarashtra would give his consent to the proposal. He said, "King Dhritarashtra is already very unhappy at the distress of the Pandavas in the forest. He will certainly not agree to our going to Dwaita forest lest any confrontation should arise with the Pandavas who are now equipped with divine weapons particularly if he could come to know of our real intention. We shall have to find out some acceptable alibi to go there." Karna then suggested they could go to inspect the neighbouring Ghoshpalli (village of the Ghosh community whose profession is rearing of cattle) and this might not be objected to by the king. The suggestion being agreed upon the next day, Shakuni and Karna met king Dhritarashtra and told him, "*Maharaj*, Duryodhana is eager to visit Ghoshpalli for hunting and also to ascertain with his men, the age, number etc. of the cattle there. This work is long overdue. Moreover Ghoshpalli is a beautiful place. You may kindly approve Duryodhana's visit to Ghoshpalli."

Dhritarashtra stated in reply, "Hunting is good. It is also necessary to look after the cattle. I have heard the Pandavas are staying at a place not far from Ghoshpalli. They are all virtuous and great warriors. Moreover Arjuna has recently returned from *swargarajya* equipped with divine weapons. The Pandavas are now invincible. A dangerous situation will arise if any harm is caused to the Pandavas in course of the hunting. In the circumstances, I cannot allow Duryodhana to visit Ghoshpalli. Let some reliable persons be deputed to look after the cattle.' Shakuni assured Dhritarashtra they had no intention to harm the Pandavas and even their hermitage would not be visited.

On the insistence of Shakuni and Karna, king Dhritarashtra reluctantly agreed to Duryodhana's visit. On getting the permission, Duryodhana accompanied by Shakuni, Karna, own brothers and wives arrived at the Dwaita forest with a large army. At the Dwaita forest, the Kauravas were involved in a fierce battle with the Gandharvas when they went to the garden and the lake occupied by the latter and were defeated. Duryodhana became a prisoner at the hands of Gandharva king Chitrsena. Shakuni, Karna and other Kaurava warriors fled away to safety. Yudhisthira soon got details of the incident. On his order, Arjuna rescued Duryodhana and other Kaurava warriors after defeating the Gandharvas. Such was the irony of fate that the Kauravas who had come to Dwaita forest to derive sadistic pleasure at the plight of the Pandavas, had the misfortune of being rescued at the intervention of Yudhisthira. Duryodhana thus suffered the worst humiliation and harassment of his life. He, however, by way of repaying his gratitude to Arjuna, his rescuer, requested him to seek any thing from him. Arjuna promised to do so later. We have earlier mentioned how on Krishna's advice, Arjuna one night, during the Mahabharata war, went to Duryodhana's camp, obtained his crown against his promise given at Dwaita forest and in the guise of Duryodhana wearing his crown, managed to procure from grandfather Bhishma five sanctified arrows meant for killing the Pandavas thus frustrating the Kaurava's plan to destroy them. In the incident of Dwaita forest, the greatness of Yudhisthira was again evident. He could not countenance the imprisonment of Duryodhana, a Kuru prince and his own cousin brother at the hands of the Gandharvas. The honour of their glorious dynasty took precedence over his enmity with the Kauravas. After rescuing Duryodhana, he allowed him and other Kaurava warriors to return to their camp unharmed despite the fact that the present sufferings of the Pandavas were entirely due to his heinous conspiracy. Duryodhanas greatness was also no less significant in that later he readily handed over to Arjuna his own crown when sought by him though he could understand this would seriously harm his interest.

In the incident at Dwaita forest the stupidity and imprudence of the Kauravas was nakedly exposed once again. They seemed to have lost all power of judgement and were carried by sheer flippancy. It is a grotesque idea to derive pleasure by vaunting their wealth and prosperity before the Pandavas who were living in distress in the forest. Though denied to Dhritarashtra, the Kauravas actually planned to at least come in sight of the Pandavas. This had the potentiality of causing a confrontation between the two sides. Dhritarashtra, it may be recalled, feared such a possibility and warned Shakuni and Karna accordingly. That the Pandavas were now invincible with acquisition of divine weapons by Arjuna, was known only to the Kauravas. Even then they undertook the visit with inadequate preparations just like fickle-minded inexperienced boys with no thought about the consequences. The Kauravas also seemed to have no information about the presence of the Gandharvas in the Dwaita forest and that there was a taboo against entry into their area without permission. Even if they had the information, they completely ignored it believing that none would dare to face them – so intoxicated they were with pride. All this was against the principles of war. Had they calmly assessed the situation, they could have easily understood the ground reality as it was known that the Gandharvas were a powerful community. The Kauravas were rightly served for their arrogance with their defeat at the hands of the Gandharvas and their subsequent rescue and release by the Pandavas, their enemy.

As depicted in the Mahabharata, Duryodhana being overwhelmed with humiliation at the Dwaita forest decided to give up his own life at Ghoshpalli itself. All efforts by Shakuni and Karna to change his decision went in vain. The *danavas* who were living in hell on being defeated by the gods, were perturbed on knowing the decision of Duryodhana. In an effort to change his mind, they performed a *yajna* from which appeared an odd-looking god. On the order of the *danavas* he brought Duryodhana before them. Consoling Duryodhana they told him, "*Maharaj*, in the past you have subdued many enemies by displaying supernatural power. You are born in this world on the blessings of Lord Mahadeva. Your body is not like that of an ordinary human being. Forget your sadness. All the *Khashtriyas* armed with divine weapons will come forward to destroy your enemies. We shall influence the Pandava well-wishers Vishwa, Drona and others to fight for you. We all *daityas* and *danavas* shall destroy your enemies in the battlefield. We are all with you as *devatas* have sided with the Pandavas. Kindly return home without any anxiety whatsoever. You are sure to become the lord of the universe after destroying the Pandavas."

Duryodhana calmed down somewhat at the words of the *danavas* and came back to Ghoshpalli where at the request of his well-wishers he gave up the decision of committing suicide. Karna vowed he would kill Arjuna in the battlefield. On return to Hastinapura, Karna in order to please Duryodhana went on expedition, conquered many countries and brought huge wealth for himself. With the change of situation the morale of the Kauravas greatly improved. Duryodhana decided to perform *Rajasuyayajna* following the example of Yudhisthira. The royal priests, however, opined Duryodhana was not eligible to perform *Rajasuyayajna* as Yudhisthira of their family had already performed it. Moreover, father Dhritarashtra was still alive. Then as suggested by the priests, Duryodhana performed *Vaishnavayajna* which was equal in importance to *Rajasuyayajna* with great pomp and grandeur. The Pandavas declined the invitation of Duryodhana to attend the ceremony. While congratulating Duryodhana on completion of the *Vaishnavayajna* Karna said, "*Maharaj*, you shall perform *Rajasuyayajna* after the death of the Pandavas. I am again taking the vow I shall not even drink water until I kill Arjuna in the battlefield." Soon the Pandavas came to know of Karna's vow. Yudhisthira became worried at the thought that Karna was covered with an impenetrable natural armour for which he was invincible. He decided to shift their hermitage to a new place.

25.

Duryodhana's devious mind was always busy devising new plans to harm the Pandavas. This time he hit upon a novel plan against them. One day when sage Durvasa accompanied by ten thousand disciples appeared at Hastinapura, Duryodhana, out of fear of curse from him, engaged himself at his service. Satisfied with his service, sage Durvasa asked Duryodhana for a boon. Duryodhana accordingly, in consultation with Shakuni and Karna, said, "O great sage, virtuous Yudhisthira is now living in the forest. I shall be happy if you kindly accept his hospitality." Duryodhana's belief was that Yudhisthira in their present condition in the forest, would not be able to entertain sage Durvasa with so many disciples thus inviting severe curse from him and as a result the Pandavas would be thrown into greater misery.

Accordingly, sage Durvasa accompanied by his disciples came to the hermitage of the Pandavas at Dwaita forest and became the guest of Yudhisthira. In Draupadi's kitchen at that time there was no food with which she could entertain so many guests. She as such became apprehensive of a serious curse from sage Durvasa. Finding no other way she remembered Krishna and as described in the Mahabharata, Krishna, the incarnation of God, immediately appeared there and asked Draupadi for some food saying he was very hungry. Draupadi then brought the empty cooking pot before him indicating she had got nothing to offer him. Krishna looking into the pot found a grain of rice mixed with little herb and swallowed it with great relish uttering the words, "Let the soul of the universe be happy and contented." He then asked Bhimasena to invite sage Durvasa and his disciples for food. Sage Duvasa and his disciples were then taking bath in the nearby river. As they got up to the shore, they all felt fully contented as if they had taken a sumptuous meal. Some even felt like vomitting as is in the case of excessive eating. They left the place without returning to the hermitage for food. On Krishna's divine intervention the Pandavas could evade the curse of sage Durvasa. Duryodhana's evil design to harm the Pandavas failed miserably.

In his request to sage Durvasa to seek hospitality of Yudhisthira in the forest with his disciples, we find a sense of desperation on the part of Duryodhana. All his steps to harm the Pandavas having failed thus far, he naturally became very much dejected. He was, therefore, keen to take advantage of every opportunity to serve his purpose. This opportunity came when sage Durvasa, with his disciples, visited Hastinapura. The strange character of Durvasa, a sage of supernatural power, was well-known. It was not easy to satisfy him. He used to curse even his hosts if there was any slightest error and omission on their part. For this he was feared by everybody. Duryodhana was certain the Pandavas would invite Durvasa's wrath as it would be impossible for them to entertain him and his large retinue of disciples. This sort of idea on the part of Duryodhana is indicative of his utter immaturity. He seemed to be oblivious of the fact that Yudhisthira was endowed with supernatural powers and also that Krishna, a person of divine power, is the friend, philosopher and guide of the Pandavas. In the past they had given enough evidence of their powers. How could Duryodhana forget the vow of Krishna in their hermitage in the Dwaita forest that he would protect the Pandavas in all circumstances? He also did not give any importance to Dhritarashtra's warning that the Pandavas were now invincible with Arjuna's acquisition of divine weapons. It was childish to think that the Pandavas could be so easily vanquished on such an ordinary issue of the Pandavas' inability to entertain sage Durvasa and his disciples. Even if Krishna did not intervene, Yudhisthira would have handled the situation in some form or other with no harm coming to them from sage Durvasa. Moreover, with virtuous Yudhisthira explaining the real motive of Duryodhana in directing him and his disciples to their hermitage in their present distress, sage Durvasa might have got annoyed with him with all dreadful consequences. His vicious curse would have then fallen on Duryodhana himself - a possibility about which he had no forethought at all. Krishna's divine intervention in fact saved Duryodhana from the inevitable curse of sage Durvasa.

The Kauravas, aware of the increasing power of the Pandavas even during their exile, should have maintained a close watch on their activities and prepared themselves to face their challenge in the future. Without doing so, they frittered away their time and resources on flimsy matters. They showed fickle-mindedness when they were supposed to deal with the situation with objectivity and equanimity. The Kauravas obviously lacked leadership qualities capable of meeting the challenge of the formidable Pandavas.

26.

In the mean time, the Pandavas had shifted their hermitage to Kamyaka forest. One day, when Draupadi was staying alone at the care of priest Dhoumya in the absence of the Pandavas out on hunting in the forest, Souvikraj Jayadhratha, husband of Duhshala, Dhritarashtra's daughter appeared at the hermitage with a large army. After exchange of greetings, Jayadhratha enamoured at the beauty of Draupadi asked her to accept him as her husband. On Draupadi's refusal to this evil proposal with utter contempt, Jayadhratha forcibly took her to his chariot and departed. Priest Dhoumya while cursing Jayadhratha, followed his troops from behind.

In the forest, the Pandavas on seeing various evil omens hurriedly returned to the hermitage and came to know of the incident from the other inmates. They immediately proceeded towards the direction Jayadhratha had left and overtook him. In the ensuing battle Jayadhratha was defeated and severely beaten up by Bhimasena. Later Yudhisthira released Jayadhratha with the consent of Draupadi for the sake of their sister Duhshala. As a punishment for his abominable offence Jayadhratha's head was shaved before release.

Out of shame Jayadhratha did not return to his capital. For the expiation of his sin he sat down to meditate on Lord Mahadeva on the bank of the Ganges. When Mahadeva on being satisfied with his austerity asked him for a boon, Jayadhratha prayed to have the power to defeat the Pandavas in the battlefield. Mahadeva informed Jayadhratha he would be able defeat all other Pandava brothers except Arjuna who was endowed with divine weapons.

In the incident of abduction of Draupadi, we find Jayadhratha's utter moral degradation and lack of foresight. The forcible abduction of unmarried girls for the purpose of marriage was an accepted convention in those days. The abduction of married women was, however, rare. There is no word to condemn the action of Jayadhratha. We fail to understand how a powerful king like Jyadhratha possessing many qualities, could lose all sense of judgement in abducting Draupadi who happened to be his closest relation. Apparently he was completely overwhelmed by the beauty of Draupadi. The absence of the Pandavas seemed to have also influenced his evil decision. His passion rose to such heights that he completely ignored the consequences of his action being oblivious of the invincibility of the Pandavas. This was another example of violation of the basic principles of war which stipulate that any direct confrontation with the stronger enemy should be avoided. His reckless act of abduction led to his inevitable defeat and humiliation. Jayadhratha could save his life only due to the magnanimity of Yudhisthira.

27.

Meanwhile, the twelve-year period of exile of the Pandavas in the forest was about to end. Devaraj Indra decided he would rob Karna's impenetrable armour and earrings in order to assure Arjuna's victory in the coming war. Suryadeva (Sun God) got this information in a divine dream and advised Karna, his son, not to part with his armour and earrings to Indra. He said because of these armour and the earrings he was invincible. Karna stated in reply, "I am promise-bound I can give even my life if any *Brahmin* asks for it. If Devaraj Indra wants my armour and the earrings in the guise of a Brahmin, I must hand them over to him. Otherwise my disgrace would spread throughout the entire world. I do not want to live in this world as a disgraceful person." Suryadeva on this said, "O, great warrior Karna, Arjuna is your main rival. He will appear in the battlefield against you. If your body remains covered with your natural armour and earrings, Arjuna even with Indra's help would not be able to defeat you. You shall invite your own death if you part with your armour and the earrings. If at all you are to part with them for the sake of your promise, you must ask for an infallible arrow capable of killing one of your enemies of Indra."

At the proper time Devaraj Indra appeared before Karna in the guise of a *Brahmin* and asked for his armour and the earrings. As advised by Suryadeva, Karna prayed for the infallible arrow from Indra in exchange for the armour and the earrings. While giving the divine arrow Indra warned Karna not to use this arrow if his purpose was served with other weapons; otherwise this arrow would fall on his body and destroy it. After this, Karna with the help of a sharp weapon cut his armour and the ear-rings from his body and handed them over to Indra. Karna's face showed no sign of discomfort during performance of such a painful act.

We are aware of the mystery of birth of Karna and the five Pandavas. It is quite natural that Suryadeva and Devaraj Indra would come to the help of their respective sons Karna and Arjuna in the impending war between the Kauravas and the Pandavas. The gods were no less adept in intelligence work than the humans. Their methods were, however, somewhat different. They were endowed with supernatural powers, with which they could easily resort to various methods like meeting any person in dream, disguise, change of place by wish, assumption of ethereal body, penetration into human body etc. Many sages could also acquire these powers through *yogic* exercises. We have noticed how Suryadeva and Devaraj Indra utilised their supernatural powers in collecting information about each other's intentions in aid of their sons Karna and Arjuna. Suryadeva rested assured of certain death of Arjuna in the battlefield at the hands of Karna with the divine arrow gifted to him by Devaraj Indra at his instance. We shall see later how Suryadeva's entire plan was scuttled in the Kurukshetra battlefield at the machination of Krishna when instead of Arjuna, Bhimasena's son, Ghatotkacha was killed with that divine arrow shot by Karna and on Krishna's treachery unarmed Karna himself got killed by Arjuna.

28.

The Pandavas had again returned to Dwaita forest. One day a *Brahmin* appeared before them and complained that their two pieces of wood meant for igniting sacrificial fire, had been taken away by a deer by its horn and requested Yudhisthira to get them retrieved immediately as they were unable to perform their prescribed *yajna.* Then the Pandavas went out in search of the deer but could not find him despite all efforts. While discussing about their failure, Nakula asked Yudhisthira about the reasons for their sufferings and failure. Yudhisthira replied, "Danger comes in various forms reasons for which are unknown. Only Dharma determines the results of sin and virtue." Bhimasena then observed that they were suffering because he did not kill Duhshasana during the dice-game despite his humiliation of Draupadi. Arjuna said he must blame himself for their present distress as he had tolerated Karna's invectives on Draupadi. Sahadeva observed that their sufferings were due to his failure to kill Shakuni for defeating them in the deceitful dice-game.

The Pandavas, in course of the chase, became tired and thirsty. On Yudhisthira's order Nakul, Sahadeva, Bhimasena and Arjuna went to the nearby lake one by one to fetch water: but none of them returned. Yudhisthira was worried and himself proceeded to the lake to see as to what had happened to his brothers. At the bank of the lake he saw all his brothers lying unconscious as if they were dead. He suspected Shakuni, on the order of Duryodhana, might have created this lake by dint of magical powers and mixed poison in the water in order to kill them: or the spies of Duryodhana might have caused this mischief. He found no deformity in the bodies. Their faces also looked cheerful as before. With various thoughts in the mind as he went down to touch the water he heard the following message from the sky. "I am a moss- and meat-eating crane. This lake belongs to me. I have myself taken the lives of your brothers. If you fail to answer my questions, you shall meet the same fate as your brothers." Yudhisthira stopped and said, "This work cannot be done by any bird. You may disclose your true identity." On this came the reply, "I am not any aquatic bird. I am *Yakshya*. First give reply to my questions and then touch the water." Then Yakshya asked Yudhisthira several questions. On Yudhisthira giving correct replies to all the questions, *Yakshya* being satisfied brought back the brothers into life. After this Yakshya disclosed, "Son, I am Dharma, your father. In the guise of the deer I removed the wood pieces of the *Brahmins* in order to test you." After saying this, Dharma returned him the two wood pieces. Yudhisthira requested for a boon so that the Kauravas could not get any information about their one-year incognito stay. Dharma granted the prayer and advised Yudhisthira to proceed to Virata kingdom to live incognito.

Yakshya-Yudhisthira's questions and answers form one of the most important episodes of the Mahabharata. The facts revealed in these questions and answers, in a novel method, contain many truths which are fundamental and universal in character. These pertain to, among others, *sanatanadharma*, general knowledge and means to happy life. Here are the questions asked by Yakshya and the answers given by Yudhisthira.

Yakshya: Who has held the sun high? Who travels round the sun? Who brings about the sunset? Where is he installed?

Yudhisthira: Brahma has held the sun high. The gods travel round the sun. Dharma causes the sun-set. He is installed in truth.

Ya: How do the *Brahmins* attain godliness? For which religion do they become virtuous? Why do they have human nature? What makes them dishonest?

Yu: *Brahmins* attain godliness by studying the *Vedas*. They become virtuous from the practice of austerities. They are humans because they are certain to die. Vilification of others makes them dishonest.

Ya: What is the godliness of the *Kshatriyas?* What is honest conduct? What is human state of mind? What is the dishonest state of mind?

Yu: Proficiency in the use of weapons is the religion of the *Kshatriyas*. Performance of *yajna* is the honest conduct. Fear is the state of mind of the humans. To forsake those seeking protection is dishonesty.

Ya: Who is greater than the earth? Who is higher than sky? Who is faster than wind? What is lighter than grass?

Yu: Mother is greater than the earth. Father is higher than the sky. Mind is faster than wind. Thought is lighter than grass.

Ya: Who does not close eyes while asleep? Who does not palpitate even after birth? Who has no heart? Which does grow by speed?

Yu: Fish does not close eyes while asleep. Egg does not palpitate after birth? Stone has no heart. River grows by speed.

Ya: A person living abroad, a person living in his own house, a sick person and a dying person – who are their friends?

Yu: A companion is the friend of the person living abroad, wife is the friend of the person living in his own house, physician is the friend of the sick person, charity is the friend of the dying person.

Ya: Abandonment of which brings in popularity? Abandonment of which alleviates grief? Abandonment of which makes man rich? Abandonment of which makes man happy?

Yu: Abandonment of pride makes man popular. Grief subsides with abandonment of anger. Abandonment of desire makes a person rich. Abandonment of greed makes man happy.

Ya: What is the message for mankind? What is most surprising? What is the path? Who is happy?

Yu: Under the influence of all-pervading illusion, time is driving lives on the earth in a whirlpool. The sun is their fire. Day and night are their fuel. Months and seasons are their ladle for stirring. This is the message. Everyday man is dying. Yet all others want to be immortal. What can be more surprising than this? Vedas are different. *Smriti shastras* are different. There are no sages who hold the same opinion. The essence of *dharma* is merged in mystery. That is the path which has been traversed by the wise men. The person who is without debt, does not live in a foreign country and is satisfied by eating only rice with herbs in the evening in his own house, is alone happy.

Ya: Who is a man? Who does possess all the wealth?

Yu: The news of good work spreads throughout the world and the heaven. When one's song of praise vibrates all around, he is known as the best of men. He who treats good and bad, pleasure and pain and past and present as equal, is the possessor of all wealth.

Yakshya being satisfied with the answers of Yudhisthira, asked him to name one of his brothers whom he wanted to see alive. Yudhisthira uttered the name of Nakula. On this Yakshya asked him why he had wanted to see alive his step brother Nakula disregarding Bhimasena and Arjuna who happened to be his mainstay. Yudhisthira stated in reply, 'If I disown *dharma,* I shall be destroyed by Dharma. I shall never forsake *dharma.* Both Kunti and Madri are my mothers. By bringing Nakula back to life you may kindly bless both Kunti and Madri so that they can have at least one son each.'

Yudhisthira's answers remind us that any person who is simple, honest and straightforward, has no pride and greed and remains calm in all circumstances – good or bad – can achieve success by following the path of the wise men. These qualities are worthy of emulation not only by the general people but also by the kings and the rulers. Rather these qualities have got special significance in respect of the kings and the rulers. Because on their actions and policies depend the welfare of the people at large. If they are dishonest and tyrannous, the subordinate employees and the people would develop a tendency to go astray. This has far-reaching consequences. The entire administration, which is intended to serve the interests of the people, may collapse. History bears many such instances. Only the administration which is just and fair, is capable of doing good to the people. Truth and virtue are the pillars of victory. Yudhisthira, being the son of Dharma, naturally gave vent to such fundamental principles in his answers to Yakshya. Dharma in the guise of Yakshya being assured of his son Yudhisthira even in their present deep distress, continued to adhere to the basic principles of truth and morality, himself came forward to help him. He blessed him with the boon that the Pandavas would be able to successfully complete their incognito stay.

29.

The twelve-year period of exile of the Pandavas in the forest untimely ended. Now according to the conditions of the dice-game, they would have to stay incognito for one year. This was, no doubt, fraught with many dangers. The Kauravas by despatching spies to different directions were keeping a close watch on the movements of the Pandavas. From now on we find Yudhisthira in the centre-stage directing all actions and movements of the Pandavas. After discussions among themselves, the Pandavas decided to spend their period of incognito stay in disguise in Viratnagar, capital of the kingdom of Matsya. It was agreed that Yudhisthra introducing himself as an expert in the dice-game, would become a courtier of Virataraja. Bhimasena who was expert in cooking, would take up the job of a cook in the royal kitchen with the assumed name of Vallava. Arjuna now an eunuch would teach dance and music to the royal inmates in the name of Brihannala. Nakula with experiences about horses would take up the responsibility of the royal stable in the name of Granthika. Sahadeva with his knowledge in cattle would become the head of the royal cattle-shed in the name of Arishtanemi, while Draupadi introducing herself as an expert in hair dressing would engage herself in the service of queen Sudeshna. The Pandavas thus very correctly decided to take up jobs in disguise under Virataraja completely in conformity with their respective knowledge and inclination as is done in any intelligence operation. This would help them to remain in good books of the king by showing due proficiency in their declared professions thus dispelling any doubt about their statement. This indeed actually happened with no doubt arising in the king's mind about their identity till the end of the period of the incognito stay.

Before proceeding to Viratnagar, Yudhisthira directed charioteer Indrasena and other inmates of the hermitage to take shelter at Dwaraka which was the domain of Krishna. They were warned not to disclose Pandavas' next place of stay to any one else. Thereafter priest *Dhoumnya* briefed the Pandavas about their conduct in the court of Virataraja. He said, "This period of one-year incognito stay is extremely important for you. You shall have to pass this period in complete disguise in the midst of all praises and insults. You should always take the prior permission of the king before leaving your place of stay. Do not believe any body in regard to any mysterious discussions. Always stay in a safe place. Always remember, the enemy is keeping a sharp eye all around in search for you. Always avoid the company of the wicked people. Never sit on the bed or mount on the elephant or the chariot used by the king. Do not give any advice to the king unless asked for. Serve the king silently. Do not indulge in unnecessary talks with the royal inmates. Always remember to cultivate friendship with the king's enemies is extremely improper. Perform even a small work with all eagerness in the presence of the king. Talk only subjects which are dear and beneficial to the king. Never contradict the king in course of discussions. Remember, the king becomes annoyed of false statements. He also hates any self-advertisement of knowledge. Never boast about your own bravery and intelligence before the king. Remember, you can gain the trust of the king only by performing his dear and beneficial works.

"Now, I shall tell you about your personal conduct in presence of the king. While taking your seat in the royal court, you should never make any unnecessary movements of your hands and feet. Always remain calm and composed. Do not speak loudly. Spitting and passing of wind should be done very secretly. Mildly smile during discussions of any humorous subject in the royal court. Loud laughter or complete silence both are undesirable. Never dress up like the king. Always wear clothes and ornaments gifted by the king. In this way, stay in Viratnagar with a restrained mind. After winning your own kingdom you shall be able to behave independently."

Yudhisthira assured priest Dhoumnya that the Pandavas would always remember his advice. On his request Dhoumnya then performed *yajna* for the welfare of the Pandavas. Thereafter the Pandavas proceeded to Viratanagara and the others to Dwaraka.

The advice given to the Pandavas by priest *Dhoumnya* was timely and practical. It was not simple to stay at one place incognito even in disguise and in assumed names for such well-known persons like the Pandavas evading the spies of Duryodhana. Naturally, priest Dhoumnya warned the Pandavas about the danger of their incognito stay. The essence of the advice was that the Pandavas could successfully complete their incognito stay only by cultivating excellent relations with the king by faithfully serving his interests and by avoiding the company of undesirable persons. We shall see later that the Pandavas, under Yudhisthira's guidance, showed exemplary patience, courage and intelligence and kept their consultations completely secret during this long period of their one-year incognito stay. Duryodhana's spies could not detect their presence at Viratnagar. It is a rare event not witnessed in the entire world history.

Along with Draupadi on way to Viratnagar the Pandavas kept their weapons concealed in a road side mango tree. After keeping a dead body tied to the branches, they told the local people they had kept the body of a dead woman in the tree according to their established family custom. Their intention was to scare away the people from the tree in order to ensure that the weapons were not detected by any one. After this, on Yudhisthira's advice, the Pandavas took up secret names such as Yaya for Yudhisthira, Yayanta for Bhimasena, Vijoya for Arjuna, Yayatasena for Nakula and Yaydvbala for Sahadeva for use only among themselves and entered Viratnagar in the guise of *Brahmins*. On entering Viratnagar, Yudhisthira worshipped Goddess Durga, who on being satisfied appeared before him and assured that their identity would remain undisclosed during their incognito stay.

At the proper time, Yudhisthira appeared before the king and introducing himself as a *Byaghrapadi Brahmin* by name Kanka said, "I have come to seek your favour for my livelihood. Earlier I was a dear friend of Dhrarmaraj Yudhisthira. I have got considerable proficiency in dice-game." The king being satisfied with his behaviour and talks agreed to appoint Yudhisthisthra as one of his courtiers saying he himself was a great lover of dice-game. Thanking the king for the offer Yudhisthira said, "*Maharaj*, I have a condition. I shall never join the low-caste people in the dice-game. All the money earned after winning the game must belong to me. None would have any claim on it." The king accepting the condition gave out that he would not hesitate to kill any one doing harm to him. Thereafter Yudhisthira started living in the palace of Virataraja and none could know his true identity.

After a few days, Bhimasena appeared before the king and said, "*Maharaj*, my name is Vallava. I am an expert cook. I was previously appointed in the kitchen of king Yudhisthira. I am also second to none in physical strength. I am even capable of fighting the animals like elephants and tigers. Now I am eager to perform some good work for you." The king said in reply, "You do not look like a cook. It appears you are capable of conquering the entire world by your own strength. In any case I am engaging you as the head cook of the royal kitchen." After taking over the charge of the kitchen, Bhimasena satisfied the king and other members of the royal family with delicious dishes prepared by him. His identity remained undisclosed.

Draupadi in dirty apparel while proceeding along the path adjoining the palace, came in sight of queen Sudeshna. She, out of pity, called her to the palace and enquired about her identity. In reply Draupadi said, "My name is Sairendri. I have some skill in hair-dressing, making of garlands etc. I was first engaged to serve Satyabhama, wife of Krishna. Later I served Draupadi, the most beautiful woman of the *Kuru* clan. Now I am before you falling in bad time." Sudeshna said, "O charming woman, I cannot think of employing as my maid such a beautiful woman like you with signs of all the good qualities. Moreover, I have the fear that Virataraja might get attracted by your beauty and take you as his queen after abandoning me." Draupadi assuring Sudeshna said, "Virataraja or any other person will not be able to gain me as five very powerful Gandharvas happen to be my husbands. They are protecting me secretly." Believing Draupadi, Sudeshna engaged her as her maid. In this way, Draupadi started her incognito stay in the palace keeping her real identity completely undisclosed.

Then Sahadeva appeared before the king dressed as a cow-boy and said, "*Maharaj*, I am a *Vaishya* by name Arishtanemi. Earlier I used to look after the cattle of the Pandavas. Following the disappearance of the Pandavas I am passing my days in extreme distress without any job. I shall be grateful to be appointed under you." Virataraja at first did not believe his statement. As he wanted to know his true identity, Sahadeva said, "*Maharaj*, I was in-charge of the counting of the cattle of the Pandavas. I am also an expert in cattle disease. Besides, I can tell the events of the past and forecast those of the present and the future. For my various qualities the king of Ayodhya used to look upon me with great love and affection." On being satisfied with his words, Virataraja engaged Sahadeva to look after the royal stable. In this way Sahadeva began his incognito stay keeping his identity undisclosed.

Soon, eunuch Arjuna in a woman's dress appeared before Virataraja. The entire royal court was surprised to see such a strong-built tall person in the woman's dress. The king asked him, "O great man, you have put on woman's dress; but your body bears many signs of carrying weapons. You do not appear to be a eunuch." Arjuna said in reply, "*Maharaj*, I know music and dance and can also play the musical instruments. Kindly appoint me as the dance teacher of princess Uttaraa. My name is Brihannala. I get merged into deep sorrow when I remember the circumstances which have brought about my present misfortune." The king being satisfied with his words, appointed Arjuna as the dance teacher of princess Uttara. Soon Arjuna became dear to the royal inmates. None showed any interest about his true identity.

Lastly, Nakula appeared before the king and said, "*Maharaj*, I have all the knowledge of horses. Previously I was in-charge of the stable of king Yudhisthira. My name is Granthika. I am eager to be the keeper of your horses." The king said in reply, 'Horse-keeping does not seem to be your suitable job. In view of your eagerness, I am, however, appointing you as the head of the royal stable." Thus, Nakula also started his incognito stay at Viratanagara.

On becoming the member of the royal court, Yudhisthira within a few days became a favourite of the king, the royal prince and the fellow courtiers. He used to secretly send his brothers the money earned by defeating his competitors in the dice-game. Bhimasena used to send his brothers various items of food from the kitchen. Arjuna secretly distributed among the brothers old clothes collected from the inner apartment on the plea of sale outside.

Sahadeva used to send the brothers milk products from the cow-shed while Nakula started sending the money he got as salary from the royal court. Draupadi used to watch the activities of the Pandavas without anybody's knowledge. In this way, the Pandavas with mutual help, without, however, maintaining any direct contact among themselves, were passing their days at Viratnagar. They at the same time kept a sharp eye on Draupadi so that no harm was caused to her from the Kauravas or from any other quarter.

In the fourth month, on the occasion of the festival of *Bhrahma-mahotsava* a wrestling competition was organised in the capital. In the competition many wrestlers of the kingdom including the strongest wrestler Jimuta came to participate. When none of the wrestlers dared to challenge the formidable Jimuta, the king asked Bhimasena to fight with him. Bhimasena did not like to show his wrestling valour publicly as this might give out the identity of the Pandavas. At the same time he felt it would be quite improper to disregard the command of the king. He accordingly, with considerable reluctance, joined the competition. Jimuta as also other wrestlers were easily defeated by Bhimasena. On the death of Jimuta, the king became happy and rewarded Bhimasena handsomely. Thereafter, on the command of the king, Bhimasena fought with lions, tigers and elephants in the presence of queen and other females in the inner apartment for their great amusement.

In this way, the Pandavas spent ten months of their incognito stay by performing their respective duties to the complete satisfaction of the king, the queen and the other courtiers. One day queen Sudeshna's brother and the commander-in-chief of the king's army Kichaka, a great warrior, being enamoured of Drapaudi's beauty expressed his desire to marry her. Draupadi contemptuously dismissed his evil proposal warning he would lose his life at the hands of her five husbands who were all very powerful Gandharvas if he did not restrain himself. Having failed to change the mind of Draupadi, Kichaka sought her sister Sudeshna's help. Sudeshna accordingly brought Draupadi to her chamber on the plea of bringing for her a glass of wine when Kichaka who was hiding there, tried to draw her to him by pulling the wearing apparel. Draupadi immediately pushed him to the ground and hurriedly came to the royal court. Kichaka followed Draupadi to the court, pulled her by the hair and kicked her around in presence of the king and other courtiers including Yudhisthira. Bhimasena who was also present there became so enraged at the insult of Draupadi that he was about to get up from his seat with the intention to kill him. Yudhisthira understanding Bhimasena's intention very tactfully restrained him, lest their identity should get disclosed, by touching his body and stating he could easily collect wood from outside. (Bhimasena was then actually looking outside for a big tree with which he could strike Kichaka.) Bhimasena understood the real meaning of Yudhisthira's words and remained seated.

The king and the other members of the court took no steps to restrain Kichaka even after hearing the piteous prayer for help from oppressed Draupadi. Yudhisthira and Bhimasena also remained silent with their heads cast down. Draupadi then sharply rebuked the king denouncing him as unrighteous. On this the king pleaded his inability to intervene in the matter as according to him the cause of dispute between Draupadi and Kichaka was unknown to him. It was apparent that he did not have the courage to go against Kichaka. Yudhisthira consoled Draupadi and asked her to go to the queen. Before leaving the court Draupadi said, "I have always performed religious rites for those who have suffered so much for the dice-game of their eldest brother. They will certainly kill all the wicked people and remove my sorrow." Draupadi, thus very tactfully conveyed the message to Bhimasena and the other brothers to take steps to kill Kichaka and others to avenge her humiliation.

Queen Sudeshna, on hearing the incident, observed that wicked Kichaka blinded by lust had insulted Draupadi and if Draupadi so wished she would have him killed. On this, Draupadi told the queen that Kichaka would possibly be destroyed this night itself.

The same night Draupadi secretly met Bhimasena and after narrating the background of the incident expressed her deepest regret that Kichaka could dare to insult her in the open court in his very presence of Dharmaraj. She gave out that she would take her own life if Kichaka, her tormentor, was not killed by him. Consoling Draupadi, Bhimasena told her he had already decided to kill Kichaka. Giving out his plan he said, "Yajnyaseni,(Draupadi's another name) you may tell Kichaka about your change of mind and your willingness to meet him in the night in the royal dancing hall. Nobody stays in the dancing hall in the night. A comfortable bed has been kept ready there. You may bring Kichaka to the dancing hall by suitable allurement I shall kill him there." Draupadi agreed to act according to Bhimasena's advice.

In the night Bhimasena in the guise of a woman remained lying on the bed in the dancing hall. At the dead of night Kichaka, maddened with lust, came to the dancing hall and embraced Bhimasena in the bed thinking him to be Draupadi when a duel ensued between the two. In the duel Kichaka was killed and his body was transformed into a lump of flesh. During the duel, Arjuna was playing on his drum in order to overwhelm its sound outside. The palace guards and the others on hearing the sound of the drum thought some musical programme was being held in the dancing hall. None suspected anything wrong. On completion of his job Bhimasena retuned to his apartment. In the morning Draupadi announced in the royal court Kichaka had been killed by the Gandharvas.

Kichaka's death created a huge commotion in the capital. The followers of Kichaka held Draupadi responsible for his death and decided, with the consent of the king, to burn her alive along with Kichaka's dead body. Accordingly, they tied Draupadi with the dead body of Kichaka and proceeded toward the cremation ground with great exultation. Draupadi realising her imminent death called the Pandavas by their secret names for help. Hearing Draupadi's lamentation, Bhimasena flew into a rage and immediately pursued Kichaka's followers. Near the cremation ground he attacked them with a big tree he uprooted from the wayside. On seeing Bhimasena's dreadful sight with the tree in his hand, most of the Kichaka's followers fled away out of fear leaving Draupadi there. Some of them lost their lives at Bhimasena's hands. On being released, Draupadi returned to the palace on instruction from Bhimasena. At the gate of the palace Draupadi again met Bhimasena and told him in a coded language," I pay my obeisance to the Gandharvas who have saved my life.' Bhimsena also replied in the coded language saying "The Gandharvas who are always obedient to her, are now free from debt by keeping their promise."

At her chamber, queen Sudeshna told Draupadi, "Sairendri, you must immediately leave the palace. This is the order of the king. The king has been gripped with fear at the activities of the Gandharvas. Moreover, your beauty and charm have caused deep disquiet in the minds of the male folk here. For this you should not stay in the palace any further." Draupadi on this humbly said, "The Gandharvas will successfully complete their work within the next thirteen days. Kindly allow me to stay here for these few days only. The king will also gain immensely at the success of the Gandharvas." Sudeshna agreed.

30.

At Hastinapura, Duryodhana became worried when he did not get any information from his agents about the whereabouts of the Pandavas during their incognito stay. He, however, got from them the news of death of Kichaka at the hands of the Gandharvas. At his instance a meeting of the royal court was held to discuss the matter. Explaining the situation before the courtiers Duryodhana said, "Only a few months are left before the end of the incognito stay of the Pandavas. On completion of the incognito stay the Pandavas will proceed with all their might against us. We are to make all efforts to secure our kingdom by sending the Pandavas again to the forest. I would, therefore, call upon you to make renewed efforts to collect information about their whereabouts."

Karna suggested immediate despatch of reliable agents in disguise to all prosperous places, assemblies of persons, holy places etc. to search for the Pandavas. He also suggested the despatch of a select group of well-dressed agents who had known the Pandavas from before, to the river banks, parks, hermitages and similar other places to search for them.

Duhshasana agreed with the suggestions of Karna. He observed that the Pandavas might be hiding in a very secret place or it might be they had been killed in some natural calamities. He told Duryodhana not to worry.

Dronacharya said, "I firmly believe the Pandavas have not died. They must be staying at a secret place with extreme alertness only to come out at an opportune moment. The virtuous Pandavas are unparalleled in strength and courage. It is not easy for ordinary persons to search them out. I suggest only those *Brahmins* and saintly persons, who are fully conversant with the characteristic distinctions of the Pandavas, may be engaged for the searching operation."

Agreeing with Dronacharya, grandfather Bhishma said, "The Pandavas possess auspicious signs and are well-versed in scriptures. They are also devoted to truth and have wide experience in warfare. They are certainly waiting for good time with devotion to Krishna. They are constantly being protected because they have both virtue and strength. None can cause any harm to them. I am giving you some advice regarding the Pandavas. Listen carefully. I do not agree with the suggestions earlier put forward with regard to the determination of the place of stay of the Pandavas. *Maharaj* Yudhisthira is an extraordinary person. The king in whose kingdom he would live must also be endowed with all the virtues. No wrongs will be committed by him. It would be a kingdom of peace and prosperity. The people there will not be influenced by greed, violence, hatred and other evil vices. If you think there is truth in my words, you may decide your course of action accordingly."

Fully agreeing with Bhishma, Dronacharya told Duryodhana, "My son,, while making efforts to determine the place of stay of the Pandavas, you should simultaneously take steps which are helpful to you. It would not be proper to ignore even your weakest enemy, not to speak of the powerful Pandavas. On fulfillment of their promise they would appear with great enthusiasm. For this you shall have to make an all-out effort to increase your own strength. Take steps to increase the strength of your army in consultation with your allies. If the situation turns unfavourable, you may have to make peace with the Pandavas. This aspect will also have to be kept in mind. Follow the principles of conciliation, gift, division and punishment in bringing under control your strong and weak enemies. Keep the allies consoled with sweet words. Also ensure your army remains contented and in high morale. Adequate attention has to be paid to the collection of revenue. In this way you should prepare yourself for the war by increasing your wealth and power." The Kauravas listened to him silently without any comments.

Meanwhile, there developed a new situation which ultimately proved disastrous to the Kauravas. Trigartaraj Susharma on being earlier defeated by Kichaka had been staying at Hastinapura under the protection of the Kauravas. Now following the death of Kichaka the situation underwent a complete change. Keeping this in mind Susharma told Duryodhana, "His Majesty, Virataraja with the help of Kichaka, his heroic commander-in- chief has occupied my kingdom. Now Kichaka is no more. He has been killed by the Gandharvas. Virataraja on losing his commander-in-chief must be very weak and dejected. I think this is the best time to attack his kingdom. Your strength will also further increase with the capture of his wealth, cattle etc. after his defeat"

Supporting Susharma's suggestion, Karna said,"We should immediately attack the Matsya kingdom. It is no use wasting our money, resources and manpower in search of the Pandavas who are now without any resources and friends." Accordingly, Susharma and Duryodhana, on alternate dates, attacked Matsya kingdom with two separate armies. Susharma launched the attack first. Virataraja was defeated and made a prisoner. On Yudhisthira's order he was subsequently rescued by Bhimasena. On being defeated at the hands of Bhimasena, Susharma agreed to serve as a slave under Virataraja. On Yudhisthira's order he was, however, released. As Bhimasena was in disguise, none could know his true identity. The next day a large Kaurava army commanded by Bhishma, Duryodhana, Karna, Duhshasana and other great warriors attacked Matsya kingdom and captured many cattle. On getting this information, Arjuna secretly met Draupadi and asked her to tell prince Uttar that earlier Brihannala had successfully acted as a charioteer of the Pandava army and as such she was the only person suitable to be his chariot-driver in the present situation. After a lot of hesitation, Uttar with Brihannala as his charioteer proceeded towards the battle-field to face the Kaurava army. On seeing a huge Kaurava army he, however, became nervous and wanted to retreat. Brihannala gave him courage saying he could safely rely on her. Arjuna on the way collected the weapons kept concealed in the mango tree and disclosed the true identity of the Pandavas with the reasons behind their disguise. He then armed with divine weapons proceeded towards the Kaurava army with prince Uttar as his chariot-driver. In the battle Arjuna completely defeated the Kaurava army. He even cut away a portion of the wearing apparels of the Kaurava warriors lying unconscious on the ground for presentation to princess Uttaraa. He also rescued the cattle captured by the Karauvas.

While returning to the capital after the victory, Arjuna warned prince Uttar not to disclose the incognito stay of the Pandavas at this stage to any one else. He advised him to give out that he (the prince) himself was the architect of the victory against the Kauravas. Prince Uttar returned to the capital with Brihannala as his charioteer and was given a rousing reception for his victory.

31.

After prince Uttar left the capital with Brihannala, there were some startling developments. The king expressing his anxiety for Uttar said, "It is certain that the prince would not return alive from the battle when the eunuch Brihannala has gone with him as his charioteer." Assuring the king, Yudhisthira said in reply, "*Maharaj*, you need not worry at all. Your son will certainly be able to defeat the enemy under the charioteering of Brihannala." In the midst of this conversation the messenger brought to the king the news of victory of prince Uttar. Highly elated at the news, the king arranged a grand reception for the prince and thereafter sat down to play dice with Yudhisthira. During the dice-game the king several times referred to the prince's victory against the Kauravas. On this Yudhisthira observed, "Any one who will take Brihannala as his charioteer, is bound to come out victorious." Annoyed at this frequent praise of Brihannala the king said, "Kanka (Yudhisthira's assumed name) you are insulting me by not praising my son. You have forgot ten how to speak to a king. I am forgiving you this time." Paying no heed to the king's words, Yudhisthira again praised Brihannala and said. "*Maharaj*, there is none who is equal to Brihannala in physical strength. She is capable of defeating gods, demons and humans together." At the repeated praise of Brihannala, the king lost his patience and caused bleeding injury in the nose of Yudhisthira by hitting him with a dice. Draupadi who was standing nearby immediately held the blood in a gold bowl preventing it from dropping to the ground.

On return from the battle-field, prince Uttar was pained to see Yudhisthira smeared with blood. He angrily enquired of his father about the perpetrator of this heinous crime. On hearing the details from the king, Uttar said, "*Maharaj*, you have done a contemptible deed. You will be destroyed by the Brahminical curse, if he is not pleased and cheerful. When the king begged for pardon, Yudhisthira said, "I have already pardoned you. You and your kingdom would have been destroyed if my blood had fallen on the ground."

At this moment Brihannala appeared there. When the king congratulated her for the victory of his son, Uttar said the son of an angel had appeared at the battle-field. He alone had accomplished this impossible task. When the king wanted to see him, Uttar said that he would be appearing within a few days. The king thus could not come to know anything about Arjuna. Thereafter, the Pandavas in a secret meeting with prince Uttar decided their future course of action.

The next day Yudhisthira in royal robes took his seat on the throne in the presence of prince Uttar, Draupadi and other Pandava brothers. As the king entered the throne room, Yudhisthira introduced his brothers and Draupadi to him. Uttar introducing Arjuna to the king said he was the son of the angel who alone with indomitable courage and strength, had defeated the powerful Kaurava army. The king on hearing the facts was struck by utter surprise. He formally received Yudhisthira with all honour and dignity, and offered him his entire kingdom. The king then proposed the marriage of princess Uttaraa to Arjuna who, however, was agreeable to accept Uttaraa as his daughter-in-law. This being approved by Yudhisthira, Uttaraa's marriage with Abhimanyu, son of Arjuna, was solemnised in presence of Krishna and many other dignitaries at Viratnagara with great pomp and grandeur. Thus ended the full period of exile including the one-year incognito stay of the Pandavas in compliance with the promised conditions of the dice-game.

32.

Duryodhana on getting the information of their public appearance, raised objection that the Pandavas before completion of their one-year incognito stay, had openly fought on behalf of Virataraja against the Kauravas and for this they had broken their promise. He demanded the Pandavas would have to go to exile again in compliance of the conditions of the dice-game. On calculation, Duryodhan's objection was found to be without any basis. Bhishma and the other elders gave the opinion the Pandavas had actually completed their one-year incognito stay. The Kauravas were not satisfied with this verdict.

The Kauravas and the Pandavas were involved in a serious war of nerves over the incognito stay. The Kauravas tried to find out the whereabouts of the

Pandavas by sending their agents to various places. On the other hand the Pandavas were determined to keep their place of stay unknown to any body else. And this success of Pandavas showed the utter incompetence of the Kaurava agents in getting any information of the enemy even during that long one-year. In fact, the Pandavas under the leadership of Yudhisthira achieved their success by scrupulously following the principles of intelligence in maintaining secrecy in all their activities. Their secrecy was so fool-proof that the Kaurava agents, who were present at Viratanagara, were completely hoodwinked. They also hopelessly moved about without achieving anything tangible.

As earlier indicated, Yudhisthira himself devised the details of the plan to be adopted during the incognito stay. Here we find Yudhisthira as a shrewd intelligence operator. Yudhisthira was the embodiment of truth and virtue. He was against taking any unfair means to achieve his objective. He knew very well that it was extremely difficult to stay incognito for such a long period particularly when the Pandavas were all very well-known personalities. Moreover, Duryodhana's spies were actively searching for them. In this regard, Bhimasena's fear was always fresh in his mind. This was why he proceeded in the matter very cautiously by safeguarding all sides. Yudhisthira had complete confidence in himself. Though he knew full well that success was essentially the result of one's own efforts, he being a highly religious person was equally conscious of the fact that divine grace was also required for such success. He accordingly, besides chalking out the plan of action during the incognito stay, obtained on the eve of their journey for Viratanagara, the blessings of father Dharma, priest Dhoumnya and many other sages for the success. He even satisfied Goddess Durga with his prayer and obtained her boon. Yudhisthira, thus entered into the uncertain and dangerous period of incognito stay on the strength of his own power and judgement while invoking the divine grace.

We know that Yudhisthira decided to spend the period of their incognito stay in Viratanagara on the advice of father Dharma. This advice was fully to his liking. Virataraja was known to be a highly religious person, and the virtuous Pandavas were only expected to seek refuge in the kingdom of such a king. It may be recalled that Bhishma and the other elders advised Duryodhana to search for Yudhisthira only in the territories of truly religious kings. Search in other places, they warned, would serve no purpose. Thus selection of Viratanagara as the place of the Pandavas' incognito stay was completely justified. The virtuous bearing of the Pandavas helped secure their easy acceptance by Virataraja. It is apparent that the Pandavas would have encountered serious difficulties had they decided to stay incognito in an ordinary place. Even their success might have been jeopardised.

The advice received from priest Dhoumya on the eve of their departure to Viratanagar proved extremely useful to the Pandvas. By scrupulously following this advice, they remained patient in the face of all provocations and earned the goodwill of the king and the other courtiers by performing all their good works in disguise with their identity kept secret. Here the Pandavas as also Draupadi performed their respective roles adroitly. All this was possible because of sound leadership of Yudhisthira. He was constantly watching the activities of his brothers so that they, particularly Bhimasena known for his hot-headedness, did not do anything that would jeopardise their identity. We have seen that Yudhisthira's patience at the humiliation of Draupadi at the hands of Kichaka and his tactful prevention of Bhimasena when he was about to uproot a tree for the purpose of killing Kichaka thus averting the premature disclosure of their identity. His decision to send Draupadi to the queen was also very timely as it helped in mitigating the tension in the royal court over Draupadi's humiliation by Kichaka. Otherwise her continued humiliation would have certainly proved unbearable for Bhimasena, and Yudhisthira himself would have been unable to restrain him. Yudhisthira's wisdom, patience and foresight thus prevented a serious catastrophe.

The entire plan to kill Kichaka was the brain-wave of Bhimasena. Though there is no mention in the Mahabharata, it seems likely that Yudhisthira had full knowledge of the plan. Draupadi showed exemplary courage and intelligence in alluring a great warrior like Kichaka to the royal dancing hall in the night as advised by Bhimasena. Here, we also get another example of her acting capability. By exuding all her charm she was able to convince Kichaka of her change of mind. Her proposal for union in the dancing hall raised no suspicion whatsoever in his mind and he was easily led to his death trap. Her distress call for help from Bhimasena by the secret name when she was being forcibly taken away towards the cremation ground, gives evidence to her great presence of mind and mental equanimity in the face of grave danger, ultimately leading to her rescue along with the defeat of Kichaka's followers. She intelligently created confusion in the mind of the king and other courtiers by announcing Kichaka's death at the hands of the Gandharvas. Her action while serving the purpose, kept the identity of the Pandavas undisclosed. She also showed rare presence of mind when she held the bowl to prevent Yudhisthira's blood from falling to the ground following the injury caused to him by Virataraja. She knew Arjuna had a vow that he would kill anyone who would dare to spill Yudhisthira's blood to the ground except in the battlefield. Draupadi's timely action thus saved life of Virataraja from the hands of Arjuna. We know that the entire matter ended peacefully when Virataraja sought pardon from Yudhisthira. The solemnisation of the marriage of Uttaraa with Abhimanyu forged a strong alliance between the Pandavas and the Viratas. This alliance played a significant role in the Mahabharata war.

Draupadi and the Pandavas selected their own assumed names and professions. Yudhisthira did not impose his own decision on others in this regard. This was indeed a very correct decision. He knew that any outside interference would have only affected their natural professional competence. Yudhisthira was fond of dice play. He accordingly became the king's dice player. Bhimasena was a voracious eater and an expert in cooking. For these qualities, he was appointed as the head cook of the royal kitchen. He was physically strong and had great competence in wrestling. He was as such engaged by the king in wrestling competition and also in fighting with animals. Arjuna learned music and dance in the court of Indra and was also a eunuch. He, accordingly, became the dance and music teacher in the inner apartment. Nakula and Sahadeva for their qualifications were appointed as head of the royal stable and the cattle farm respectively. Draupadi, as the royal princess, knew the art of hair dressing, and accordingly there was no difficulty for her to become the queen's maid. We are all surprised to see the self-confidence and the acting competence of Draupadi and the Pandavas. Right selection of the professions in disguise in conformity with the principles of intelligence operations, mainly contributed to the Pandavas' successful completion of their incognito stay. This success proved beyond doubt that the Pandavas were more intelligent, clever and skilful than the Kauravas.

There is no excuse for the failure of the Kauravas in detecting the place of incognito stay of the Pandavas. Duryodhana was aware that the Pandavas were armed with divine weapons and they would fiercely confront them with the help of Krishna and other allies on completion of the incognito stay. To the Kauravas like the Pandavas this incognito stay was a life and death question. Duryodhana, no doubt tried to obtain information of the Pandavas' movements and activities through his agents. Some of the agents reported to him at Hastinapura that they had no information about the whereabouts of the Pandavas because of loss of contact with them due to sudden advent of rain and storm during the last leg of their exile in the forest. In fact, when the Pandavas were on their way to Viratnagar through the forest, Draupadi one day noticed some people moving suspiciously some distance away. Arjuna on getting this information understood they were Duryodhana's agents engaged to watch their movements. He, immediately with the help of his divine arrow, created rain and storm thereby causing optical illusion which prevented them from pursuing the Pandavas any further. Apparently, Duryodhana had no contingency plan to deal with such unforeseen developments. The Pandavas thus could deceive Duryodhana's agents under the cover of natural calamities to proceed safely to Viratanagara.

Duryodhana's agents did not correctly follow the principles of surveillance. They should have maintained visual contact with the Pandavas from adequate distance. This, apparently they did not do and they prematurely exposed their presence out of exuberance by coming too close to the Pandavas. Having lost sight of the Pandavas in the midst of storm and rain the agents got no idea in which direction they had gone. This is no doubt the first and the most serious failure of the agents in detecting Pandavas' incognito place of stay which was the most dangerous period of their exile.

Almost simultaneously, the Pandavas and Draupadi took up their jobs in the palace of Virataraja. They of course were all in disguise with assumed names and false credentials. They, however, were all highly polished in their talks and behaviour. The five Pandava brothers appeared graceful even in their disguise. Draupadi in the guise of an ordinary maid also looked as charming and beautiful as before. The king and the queen were convinced of their superior lineage and engaged them without much hesitation in their respective jobs as prayed for. This arrival at the capital of so many unknown persons, including a beautiful lady at a time, did not surprisingly cause any suspicion in the minds of Duryodhana's agents. The killing of Jimuta, kingdom's best wrestler, fighting with the fierce animals and rescue of Draupadi after defeating the followers of Kichaka with an uprooted tree by Bhimasena masquerading as Gandharva also caused no suspicion with regard to his true identity. Even though the agents were aware that such extraordinary deeds could only be performed by Bhimasena.

Does this failure of Duryodhana's agents indicate that they were professionally incompetent? We do not think so. The incidents were so serious that even the superficial observers must have been inquisitive about the identity of the perpetrators of these extraordinary deeds, not to speak of the trained agents of Duryodhana. Is it that the agents were actually Vidura's men who intentionally on his instructions remained indifferent to these serious happenings and refrained from reporting anything to Duryodhana? Though there is no mention in the Mahabharata, circumstances seem to justify this presumption. The abject failure of the agents cannot be explained in any other way. We have got enough evidence of Vidura's competence as a shrewd intelligence operator. As a well-wisher of the Pandavas, it is reasonable to believe that he was keeping a track of their movements and activities during the exile and their staying incognito at Viratnagar. It appears, he secretly infiltrated his own reliable persons among the agents employed by Duryodhana to keep watch over the Pandavas and they misguided them at every step so as to keep Duryodhana in the dark about the developments at Viratnagar since the arrival of the Pandavas there. Our suspicion about Vidura becomes stronger in this regard when we find that he refrained from giving any opinion about the possible place of Pandavas' incognito stay like Bhishma and Drona. If our presumption is correct (and correct it is as analysis of the events indicates), Vidura's meticulous counter-intelligence operation is indeed rare even in modern times when intelligence operation has acquired tremendous sophistication. Krishna might also have had a hand behind Vidura's efforts to scuttle Duryodhana's steps to detect the incognito stay of the Pandavas.

Duryodhana's agents of course informed him about the death of Kichaka at the hands of the Gandharvas. There was, however, nothing new in this information. Their information was based on the open announcement by Draupadi that Kichaka had been killed by the Gandharvas and the resultant severe tension in the capital. The agents were still in the dark about the real facts. On getting the news of Kichaka's death, Duryodhana had the suspicion that Bhimasena might be the perpetrator of the murder, as such a heroic person like Kichaka could only be killed by heroic Bhimasena. But it had been too late. By that time, moreover, Duryodhana made no efforts to find out the real identity of the Gandharvas. It was known after their public appearance, on completion of the one-year incognito stay that the Gandharvas were none other than the Pandavas. The Kauravas were thus completely outwitted by the Pandavas.

We are aware that Duryodhana, without getting any information of the Pandavas first, decided to again depute his agents to different places to search them out. We know Bhishma (as also Drona) disagreed with him and advised him to concentrate his search only in the kingdoms of those kings who were virtuous. He also suggested deputing suitable *Brahmins* and other saintly persons as agents. Duryodhana, however, did not give any importance to this valuable suggestion, and he instead on the advice of Karna, in coordination with Susharma, attacked the kingdom of Virataraj and met humiliating defeat. Had Duryodhana complied with Bhishma's advice, developments might have taken a different turn.

We have seen in the story of Nala and Damayanti, how Damayanti alone, with the help of *Brahmin* agents, found out her missing husband Nala. What was possible for Damayanti alone and unaided, was not possible for Duryodhana with his huge resources and manpower, to find out five very distinguished well-known persons like the Pandavas and Draupadi, a lady of exquisite beauty- all living in the same palace compound – during the long one-year period. What could be more shameful for Duryodhana than this?

33.

Soon after their public appearance, a meeting was held at the court of Virataraja to decide the future course of action of the Pandavas. The meeting was attended, besides the Pandavas, by Virataraja, Panchalraja (Draupadi's father), Krishna, brother Baldeva and Jadava warrior Satyaki. Initiating the discussion, Krishna said, "The Pandavas on being defeated by the Kauravas in the deceitful dice-game have fulfilled their promise by undergoing immense sufferings for thirteen long years. They are now justifiably entitled to get back their lost kingdom. We are, however, not aware of the intention of Duryodhana. I suggest, let a religious person be deputed to Hastinapura for a settlement by asking for the return of the kingdom."

Agreeing with Krishna, Baldeva said, "It is true that the Kauravas have captured the wealth and kingdom of the Pandavas by deceit, but even then they should not be unnecessarily antagonised. We should not forget that Yudhisthira disregarding the advice of his well-wishers, willingly joined the dice-game out of sheer recklessness. He knew Shakuni is an expert dice-player. Even then he started playing with him though his own knowledge of the game was limited. In this I find no fault of Shakuni. I believe *Maharaj* Dhritarashtra will not ignore any proposal of peaceful settlement with the Pandavas. It is always preferable to obtain money and property by peaceful means. Use of force to obtain money and property is undesirable. Let some wise person be deputed to *Maharaj* Dhritarashtra with the settlement proposal."

Sharply criticising Baldeva, Satyaki said, 'Expert dice-players invited Yudhisthira to the dice-game and defeated him knowing fully well that he has no experience in the game. How can it be justified? If Yudhisthira had himself invited the Kauravas to play the game and got defeated, we could have considered it to be justified. Now why would the Pandavas bow down to the wicked Kauravas when they are free of the bond of promise of the dice-game? The Pandavas should by force recapture their lost wealth and kingdom. We are not short of power and resources."

King Drupada said, "Duryodhana will never willingly hand over Yudhisthira's kingdom to him. It would also not be possible to win over Duryodhana by any conciliatory words. It appears war is inevitable. We shall have to make preparations for war right from now. Let messengers be sent to our allies praying for help. It is certain that Duryodhana will also seek help of the different kings by sending his own messengers. According to the prevailing custom he who sends the messenger first, gets the promise of help. We should not, therefore, make any delay in the matter. My *Brahmin* priest, who is clever and intelligent, may proceed to the Kaurava court with our demand."

Krishna said, 'The suggestion of Drupadaraj is quite reasonable. We are to act according to his advice. We, the Yadavas, however, are equally related to both the Kauravas and the Pandavas. The Kauravas did never misbehave with us. In case Duryodhana out of greed for power, rejects the peace proposal, messengers may first be sent to the different kingdoms for help. After that our help may be sought.'

After the meeting was over, Krishana left for Dwaraka. Yudhisthira then started deputing messengers to the different kingdoms. Soon many kings with their armies assembled at Viratnagar. On getting this information, Duryodhana also became active in mobilising his forces. On his invitation many kings began to assemble at Hastinapura with their armies. In the mean time, Drupada's priest along with his disciples left for Hastinapura with the peace proposal.

Before his departure for Hastinapura, the priest was given a few tips by the king. Addressing the priest the king said, "You are aware of the present relations between the Kauravas and the Pandavas. With the knowledge of king Dhritarashtra, his sons have captured the kingdom of the Pandavas by defeating them in deceitful dice-game. On arrival at Hastinapura, your duty would be to satisfy Dhritarashtra by explaining to him the tenets of religion so that he is encouraged to take steps to change the mind of his principal warriors. My belief is that Pandava's well-wisher Vidura on hearing you, would try his best to spread anti-Kaurava sentiments among the principal courtiers like Bhishma. Duryodhana will be worried if dissensions crop up among the senior leaders on whose active support he is preparing for war. Naturally, he will have to make special efforts to iron out the differences resulting in unnecessary loss of time and energy. In this opportunity the Pandavas will be able to complete their war preparations. At the same time, you should intelligently try to sow discontent and dissension among the enemy's army commanders. In order to rouse sympathy for the Pandavas you may very skilfully narrate their sufferings and privations during the period of exile to the king and other senior courtiers. To the elders, you may explain the traditional family customs and practices. This will help create sympathy for the Pandavas while causing dissensions among the Kauravas. You are a *Brahmin* well versed in the Vedas. Moreover, you are our messenger on a peace mission. You have nothing to worry."

It would appear Drupadaraj's assessment of the situation was correct and this was accepted by Krishna and other dignitaries present in the meeting. Baldeva's discordant statement was brushed aside. In view of the known arrogance and greed of Duryodhana, all on the Pandava side seemed convinced that their lost kingdom could not be retrieved by peaceful negotiations and that they would have to take recourse to war to achieve their objective. While keeping the door of negotiations open, they were realistic enough to start their war preparations without any loss of time. Duryodhana was also equally active in mobilising forces indicating his rejection of the path of peaceful settlement. In the context of war hovering on the horizon, the spy network of both the sides was specially activated. In this regard, the shrewdness of Virataraja utterly surprises us. His briefing to his priest on the peace mission indicates he was no less competent as an intelligence operator. From his long experience in governing the kingdom, he was aware that the enemy must first be weakened through internal dissensions before waging the war. With this end in view, he suitably briefed his priest about his real duty at Hastinapura under the cover of peace mission. We shall see later how his visit greatly bolstered up the dissensions in the Kaurava court over Duryodhana's actions and policies and weakened his war efforts.

Immediately after the departure of the priest to Hastinapura, Arjuna on Yudhisthira's direction arrived at Dwaraka to seek Krishna's help in the war. On getting information from his agents about Arjuna's visit to Dwaraka, Duryodhana also arrived at Dwaraka in a fast-moving chariot to meet Krishna. Both Arjuna and Duryodhana arrived simultaneously at Dwaraka and entered Krishna's chamber only to see him asleep. Duryodhana entering first took his seat by the side of his head. Arjuna entering after Duryodhana was seated by the side of Krishna's feet. Krishna rising from sleep after some time first saw Arjuna and then Duryodhana and wanted to know the purpose of their visit. Duryodhana speaking first said, "In this war I am eager to have you on our side. I have come first and as such according to the custom, we are entitled to get your help." Krishna said in reply, "O great warrior, there is no doubt you have come to me first: but my sight first fell on Arjuna, accordingly I shall help both of you. Let one side get my Narayani army and the other side only myself. In this war I shall remain neutral and unarmed." Arjuna cordially welcomed Krishna, while Duryodhana got the Narayani army. He came out of Krishna's chamber greatly elated at his achievement. Duryodhana could not realise Krishna, endowed as he was with divine power, was alone above all mundane powers, not to speak of his own army.

Thereafter, Duryodhana came to Baldeva and sought his help. Baldeva, however, pleaded his inability to help him saying on Krishna's advice he had decided to remain neutral. Duryodhana then came for help to Jadava warrior Kritavarma, who readily agreed to join the Kaurava side with his one *akshouhini* strong army. Duryodhana returned to Hastinapura greatly satisfied with the success of his mission at Dwaraka.

Later Krishna asked Arjuna why he had welcomed him to the Pandava side despite his aversion to war. Arjuna said in reply, "O God, you are alone capable of destroying the Kauravas. Your achievements are well-known throughout the universe. But my wish is that I shall establish my fame in the world by destroying the Kauravas all alone. This is why I have welcomed you to our side though you have decided to remain neutral in the war. My request is that you may kindly agree to be my chariot driver." Krishna said in reply, "Arjuna, I know you are equal to me in power and strength. I shall fulfill your wish. I am ready to become your charioteer." Arjuna returned to Viratnagara fully satisfied.

Madraraj Shalya, on getting information about the impending war between the Kauravas and the Pandavas left for Viratanagara with a large army to join the Pandava's side. Shalya was the brother of Madri, the second queen of king Pandu and the maternal uncle of Nakula and Sahadeva. As such, he was also the maternal uncle of the other Pandava brothers. Naturally he had sympathy for the Pandavas. In India, at that time there was no warrior matching his valour and strength. Duryodhana was thus eager to secure his help in the war as the side he would join would obviously become stronger. Knowing his sympathy for the Pandavas, Duryodhana devised a novel plan to win him over. He got a beautiful palace con-structed on the route to Viratanagara and lavishly entertained him and his army there. Duryodhana first did not appear before the Madraraj, who thought all these arrangements had been made for him by Yudhisthira. Being enamoured of the architectural beauty of the palace, Madraraj expressed his desire to reward the architects. On getting this information from his men, Duryodhana in disguise appeared before him. Thinking him to be one of the architects, Madraraj asked him to pray for some gift from him for his artistic skill. Immediately Duryodhana disclosed his identity and said, "Uncle, your words cannot be untrue. You have promised to give me anything I want. My request is that you may very kindly become the commander of my army. This is the only boon I seek from you." Being bound by promise, Madraraj acceded to the request of Duryodhana and left for Viratanagara saying he had some important discussions with Yudhisthira. He promised to return soon.

On reaching Viratanagara, Madraraj Shalya told Yudhisthira, "*Maharaj*, you all are now free after undergoing immense sufferings during the exile. There is no happiness for the king without his kingdom. Your evil days have ended. Now is the time for you to enjoy the kingdom after destroying the enemy." On saying this he narrated his meeting with Duryodhana *en route* and the circumstances under which he had agreed to join the Kaurava side. On hearing all details, Yudhisthira said, "Uncle, you have done the correct thing by giving the promise of help to Duryodhana. But you shall have to perform for my sake a mischievous deed. You are equal to Vasudeva (Krishna). No work is impossible for you. It is my fervent prayer after agreeing to become the charioteer of Karna, you may kindly save the life of Arjuna during their chariot combat and also weaken the power of Karna. I know this is wrong. But you shall have to do it for our good." Madraraj said in reply, "I am giving the promise I shall weaken Karna's pride and power by giving him wrong and harmful advice in the battlefield. Then it will be possible for you to kill Karna easily. All works dear to you will be accomplished by me." Yudhisthira felt assured at the promise of Madraraj.

There is no mention in the Mahabharata whether Duryodhana could get any information about this significant decision in the meeting between Madraraj Shalya and Yudhisthira. We shall see later Madrarja's betrayal cost Duryodhana dearly during the war. Had he known the fact of change of mind of Madraraj in time, Duryodhana could have taken suitable counter measures to neutralise him. This was indeed a very costly failure on his part. On the other hand Madraraj true to his promise to Yudhisthira, very skilfully played his part as an enemy of the Kauravas under the garb of friendship without raising any suspicion.

On the invitation of Yudhisthira and Duryodhana almost all the kings and warriors, with their armies, joined the two sides. At the end, a total of eighteen *akshouhinis* were mobilised– eleven *akshouhinis* on the Kaurava side at Hastinapura and seven *akshouhinis* on the Pandava side at Viratanagara. The preparations for war were thus virtually complete. Innumerable near and dear ones like elders, brothers, relatives, kinsmen and friends on being divided into the two sides were now waiting with the determination to kill one another on the commence-ment of the war.

34.

In the mean time, the Drupada-priest on arrival at Hastinapura was cordially received by king Dhritarashtra, Bhishma and Vidura. Later addressing the king's courtiers, the priest said, "O Kauravas, Dhritarashtra and Pandu are the sons of the same father. They have got equal rights to their ancestral property. But the Kauravas are enjoying that property by deceiving the Pandavas. Does it conform to the tenets of religion? You are aware that earlier king Dhritarashtra deprived the sons of Pandu of their ancestral property by taking advantage of their inexperience as minors. Dhritarashtra's sons even tried to kill them. With permission from Dhritarashtra, Shakuni won their kingdom and wealth for the Kauravas in a deceitful dice-game. In the open court Draupadi has been humiliated. You are not unaware that the Pandavas and Draupadi have undergone immense sufferings during their exile. Even then they are prepared to arrive at a peaceful settlement with the Kauravas. This settlement proposal is not out of any weakness. The Pandavas possess unlimited power and strength. They are only eager to get back their lost kingdom and wealth peacefully. You may take steps to return their kingdom and wealth by following the path of religion and justice. There is still time."

Bhishma supporting the settlement proposal said, "O Brahmin, there is no doubt about the justifiability of your proposal. Fortunately the Pandavas even without having friends and resources have remained faithful to the path of religion. That is why they shunning the path of war have prayed for peaceful settlement of the dispute. The Pandavas are now justifiably entitled to get back their ancestral property. Arjuna now endowed with divine weapons is even invincible to the gods."

Expressing strong reaction to Bhishma's observation, Karna said, "Yudhisthira of his own accord agreed to play the dice-game with Shakuni and got defeated. He went to the exile in fulfillment of his promise. Now like a fool in violation of the promise he is demanding the return of his ancestral property with the help of others. If the Pandavas are really interested to get back their property, they shall have to go to exile in the forest again for the fulfillment of their promise. They should be careful enough not to embark on an unholy war like fools."

Rebuking Karna for his derisive remarks against the Pandavas, Dhritarashtra said. "The opinion of grandfather Bhishma is justified in all respects. The entire world will be happy if the dispute can be solved amicably. Today itself I am sending Sanjaya, my charioteer to Yudhisthira to discuss the settlement proposal."

After the departure of the Drupada-priest, Dhritarashtra called Sanjaya to the court and told him. "Sanjaya, you immediately proceed to the Pandavas at Viratranagara. The Pandavas are virtuous. Even after undergoing untold sufferings during their exile and the incognito stay, they do not harbour any ill-feeling against us. Out of imprudence Duryodhana has seized the wealth and property of the Pandavas. The Pandavas are now immensely powerful. Arjuna is armed with divine weapons. Krishna who is the greatest and the only one in the entire universe, is now the charioteer of Arjuna. Bhimasena's proficiency in the fight with clubs is well-known. In the flame of his anger, the Kauravas will be reduced to ashes. Virataraja, Satyaki and many other renowned warriors are on the side of the Pandavas. Bhishma, Drona and the other warriors of repute despite being on our side, the Pandavas, I think, are still comparatively much stronger than the Kauravas. Sanjay, I am very much afraid of the angry Yudhisthira. He is an ascetic of the highest order and he observes strict austerity. His decision is always correct and successful. As his anger is justified, I have been gripped by a terrible fear. Sanjay, you should enquire about his welfare with pleasing words. Humbly tell Krishna, king Dhritarashtra is always eager to have an amicable settlement with the Pandavas. Try your best so that peace is established."

At Viratanagara, Sanjay explaining the settlement proposal to the Pandavas said, "O Pandavas, King Dhritarashtra has strongly expressed his desire for peaceful settlement of the dispute. You are endowed with all the virtues. You are also free from anger and jealousy. It will not be proper for you to perform any mean deed. Infamy will fall upon you if you take the path of confrontation disregarding our proposal for peaceful settlement. Your very existence in the world would be purposeless on the death of the near and dear ones in the war even if the Kauravas are all destroyed and you come out victorious. The Kauravas and the Pandavas are equal in strength. Victory and defeat are thus uncertain. No side will gain anything from victory. Defeat of the enemy will also give the victor no peace. With my prayer for peaceful settlement I am seeking the blessings of Krishna and the Panchalraj (Draupadi's father)."

Turning to Yudhisthira Sanjay said, "The Kauravas shall not return your kingdom without war. But, I think, begging is preferable to the victory in war. You could have earlier destroyed the Kauravas with the help of Krishna and Arjuna. This was not done. By staying in the forest for a long period you have given enough opportunity to the Kauravas to strengthen themselves while weakening your own allies. Why would you now go to war at this inopportune moment? I think forgiveness is superior to anger. Again as you know, even after conquering the entire world, you shall not be able to overcome old age, misery and death. Better give up the path of war. Do not get smeared in sin by killing your near and dear ones. It would only be proper for a religious and intelligent person like you to follow the path of the virtuous people."

Yudhisthira said in reply, "O Sanjay, those who are engaged in good work as ordained by religion after overcoming their sufferings, are actually praiseworthy. I shall always follow the path of my of forefathers. I have no desire to live even in heaven or in *brahmaloka* by following the path of irreligion. The great Krishna is well versed in moral science. He is the well-wisher of both the Kauravas and the Pandavas. Let him say which path—war or peace—we should follow in the present circumstances."

Then Krishna addressing Sanjay said, "O Sanjay, I sincerely want a peaceful settlement of the dispute between the Kauravas and the Pandavas. *Dharmaraj* Yudhisthira is also in favour of peaceful settlement. But king Dhritarashtra and his sons are extremely greedy. It is difficult to arrive at any settlement with them. *Dharmaraj* Yudhisthira is endowed with all the qualities befitting a king. He will never take recourse to any sinful means to achieve his purpose. Justly he alone is the owner of the kingdom. But Dhritarashtra and his sons like robbers have seized his kingdom. Is it justified? The Kauravas surprisingly are considering this act in conformity with religion. Why would others enjoy the property which rightfully belongs to the Pandavas? It is always desirable to die fighting in defence of one's right. It would be wrong for the Pandavas to remain apathetic in regaining their lost kingdom. Sanjay, now you are giving religious sermons to king Yudhisthira. Where was your religion when Draupadi was being humiliated in the open court? You did not then give any advice to Duhshasana when he was trying to disrobe Draupadi in presence of the king and his courtiers. I have decided to personally proceed to Hastinapura in order to strive for a settlement with the Kauravas without, in any way, undermining the interest of the Pandavas. If my just proposal is ignored, there is absolutely no doubt that the sinful, Kauravas will meet sure death at the hands of Arjuna and Bhimasena."

From the words of Krishna, it was evident to Sanjay that his mission for a peaceful settlement with the Pandavas had failed. As he was ready for departure from Viratanagara, Yudhisthira said, "O Sanjay, you may tell king Dhritarashtra that it would be imprudent on his part to ignore the Pandavas. You may also tell him we are willing to live in a spirit of peaceful co-existence with the Kauravas. Tell our grandfather Bhishma that he may exert all his efforts to protect the Kuru clan from the inevitable destruction. Tell Mahamantri Vidura to stop this war by all means. Later you may tell Duryodhana that we have forgiven all his faults and we shall be satisfied if only five villages are given to our five brothers. We have no intention to harm the Kauravas. We are ready for both war and peace."

On hearing Yudhisthira, Krishna and other Pandava leaders, Sanjay was convinced about the justifiability of their cause. At Hastinapura, he first briefly reported to king Dhritarashtra and other Kaurava elders about his mission at Viratanagara. Frankly expressing his views he told Dhritarashtra, "*Maharaj*, out of fear of your sons you are trying to appropriate the kingdom of the Pandavas which rightfully belongs to them. This has caused you great defame throughout the world. This fratricidal war is entirely due to your fault. If you do not return the kingdom to the Pandavas, war will be inevitable resulting in the complete destruction of the Kauravas. You are being guided by some unscrupulous people. Later I shall report to you all details."

The next day Sanjay again met king Dhritarashtra and other Kaurava elders in the court. Giving his assessment he said, "*Maharaj*, Arjuna, armed with his powerful *gandiva* bow with the help of Krishna, his charioteer, is determined to destroy the Kauravas along with his brothers if their kingdom is not returned to them. The Pandavas are fully prepared for war. They are in high morale. Even the horses of the chariots, elephants etc. are swinging their bodies in excitement for war. Surprisingly even the arrows are trying to fly to the sky in order to strike the enemy."

Bhishma, on hearing Sanjay expressed his views in favour of peaceful settlement with the Pandavas by returning their kingdom. Karna strongly protested against Bhishma's suggestion of peaceful settlement and declared that he would himself destroy all the Pandavas in the battlefield. Bhishma then referring to the incidents at Ghoshpalli and Viratanagara, from where Karna cowardly fled away without any fight told Dhritarashtra, "All self-applauding persons always take recourse to falsehood. Karna is not even one sixteenth part of the Pandavas in strength." Drona agreeing with Bhishma observed as an archer Arjuna was second to none.

Without giving any importance to the opinion of Bhishma and Drona, Dhritarashtra enquired of Sanjay about the war preparations of the Pandavas. Sanjay in reply mentioned the skill in warfare of Bhimasena, Arjuna and other warriors and gave out that Yudhisthira had made extensive preparations for the war by mobilising hundreds of kings from the east and the west. Getting an idea of the Pandavas' war preparations, Dhritarashtra was stricken by fear, and apprehending certain defeat in war advised his sons to come to a peaceful settlement with the Pandavas. Consoling his father, Duryodhana described the skill in the warfare of the Kaurava warriors and mentioned the Kauravas had mobilised an army of eleven *akshouhinis*. On the other hand, he said, the strength of the Pandava army was only seven *akshouhinis*. Moreover the Kaurava army was better trained.

Thereafter, on queries from Dhritarashtra and Duryodhana, Sanjay gave other details of the Pandavas' war preparations including Arjuna's chariot and its ensign, identity and the individual skill of the warriors and their rivals in the battlefield. He particularly mentioned that prince Dristadyumna (Draupadi's brother) was constantly provoking Yudhisthira to go to war.

Getting details of the power and strength and war preparations of the Pandavas from Sanjay, King Dhritarastra, grandfather Bhishma, Vidura, mother Gandhari and other elders expressed time and again in favour of peaceful settlement with the Pandavas. Vidura, while emphasising the need for peace separately, explained to Dhritarashtra the principles of ethics, the duties and responsibilities of the king, security of the kingdom and various other matters to which we have referred earlier. But Duryodhana and Karna remained firm in their earlier views. Duryodhana declared that he would not give the Pandavas even the land measurable with the point of a needle, not to speak of their kingdom. All hopes for peace were thus dashed to the ground.

35.

At Viratanagara, in the mean time, the Pandavas held a meeting at the royal court to discuss their future course of action. Initiating the discussion, Yudhisthira said, "O Krishna, it is clear from the words of Sanjay that the Kauravas would not return our kingdom without war. The destruction of our clan is inevitable in the war. At the same time renouncement of the kingdom without war tantamounts to death. O' Janardana, (Krishna's another name) you are our dear friend and well-wisher. Besides you are omniscient. You are the only person who can devise our correct path in this terrible situation."

Krishna in reply said, "I have decided to proceed to Hastinapura to bring about a peaceful settlement for the good of both the sides. If peace is established, you shall be saved from death and destruction. I myself shall also attain virtue."

Yudhisthira first did not agree with Krishna's decision apprehending his harm at the Kaurava court. On his assurance that he would not hesitate to destroy the Kauravas immediately if they tried to harm him in any way, Yudhisthira gave his consent to Krishna's peace mission. Wishing Krishna all success, Yudhisthira observed that it would be excellent if peace was established. Otherwise, he said, the Pandavas would choose the path of war.

Krishna knew Yudhisthira was essentially a man of peace. In order to harden Yudhisthira's attitude as war seemed imminent, he said, "*Maharaj*, I have heard Sanjay. I am also aware of your intention. You are a virtuous person. To you even a small gain without war is much more valuable. You must not, however, forget the *dharma* of the *Kshatriyas*. To show humility on the part of a *Kshatriya* is always condemnable. Victory or defeat in war has been ordained by God. Destroy the enemy with your *Kshatriya* valour. The Kauravas are extremely greedy. They have mobilised a huge army for the war. They are assured of their strength with the support of Bhishma, Drona, Kripa and many other kings and warriors. In the circumstances it is unlikely they would come to any settlement with you. They would not return your kingdom if you take a mild attitude. War seems a certainty. I am noticing bad omens all around. Your war preparations must continue unabated."

To the surprise of everybody present, Bhimasena told Krishna, "O Madhusudana, at the court of Hastinapura you may conduct your talks for the good of both the sides. Do not unnecessarily provoke the Kauravas in the name of war. Always try to please them by mild words. The destruction of the Bharata clan in war is not at all desirable. Rather our acceptance of Duryodhana's subordination will be more beneficial. Dharmaraj Yudhisthira and Arjuna are also not interested in war."

In an attempt to provoke Bhimasena, Krishna said, "O Bhimasena, you have always spoken in favour of war against the Kauravas. Now you are speaking in favour of a peaceful settlement with them. I think fear has gripped your mind with the approach of war. Your brothers are feeling discouraged with your words. As you are born in a *Kshatriya* clan, it is not fair for you to be afraid of war. Shun your mental weakness and be ready for war."

In reply, Bhimasena said, "O Krishna, you have spoken harshly without understanding the real meaning of my words. In the past you have got enough evidence of my valour and strength. No body will escape from my iron hands. I am not afraid of war. Only for the sake of establishing a bond of friendship with the Kauravas, I have expressed my desire for a peaceful settlement."

Congratulating Bhimasena, Krishna said, "I have uttered those words out of my love and affection for you only to know your real intention. I am not unaware of your greatness, strength and virtue. We shall have to remember both victory and defeat are uncertain in war. Even then it would be wrong to behave weakly with the enemy. I shall try to bring about an honourable settlement between the Kauravas and the Pandavas. War will break out if my mission fails. Now Arjuna and you should prepare for war."

Arjuna then told Krishna, 'It is not unjustified for you to strive for peace. I have, however, the feeling that wicked Duryodhana will never agree to any peaceful settlement. In the circumstances you may do what is good for us."

At the end, Krishna said, "It is my duty to do good to both the sides. Both victory and defeat are under my control. The great men of the olden days have said success is not possible unless human efforts are combined with divine grace. I can only make efforts to the best of my ability. I have, however, no control over divine grace. At the Kaurava court, I shall try my best with words and deeds to establish peace. But I am doubtful about my success. Earlier Bhishma's advice for a peaceful settlement has been spurned by Duryodhana. It appears Duryodhana will not be agreeable to hand over even a small part of the captured kingdom to the Pandavas."

Requesting Krishna to exercise utmost restraint Nakula said, "O Madhava, at the Kaurava court you should first speak in a soft voice. If this serves no purpose only then you may use harsh language. Do not utter any such words that may unnecessarily provoke Duryodhana's anger. I believe if the Kauravas do realise our real strength they shall shun the path of war. It is very likely that Bhishma and other Kaurava elders realising the justifiability of your words, will dissuade Duryodhana from war. It appears that your peace mission to Hastinapura will be successful with the fulfillment of all the wishes of Yudhisthira."

Differing with Nakula, Sahadeva said, "In my opinion, we must wage war against the Kauravas even if they agree to accept the terms of peaceful settlement. Without war how would we avenge the humiliation of Draupadi. I am ready to fight against the Kauravas even by forsaking religion."

Great warrior Satyaki supporting Sahadeva, asserted, "Our anger will subside only with the death of Duryodhana."

Draupadi who was carefully listening to the discussions, became apprehensive that Krishna might ultimately manage to bring about a settlement with the Kauravas thus dashing to the ground her cherished resolve of revenge against them. Speaking out her mind she said, "No mercy whatsoever should be shown to the Kauravas. Killing of someone unfit to be killed is as sinful as non-killing of one fit to be killed. O Madhusudana, it is your duty to see that the Pandavas do not become guilty of this sin. What a surprise that the Kauravas are still alive! Fie on Arjuna's bow and Bhimasena's strength. Bhimasena and Arjuna seem determined to meekly sue for peace. This will cause me no harm. My old father, brothers and sons with the help of the allies will fight the enemy. I shall have no peace of mind without seeing the beheaded body of Duhshasana. My heart is being torn into pieces on hearing Bhimasena's pleading for peace."

After saying this, Draupadi begun to weep profusely. Consoling her Krishna said, "I assure you, Kuru women on the death of their near and dear ones will also one day weep like you. I am giving the word on the order of *Dharmaraj* Yudhisthira, I shall engage myself in destroying the Kauravas with the help of Bhimasena, Arjuna, Nakula and Sahadeva. If the Kauravas disregard my advice, dogs and jackals will devour the flesh of their dead bodies. This word of mine will never be untrue. Please calm yourself. You shall see your husbands capturing their kingdom and wealth on the death of the enemy."

As decided, Krishna armed with his traditional weapons thereafter left for Hastinapura on his peace mission, after taking leave of the Pandavas. A large army under the command of Yadava hero Satyaki accompanied him. On the way some *Brahmins* joined him with a view to listening to his rich religious sermon at the court of Hastinapura. As he proceeded suddenly like a bolt from the blue natural calamities overtook him indicating evil omens. After halting in the night with his entourage at a wayside village where he was received with great honour and enthusiasm, he resumed his journey in the morning for Hastinapura.

36.

At Hastinapura, King Dhritarashtra on getting information from the emissary about Krishna's visit, got a beautiful assembly hall constructed for his reception. He, also as a token of friendship, decided to present him various rare and expensive gifts including a one-coloured horse, a chariot made of gold, an elephant with large trunks, jewelleries etc.

At the decision of offering gifts, Vidura told Dhritarashtra, "*Maharaj*, it is palpably evident that you, with a deceitful intention, are seeking to wean away Krishna with these gifts from the Pandavas by driving a wedge between them. But I know, Krishna considers Arjuna as his own life and under no circumstances will he forsake him. It would thus be improper to do anything which is not to his liking. You should do only that work which will please Krishna. Krishna is coming here on a peace mission. Now it is your duty to work according to his advice. The Pandavas consider you as their father. You should treat them as your own sons."

Agreeing with Vidura, Duryodhana said, "*Maharaj*, Krishna is devoted to the Pandavas. He thus cannot not be influenced by any temptation. Rather he will think we are offering these gifts out of fear of war. I think no special arrangements need be made for his reception."

Bhishma said, "O great hero, whatever arrangements are made for Krishna's reception, he will remain undeterred in his duty. The best course for you would be to act according to his advice. Come to a peaceful settlement with the Pandavas with Krishna's help."

Giving no importance to Bhishma's words, Duryodhana said, 'Grandfather, I have got a plan, Kindly listen. Krishna, the only stay of the Pandavas, is reaching here tomorrow. At the first opportunity I shall make him a captive. There is no doubt that the entire world along with the Pandavas will come under my control if Krishna remains with me. Now kindly devise some means so that Krishna does not get any idea about our plan"

Enraged at the irreligious plan of Duryodhana, Bhishma left the court in protest. Before leaving he told Dhritarashtra, "This son of yours is always after mischief. You also support him. I am seeing clearly this villain will perish along with others in the rage of Krishna."

The next day, Krishna on arrival at Hastinapura, was warmly received by King Dhritarashtra, Bhishma and other elders and ushered to the court. After exchanging pleasantries with all present, he conversed with them for some time in a jovial mood with humour and laughter. Thereafter, he appeared at Vidura's house where he was happy to meet mother Kunti. After exchange of pleasantries with Vidura he informed him about the happenings at Viratanagara. Overwhelmed with simultaneous joy and sorrow, mother Kunti with tears in her eyes referred to the untold sufferings of Draupadi and the Pandavas in exile and asked Krishna to see that her sons did not forgive the wicked Kauravas. She deeply regretted that she had to suffer so much despite the fact that Krishna, Balarama and great warrior Pradyumna (Krishna's son) were their patrons and that Bhimasena and Arjuna were still alive. Krishna assured mother Kunti that she would shortly see her sons regain their lost kingdom ending all her sorrows.

From Vidura's house Krishna came to the house of Duryodhana. After exchange of pleasantries Duryodhana invited Krishna to have food with him. Krishna refused the invitation saying the emissaries were supposed to take food and drinks only after completion of their assigned tasks. Expressing surprise at the words of Krishna, Duryodhana observed it was not understood why his cordial invitation was not accepted. He pointed out that he had no enmity or quarrel with Krishna. In reply Krishna said, "O Kaurava, people partake food of others either lovingly or when in distress. You have not invited me out of love for me. I have also not fallen in distress. Why then should I take food in your house? You hate the Pandavas without reason. He who hates the Pandavas, also hates me and he who is devoted to them is also devoted to me. I am not different from the Pandavas. There is certainly some ill-motive behind your invitation. I have decided to take food at the house of Vidura." Krishna then returned to Vidura's house. There Bhishma and other elders met Krishna and invited him to their house. Krishna did not oblige and stayed on in Vidura's house for food.

After food and rest, Vidura told Krishna, 'O Madhusudana, it has not been proper for you to come to Hastinapura. Bhishma, Drona, Kripa, Ashvatthama and Jayadratha are all indebted to Duryodhana for their livelihood. This is why they will not strive for peace antagonising Duryodhana. The Kauravas as also Karna firmly believe the Pandavas will never attack Bhishma and other elders in the battlefield. Duryodhana believes Karna alone is capable of destroying the enemy. The Kauravas have decided not to return the Pandavas' kingdom to them. In the circumstances there is absolutely no doubt that your efforts to bring about a peaceful settlement has no chance of success. Duryodhana has mobilised a huge army. Many kings and warriors are now Duryodhana's allies. Those kings who were defeated by you, have now sought protection of Duryodhana. They are all determined to fight the Pandavas. In this situation I do not want you to appear at the assembly of the enemies with your peace proposal."

Krishna said in reply, "O Vidura, what you have said is all justified. Duryodhana's tyranny has brought the Kuru clan to the brink of disaster. I shall try for a settlement between the two sides so that peace is established. This work conforms to the religion. Even in failure my efforts will have some results. A wise man tries to dissuade his friend from performing a misdeed even by pulling him by the hair. No blame comes to him even if his efforts end in failure. I have got nothing to lose if Duryodhana rejects my peace proposal. Rather I shall have the satisfaction I have been able to give honest advice to my relations. Otherwise I cannot be considered to be a relation of the Kuru clan. I tell you I shall not hesitate to kill those who will dare to insult me in the Kaurava assembly."

The next day, in the midst of shouts of joy from the citizens Krishna holding the hands of Vidura and Satyaki came to the Kaurava assembly in his own chariot. At the entrance he was cordially received by Duryodhana and

Karna and brought to the assembly hall. On entrance, King Dhritarashtra, Kaurava elders and the assembled kings welcomed Krishna and paid him due obesiance one by one according to age. Krishna then while standing in the assembly told grandfather Bhishma, "Look, *Devarshi* Narada and many other sages have descended on the earth to listen to the deliberations in the assembly. Kindly arrange seats for them immediately." On Bhishma's order, seats were brought without delay. After Narada and the other sages took their seats, Krishna took the seat specified for him. All the dignitaries present began to observe him with awe and surprise. There was then pin-drop silence in the assembly hall.

Krishna, after a while, looking at King Dhritarashtra said, "*Maharaj*, it is my earnest desire that the Kauravas and the Pandavas come to a peaceful settlement. I have appeared before you with the fervent appeal to stop this war so that the valiant warriors do not unnecessarily get destroyed. You are born in the great Kuru clan. You should not do anything unjust. It is a matter of deep regret that despite a person of your wisdom remaining installed in the throne, the Kauravas are engaged openly and secretly in various dishonest activities. Duryodhana and the other sons of yours are inhuman and greedy. By avoiding the path of religion they are behaving treacherously with their own relations. The Kuru clan is now faced with a terrible catastrophe. The entire world will be destroyed if you ignore this danger. Yet, you are the person who can put an end to this calamity. I believe it is still not impossible to bring about a settlement between the two sides. You take steps to pacify your sons, I shall restrain the Pandavas. The Pandavas are armed with divine weapons. It is impossible to defeat them in war. You should take steps for at an amicable settlement with the Pandavas by returning their lost kingdom.

"On advice from your sons you asked the Pandavas to settle at Khandavaprastha. There, they built their own capital Indraprastha on their own, conquered many kingdoms with their valour and placed them under your authority. With your approval, Shakuni defeated the Pandavas in the deceitful dice-game and captured Pandavas' kingdom and wealth. Even at the humiliation of Draupadi in the open court, they restrained themselves and did not deviate from *Kshatriya dharma*. On your order, the Pandavas lived in exile in the forest for twelve years and stayed incognito for another one year. During this period they underwent immense sufferings. Even then they did not break the promise. They treat you as their father. They are always subservient to you. They expect you to keep your promise by returning to them their portion of the kingdom which is due to them. As a well-wisher of both, the Kauravas and the Pandavas, I am telling you all this. *Maharaj*, the Pandavas are ready for both peace and war. Do what you think best."

The assembled courtiers and kings appreciated Krishna's passionate appeal for peace. They, however, preferred to remain silent.

Sage Narada told Dhritarashtra, "O son of Kuru, Krishna is the real friend of both the sides. A friend does his duty without expecting anything in return. For this reason a friend's advice should always be accepted. The Kuru clan, as also the entire world, will be benefited if Krishna's peace proposal is accepted."

Dhritarashtra said in reply, "O venerable sage, what you have said is no doubt justified, but it is impossible on my part to implement it." "Looking at Krishna he said, 'O Keshava, (Krishna's another name) your words are pleasing and these conform to scriptures, but I am not independent. You yourself pacify sinful Duryodhana."

Then Krishna addressed Duryodhana and said, "O brother, your father and the courtiers are all in favour of a peaceful settlement with the Pandavas. You shall terribly suffer if you disregard their friendly advice. The Pandavas are devoted to religion. Despite being subjected to many persecutions, they do not harbour any anger against you. They are your friends. It would be absolutely improper to go against them. You have embarked on a wrong path of expanding your empire in collaboration with some irreligious people. Give up this path of destruction. All your wishes will be fulfilled if the Pandavas remain satisfied. Remember there is nobody who can defeat Bhimasena and Arjuna in the war. Look at your sons, brothers, relations and friends. See they are not destroyed for your sake. Do not earn in history the dubious distinction as the destroyer of your own clan. The Pandavas will install you as the crown prince, while your father will be the emperor. Do not ignore Goddess Lakshmi who is eager to bless you. Listen to the advice of your well-wishers. Endear yourself to the friends by returning the Pandavas' kingdom to them."

Bhishma and the other elders then repeatedly advised Duryodhana to agree to the peace proposal as suggested by Krishna.

Duryodhana remained adamant and refused to listen to anybody. Addressing Krishna he angrily said, "Vasudeva, (Krishna's another name) it is a matter of extreme regret that you as also my father, grandfather Bhishma, Vidura and Drona are always engrossed in despising me though I am not guilty of anything. The Pandavas are themselves responsible for the loss of their kingdom and their sufferings. They voluntarily accepted the conditions of the dice-game. Shakuni won for us their kingdom by defeating them in the game. How can I be blamed for this? On father's order the kingdom which came to our possession, was returned to the Pandavas. They again got defeated in the game and in compliance of the mutually accepted conditions went to the exile. Here also no offence can come to us. Yet, surprisingly they are conspiring against us by joining the hands of our enemies. We are not afraid of war. Even gods will not be able to defeat Bhishma, Drona and Karna, what to speak of the Pandavas. During my life time I shall not return their kingdom. Not even the land measurable with the point of a sharp needle, will be given to them."

Krishna rebuked Duryodhana and said, "Duryodhana, it appears you are determined to lie on the death bed. Your wish will be fulfilled. War is imminent. I am warning you for the last time that you all will be destroyed if Pandavas' kingdom is not returned to them." Then turning to Bhishma and other elders, Krishna requested them to immediately capture Duryodhana, Karna, Duhshasana and Shakuni and hand them over to the Pandavas. In the midst of the prevailing tension, mother Gandhari appeared at the assembly hall and tried in various ways to persuade Duryodhana to agree to the peace proposal, but he remained firm in his stand. Then suddenly Duryodhana left the hall and began a secret confabulation with Shakuni, Karna and others. This was noticed by Yadava hero Satyaki, who suspecting something sinister, informed Krishna in the hall about his fear after alerting the accompanying army outside.

On hearing this Krishna told Dhritarashtra, "*Maharaj*, your sons have planned to oppress me. I tell you I can destroy all of them, but I shall not involve myself in any sinful act. Let Duryodhana do what he thinks best." A terrible fear gripped Dhritarashtra, and he immediately called Duryodhana to the hall and began to chastise him. Vidura also warned that all the tormentors of Vasudeva would be destroyed.

At that moment a strange supernatural scene descended in the assembly hall. Krishna stood up with a loud laugh when in diminutive form Gods like Brahma and Rudra as also the five Pandava brothers with their allies armed with various weapons, came out of his body. Also came out of his body his own weapons namely conch, mace and chakra. There was emission of fire from his nose, eyes and mouth and of rays like those of the sun from the pores of his skin. Bhishma, Drona, Vidura, Sanjaya and the assembled sages on being gifted with divine eyes by Vasudeva saw his terrible appearance and closed their eyes out of fear. Dhritarashtra who was blind from birth, also saw Krishna's Vishwarupa (one in whom the universe is represented) on being gifted with divine eyes. The assembled kings and sages began reciting songs of praise for Vasudeva. After some time Krishna reassumed his former appearance and left the hall with permission of the assembled sages. The bewildered Duryodhana and his accomplices failed to do any harm to Krishna.

From the assembly hall, Krishna accompanied by Vidura came to his house and reported the developments to mother Kunti. Expressing his decision to leave for Viratanagara, he asked mother Kunti if she had any message for the Pandavas. On this mother Kunti told Krishna, "O Keshava, tell Yudhisthira on my behalf that at this time his main duty is to come out of the present danger. For this purpose he should judiciously apply the principles of conciliation, gift, division, punishment and justice to get back the lost kingdom. Ask him to shun all mildness and wage war keeping in mind the principles of *dharma*. In no case the honour of the family should be sacrificed." Mother Kunti advised Krishna to convey similar message to Bhimasena, Arjuna, Nakula and Sahadeva.

En route to Viratanagara, Krishna met Karna and took him to his chariot. In the chariot he told him, "O Karna, I am disclosing a secret occurrence to you. Listen carefully. You are not aware of your birth history. You are born of Kunti when she was unmarried. You are accordingly the son of Pandu. You please accompany me to the camp of the Pandavas. Let the Pandavas also know you as the son of Kunti and their eldest brother. You shall be installed as the king and Yudhisthira will serve you as the crown prince. Draupadi will also cordially accept you as her husband."

In reply Karna said, 'O Krishna, I agree Pandu is my father according to the rules and laws of religion. Kunti, however, forsook me wishing my harm. Charioteer Adhiratha rescued me and handed me over to his wife Radha, who has carefully brought up and maintained me. I know Adhiratha as my father and Radha as my mother. I am married. My sons and grandsons are living. I am devoted to my own wives. Under no temptation I shall be able to forsake them. Moreover, I am enjoying my kingdom in peace and safety under the protection of Duryodhana. King Duryodhana has decided to proceed in war against the Pandavas on my support. I shall not be able to commit treachery against him under any fear or temptation. You have done a correct thing by keeping secret the story of my birth to Yudhisthira. He will not accept the kingdom if he comes to know the history of my birth. On the other hand if the kingdom is conquered by me it will be handed over to my friend Duryodhana. In the circumstances let *Dharmaraj* Yudhisthira continue to remain installed as the king."

On hearing everything Krishna said, "O Karna, I wanted to give you the entire world; but you did not accept it. Remember, it is the Pandavas who will win the war and only after a week the war will start."

"We shall meet in the battlefield", saying this Karna left Krishna's chariot and returned to Hastinapura. Krishana accompanied by Satyaki then departed for Viratanagara.

37.

In the mean time, mother Kunti became worried at the thought of inevitable destruction of her own sons in the coming war. She thought perhaps ultimately

Bhishma, Drona and Kripa would not take up arms against the Pandavas. She was not, however, sure about the attitude of Karna. His mind was vitiated by hatred towards the Pandavas. He was the closest friend of Duryodhana, the Pandavas' arch enemy. After deliberation she decided to persuade Karna to join the Pandava side. Accordingly one day, she secretly met Karna and told him, "My child, you are the son of Kunti. Radha is not your mother. Adhiratha is also not your father. You were born of me when I was unmarried. The Sun-god is your father. You leave the side of Duryodhana and join your own brothers, the Pandavas."

Rejecting Kunti's proposal, Karna said, "O respected *Kshatriya* lady, you have not performed your duty as a mother towards your son. Now for your own interest you are addressing me as your son. I shall lose my good name and reputation if I now join the Pandava side. The war is imminent. This is the time for me to show my gratitude to the Kauravas. Yet, I am giving the word I shall not fight with Yudhisthira, Bhimasena, Nakula and Sahadeva. I shall fight only with Arjuna. In the event of death of one of us, you shall continue to be known as the mother of the five Pandavas." Somewhat satisfied with Karna's words, Kunti said, "My boy, remember your promise you shall not fight with any other Pandavas except Arjuna." On conclusion of talks, Kunti and Karna returned to their respective quarters.

38.

On reaching Viratanagara, Krishna reported the happenings at Hastinapura to Yudhisthira, and said that the Kauravas would not return his kingdom without war and they had already mobilised their army at Kurukshetra.

On this information, the Pandavas also moved to Kurukshetra with their army. Grandfather Bhishma and Draupadi's brother Dhristadyumna became the commander-in-chief of the Kaurava and the Pandava armies, respectively. Bhishma was then an old man of 90-100. It is very surprising that Bhishma agreed to shoulder such a heavy responsibility at this age when his physical strength and mental alertness had visibly declined. When Duryodhana, by way of courtesy, first approached Bhishma who happened to be the senior-most member of the family, with the offer, he could have easily declined it on the ground of his old age. It is said that his acceptance of the offer was to show that he continued to be still at the helm of the affairs of the Kuru clan. We shall see later that he failed miserably as the commander-in-chief of the Kaurava army.

Bhishma had developed a halow around him that he was a great hero. We, however, do not find him fighting any great battle during his life–time. His audacious abduction of the Kashi princess from the *swayamvarasabha* involved no fighting. As it was a simple hit-and-run operation, his valour as a warrior remained untested. In no case can we equate the abduction to any heroic act like winning a great war. In the Mahabharata there is an incident of serious combat between Bhishma and Parashurama for three weeks. On being defeated in the combat,Parshurama admitted there was no warrior like Bhishma in the entire world. (We shall get the details later.) The research scholars have, however, found out that Parashurama was a warrior of the first *yuga* (epoch) of the world, while the Mahabharata is the story of the third *Dwapara yuga*. Bhishma's successful combat against Parashurama thus being an interpolation, his reputation as a great warrior does not hold good. In the battle at Ghoshpalli, it may be recalled that the entire Kaurava army under his command was miserably defeated by Arjuna alone. Bhishma also did not join King Pandu in his expedition soon after the ascendancy to the throne, indicating his reluctance to take unnecessary risks. Before the Kurukshetra war, Satyavati with her two daughters-in-law departed for the forest. Bhishma though older than Satyavati, however, preferred to stay back at Hastinapura underlying his greed for power and authority.

It was most unfortunate for Duryodhana to have got a person like Bhishma as the commander-in-chief of the Kaurava army in the Kurukshetra war. He actually did not want him to lead the Kaurava army. He expected Bhishma, on the ground of his old age, would suggest some other Kaurava warrior for this difficult assignment. When Bhishma agreed to command the Kaurava army, Duryodhana had no choice but to acquiesce. Bhishma's commandership of the Kaurava army worried both Duryodhana and Yudhisthira. Bhishma being a known well-wisher of the Pandavas and an ardent critic of the Kauravas, Duryodhana was worried about his real intention in the war, while Yudhisthira's worries arose from Bhishma's decision to take up arms as the commander of the Kaurava army against the Pandavas belying all hopes to the contrary despite his open and consistent support to their cause. We shall find the answers later.

On the other hand, the Pandava commander-in-chief Dhristadyumna was a non-controversial young warrior of indomitable courage. He was determined to fight the Kauravas to the last to avenge the humiliation of his sister Draupadi during the dice-game.

One day before the start of the war, Duryodhana sent Uluka, son of Shakuni to the Pandava camp as his emissary. Briefing him before his departure, Duryodhana said, "O Uluka, you shall tell Yudhisthira on my behalf that he always assures others of protection; but he has now embarked upon the path of destroying the entire world following the example of the proverbial cat who under the guise of an ascetic devoured all the mice after gaining their trust. In this way, he like the cat has decided to deceive his near and dear ones.

"Uluka, tell Krishna he created an illusion in the assembly hall at Hastinapura by taking resort to magic. This magic power is also known to Duryodhana; but he does not like to achieve his objective by any other means except by his own physical strength. Further tell him he was a servant of King Kangsa. For this a king like Duryodhana hates to fight with him.

"Ulaka, tell Bhimasena, he had to work as a mere cook at Viratanagara as the behest of the Kauravas. If he had the power, let him drink the blood of Duhshasana in the battlefield in fulfillment of his vow.

"Uluka, tell Arjuna, he is nothing but a frog in the well. This is why he could not realise the power and strength of the Kauravas. Tell him, Duryodhana is aware of his power. He is also aware of the fact Vasudeva is his main stay. Even then Duryodhana had sent the Pandavas to exile in the forest for thirteen long years after capturing their kingdom. Where was his power during the dice-game? Remind him that he as a eunuch was teaching music to the daughter of Virataraja. Inform him thousands of Vasudevas and hundreds of Arjunas will flee away in different directions at the unfailing marksmanship of Duryodhana."

Uluka reported everything to the Pandavas in their camp as instructed by Duryodhana. Krishna asked Uluka to tell Duryodhana everything would be done as wished by him. Bhimasena told Uluka, "O Uluka, tell Duryodhana I shall remain true to my vow and drink Duhshasana's blood in the battlefield. Besides, I shall kill your father Shakuni after killing you in his presence." Arjuna said, "Uluka, tell Duryodhana I shall give answer to his insolent words with my *gandivadhanush* tomorrow in the battlefield. Duryodhana should not think I shall not strike grandfather Bhishma. I shall first kill Bhishma on whose reliance he has embarked on this war." Yudhisthira said, "Uluka, remind Duryodhana he who robs another person's wealth and tries to protect himself with others' help, is himself a eunuch." Shikhandi, Draupadi's brother said he had been born only to Kill Bhishma. Dhristadyumna said he would do a work which was impossible for others to perform. He would kill Drona along with his army and the near and the dear ones.

Uluka reported every detail to the Kauravas on return.

39.

In the pre-war *Udyogaparva* (period of preparation) we come across application of various methods in the matter of collection of intelligence. In this regard, both the Kauravas and the Pandavas were equally active. Knowing the war inevitable, they while trying to improve their strength by additional mobilisations, maintained strict vigilance through secret agents and the emissaries about each other's war preparations. They vigorously applied various principles like conciliation, gift and division in order to weaken the enemy. In this regard the success of the Pandavas was greater than that of the Kauravas. The Pandavas were also successful in the application of the principle of damage-control.

Behind the success of the Pandavas lay Krishana's keen intellect and extraordinary far-sightedness. Yudhisthira had admitted many times that he was going to war mainly depending on Krishna. This dependence on Krishna was evident in all his activities. On the Kaurava side there was no person of Krishna's stature. Duryodhana did not receive any correct advice from Shakuni, Karna and Duhshasana who all bore deep hatred against the Pandavas like him. Duryodhana himself was very obstinate and uncompromising. For all actions he was solely guided by these sycophants without any thought about the consequences. Grandfather Bhishma and Vidura could have played Krishna's role on the Kaurava side. They actually tried their best to dissuade Duryodhana from this suicidal path of going to war with the Pandavas who were armed with divine weapons. They were, however, against all his activities and harboured deep sympathy and support for the Pandavas. Only on the ground of their obligation to Duryodhana for their livelihood, they did not forsake him. They at the same time did not come forward to actively help Duryodhana. This was in sharp contrast with Krishna's help and support to the Pandavas. With no help from them, as also due to absence of proper application of the principles of intelligence collection, Duryodhana's information gathering was faulty and inadequate. There was also no objective assessment of the gathered information. In this regard, the Pandavas with Krishna's help were in a much better position. The *Udyogaparva* bore enough indication about the results of the coming war.

An analysis of the events in the *Udyogapava* will reveal the extent of success and failure of the two sides. The first and foremost failure of Duryodhana was evident when he got Krishna's Narayani army and not Krishna on his side. We know how happy he was on getting Krishna's army. The fact that Krishna alone is much more powerful than any army as also the fact that victory would come to the side where Krishna is, as he is the incarnation of God possessing all the divine powers, could not be realised by Duryodhana. In fact Duryodhana's appraisement of Krishna was distorted. He used to hate him as an ordinary sorcerer. In this regard he disregarded the advice of Bhishma and other elders. On the other hand, we shall see later that the Pandavas with Krishna's help and advice came out of all dangers and vanquished the Kauravas in the war.

We are aware that it was Duryodhana who first went to Krishna to seek his help. His purpose remained unfulfilled due to Krishna's machination.

According to prevailing custom, Krishna was supposed to join the Kaurava side Duryodhana being the first to approach him. Krishna, however, went into deceitful sleep just before Duryodhana entered his chamber. We have seen how Krishna deceived Duryodhana. He also bewildered Duryodhana by telling him another lie. There was untruth in Krishna's statement in that he equated his Narayani army with himself remaining unarmed and neutral in the war. He even broke this promise when he became the charioteer of Arjuna during the war. In the battlefield, it may be noted, the role of a charioteer is greater than that of the warrior himself. Arjuna's success in the war was mainly due to intelligent charioteering of Krishna. Besides, as we shall see later, Krishna twice went out to fight with his famous disc when the situation in the battlefield became desperate for the Pandavas. This break of promise of Krishna drew no protest or opposition from the Kaurava side. If Duryodhana's relations with Bhishma and the other elders were normal, some redress might have been possible. None of them, however, came forward to warn Duryodhana in the matter. Duyodhana thus easily fell a victim to Krishna's deceit. In the face of Krishna's superior intellect, Duryodhana's agents also could do nothing. Krishna thus very tactfully remained on the side of the Pandavas, paving the way for their victory.

One of the serious failures of Duryodhana was that he was completely ignorant of the secret promise of help given by Madraraj Shalya to the Pandavas. We know Duryodhana obtained Madraraj's concurrence of help in the war by lavishly entertaining him on his way to Viratanagara. He, however, did not think it necessary to get any information about the secret parleys Madraraj had with Yudhisthira and other Pandava brothers at Viratnagar. Yet Madraraj's visit to Viratanagara was within his knowledge. Madraraj being the maternal uncle of Nakula and Sahadeva, was naturally sympathetic to the Pandavas. Actually he was proceeding with a large army to join the war on their side. Duryodhana, keeping this fact in mind, should have engaged reliable agents to obtain details of discussions between Madraraj and Yudhisthira. Even if he had agents at Viratanagara, they remained inactive. Here, it is suspected, the Vidura had a hand in it. Had Duryodhana known the secret promise of help to the Pandavas by Madraraj in time, he would not have accepted him on the Kaurava side. This might have changed the course of war. We shall see later how Madraraj Shalya betrayed the cause of the Kauravas in the battlefield as the charioteer of Karna in compliance of his secret promise given to Yudhisthira.

Duryodhana also had no information about Karna's promise to mother Kunti that he would fight only with Arjuna in the battlefield. He had great confidence on Karna who was his closest friend. As such he had no suspicion about his movements and activities. None should be trusted too much – this principle for the king, Duryodhana had completely ignored here in respect of Karna. Though Arjuna was his principal rival, he was supposed to fight with all the enemy warriors including other Pandava brothers. By keeping his promise, Karna thus saved the lives of the Pandava brothers. It was not difficult for him to imprison Yudhisthira in the battlefield. Had this been done, victory of the Pandavas would have been uncertain. Possibly, Yudhisthira in captivity would have agreed to end the war seeing terrible destruction all around on terms and conditions acceptable to both the sides. Apparently, as a result of Karna's promise this was not possible.The Kauravas were also not interested to know the birth history of Karna. They knew him to be the son of Adhiratha. It did not strike them how a sutaputra like Karna could possess so much power and strength befitting only a *Kshatriya*. In any case Duryodhana's failure to mount surveillance on Karna and mother Kunti which was so important in a war situation, only harmed the cause of the Kauravas.

It may be remembered here that Krishna kept secret the information about the birth history of Karna from the Pandavas. Yudhisthira would not have agreed to fight with Karna if he had known that he (Karna) was the eldest of the Pandava brothers. The Pandavas, also like the Kauravas, did not show any interest about Karna's birth history. It appears Krishna kept the information secret only to ensure destruction of the wicked Kauravas in the war. Karna, too, withheld the information from the Kauravas in order not to cause any confusion among them. Both Krishna and Karna here showed exemplary precaution in keeping their discussions and decisions within themselves though reasons were different. This, of course, only helped the Pandavas. At the mercy of Karna no harm did come to the four Pandava brothers. Karna himself, we shall see later, was killed by Arjuna in an unfair battle. Mother Kunti's damage-control policy proved entirely successful. She remained as the mother of five Pandavas as predicted by Karna.

The emissaries sent by the two sides to the rival camps for peace negotiations were also engaged in collection of intelligence regarding enemy's morale, strength and weakness of the rival warriors, alliance with the other kings, war preparations and other related matters. Efforts were made to tactfully create dissensions in the enemy ranks. The Kaurava emissary charioteer Sanjaya, taking advantage of Yudhisthira's simplicity and sense of righteousness, tried to convince him to buy peace by renouncing the demand for the return of their kingdom as war would cause unnecessary destruction of countless human lives including his own near and dear ones. Yudhisthira, we know, rejected Sanjaya's proposal; but ultimately he confined his demand to only five villages for them. In this regard Sanjaya's efforts were partially successful. He collected a plethora of useful information about the war preparations of the Pandavas. In fact, he himself was gripped with fear to see the huge mobilisation of the Pandava army and its restlessness to go to war without delay. It seems he was convinced about the rightful demand of the Pandavas and accordingly he requested Dhritarashtra on return, to hand over the Pandavas' kingdom to them. He even warned him in the event of war breaking out, that the Kauravas would be completely destroyed. The Pandavas thus got another well-wisher in Sanjaya in the Kaurava court.

Krishna knew his peace mission to Hastinapura would not be successful as he was sure Duryodhana would remain firm in his stand. Besides, King Dhritarashtra was weak and vacillating having no control over Duryodhana. There were mainly two reasons behind Krishna's peace mission. The first reason is moral. Krishna was then recognised as the most renowned person besides being related to both the Kauravas and the Pandavas. This was why he thought he owed some responsibility in preventing this fratricidal destructive war. The second reason was to collect information about the war preparations of the Kauravas and get an idea of the extent of dissensions in the Kaurava leadership. During the visit he stayed in the house of Vidura and had long discussions with him. Obviously, Krishna and Vidura exchanged valuable information regarding the war preparations of the two sides. The information collected by Krishna proved extremely useful in determining the war strategy of the Pandavas. In this respect, Krishna's mission was quite fruitful though he failed to bring about any *raprochement* between the two sides.

Satyaki was first to understand the evil design of Duryodhana against Krishna. He was an *Ingitayajna*. On seeing Duryodhana's body language and his frequent parleys with Karna and his brothers he was convinced that he (Duryodhana) was planning something sinister. We know on being warned by Satyaki, Krishna assumed *Vishbarupa* and came out of the Assembly hall unharmed. This story of Krishna assuming *Vishwarupa* as depicted in the Mahabharata seems to be an interpolation in order to dramatise the whole matter. It appears a small battle was fought with the Kauravas when the Yadava army under Satyaki tried to escort Krishna out of the hall. It may be remembered, Krishna took a large army under the command of Satyaki to Hastinapura. Krishna himself was armed with his traditional personal weapons including his famous disc, *Chakra*. This indicates Krishna apprehended some trouble during his peace mission at Hastinapura. That a battle ensued when Krishna left the hall, seems reasonable. Krishna showed a great sense of far–sightedness by apprehending his own danger during the peace mission. This was possible because of Krishna's careful assessment of the prevailing situation. The credit for his successful escape was entirely due to him.

Krishna apparently did everything to avoid war. His appeal for peace received wide support from the Kaurava elders including King Dhritarashtra and queen Gandhari. As a result Duryodhana and his supporters were completely isolated in the Kaurava court. Dissensions in the Kaurava leadership also further deepened. Considered from all aspects, Krishna's mission proved helpful to the Pandavas.

Krishna served a big purpose in disclosing Karna's birth history to him. Karna became sympathetic to his own brothers, the Pandavas. This was apparent when he gave the promise to mother Kunti that he would not fight with any other Pandavas except Arjuna. It appears mother Kunti met Karna on Krishna's advice. The non-disclosure of the promise of Karna to both the Kauravas and the Pandavas in fact weakened the Kauravas *vis-à-vis* the Pandavas in the war which was a big gain to the latter.

Karna's promise given to mother Kunti, just on the eve of the war, was no doubt an act of betrayal on his part to the Kauravas who did so much for him. On hearing that he was the eldest of the Pandavas, he was gripped with a serious mental conflict. On the one hand, there was his commitment to the Kauravas and on the other, there was the question of saving the lives of his own brothers. It was not possible to reconcile the two conflicting obligations. Karna in the midst of this dilemma, tried to strike a balance to the extent possible in deciding not to fight with other Pandava brothers as promised to mother Kunti and to fight with only Arjuna, his principal rival and the most powerful warrior on the Pandava side. Judging the peculiar circumstances in which he had to give the promise to mother Kunti, it is easily conceivable that he could not think of any other alternative (and in fact no other alternative was left). It did not even strike him that such a promise would harm the interest of the Kauravas. We cannot perhaps blame Karna for this decision considering the situation following the disclosure of his birth history. We are deeply saddened at the misfortune of Karna, a great warrior with a large heart ever ready to give away anything on asking.

One question cannot but be raised. Did Krishna sincerely try to establish peace? During discussions at Viratanagara, we have seen, he appeared to be always in favour of war. He maintained those who had humiliated Draupadi must be destroyed. He advised Yudhisthira to shun all mildness and deal with the enemy with courage and determination. By keeping secret the birth history of Karna, he actually kept the path of war wide open. During the peace mission, he should have perhaps spoken in the beginning in a more conciliatory manner and could have better avoided using such harsh words against Duryodhana at the very outset. Krishna was endowed with divine powers. Could these powers not have been used for the establishment of peace? On the failure of his peace mission he could have easily imprisoned Duryodhana. Without doing it he used his divine powers to ensure his own safe exit from the Kaurava assembly. Grief-stricken Gandhari at the end of the Kurukshetra war told Krishna this war could have been stopped by him alone; but he did not. For this failure she uttered a terrible curse that Krishna's Yadava and Vrishni clan would be destroyed just like the Kuru clan. Gandhari's curse came true. Krshna's clan was destroyed due to internal quarrel. Judged from all angles it appears Krishna undertook his peace efforts in a half-hearted manner only to perpetuate his name and fame as a man of peace. In the Geeta during the *Vishwarupa-darshana Yoga*, Krishna, the incarnate of the Supreme God Vishnu declared he had now appeared as a terrible annihilator of human lives for the establishment of *Dharmarajya*. When destruction was his declared aim, how could he be expected to try for peace? One aspect of the Krishna's peace mission was, however, clear. He, as we have mentioned earlier, under the cover of the peace mission not only collected vital information about the war preparations of the Kauravas but also managed to bolster up the dissensions in the Kaurava leadership. Krishna's peace mission was, in fact, an extension of his efforts to ensure the victory of the Pandavas in the coming war. Such a novel method of collecting information apparently under a laudable cover, was possible only for a shrewd and intelligent person like Krishna. It was indeed a classic example of a successful intelligence operation.

40.

All peace efforts having failed, the war was now imminent. The two rival armies were being mobilised at Kurukshetra. On being installed as the commander-in-chief of the Kaurava army, Bhishma called Duryodhana and said, "My boy, do not worry; I shall fight to the best of my ability and defend your army."

On this Duryodhana said, "Grandfather, you are omniscient; nothing is unknown to you. Now kindly give me an idea of the power and strength of the rival warriors."

Bhishma said in reply, "You and your brothers are all celebrated warriors fighting from chariot. Your commander Satyabana, demon Alambusha and Bhagadatta, king of Pragyotishpura are all *maharatha* i.e. *rathayuthapati* (commander of many warriors.) Bhojraj Kritavarma, Madraraj Shalya and Bhurishrava of the Kuru clan are all *atiratha* (commander of the *maharathas*.) Kripacharya and Dronacharya are also *atiratha*. Kripacharya out of affection for him would not kill Arjuna. Ashvatthama, son of Dronacharya is a *maharatha*. For his one fault I cannot recognise him as an *atiraratha*. He considers his own life very dear. Your dearest friend, Karna is neither an *atiratha* nor a full *rathi*. He is mean-minded and proud. He is always busy in vilifying others. He has lost his natural armour and earrings. His power has suffered due to the curse of his preceptor Parshurama for falsely introducing himself as a Brahmin. According to me, Karna is an *ardharatha* (half warrior.)"

Dronacharya concurred with Bhishma that Karna was an *ardharatha*. Karna burst into a rage at the words of Bhishma. He said, "Grandfather, you are hurling very harsh words on me without any fault of mine. In my opinion you yourself are an *ardharatha*. You are creating dissensions among the warriors by falsely classifying them into different categories. This will cause great harm to the Kauravas. Your conduct is suspicious." Karna then turned to Duryodhana and said, "My friend, Bhishma's intention is not good. You better forsake him. No doubt old person's words should be listened with respect; but do not listen to Bhishma who is very old and behaving like a child. I am taking the vow I shall not participate in the war so long Bhishma is living."

Immediately a serious altercation ensued between Bhishma and Karna. Duryodhana became worried. He told Bhishma, "Grandfather, war is round the corner. Kindly think how our welfare can be ensured. In the war, both Karna and you will have to perform great deeds. Now tell us about the power and strength of the Pandva warriors. On this Bhishma said, "Yudhisthira, Nakula and Sahadeva are all *rathis*. Bhimasena is equal to eight *rathis*. There is no *rathi* and warrior like Krishna's friend Arjuna in the two armies. Only Dronacharya and myself can face Arjuna in the battle-field. All the five sons of Draupadi are *maharathas*."

Narrating the comparative power and strength of the Pandava warriors, Bhishma said, "I shall not shoot any arrow at Shikhandi, son of Drupudaraj as he was a woman before and had become a man afterwards. I shall also not kill the Pandavas"

Answering Duryodhana's question why he would not kill Shikhandi, Bhishma said, "I forcibly abducted three daughters of the King of Kashi from their *swayamvarasabha* for marrying them to my step brother Vichitravirya. As the eldest sister Amba was betrothed to King Shalva, she refused to marry Vichitravirya, who then married the other two sisters Ambika and Ambalika. King Shalva, however, refused to marry Amba on the plea that I had touched her. Amba held me responsible for her misfortune and resorted to religious austerities in order to take revenge on me. Sage Parshurama on learning the plight of Amba asked me to marry her. He is my preceptor. I unsuccessfully tried to convince him that it was not possible for me to marry Amba or any other woman as I had already taken a vow of celibacy. Then a battle ensued between us and it continued for a long time. Ultimately at the intervention of Narada and other sages the battle came an end. I came to know from them that Parshurama and myself are incapable of killing each other. Parshurama then announced with satisfaction that there was no *Kshatriya* warrior like me in the whole world. Thereafter, I left the place with his permission, while Parshurama departed for Mahendra mountains.

"In the mean time Amba again engaged herself in extreme religious austerities at the bank of the Jamuna. Satisfied with her austerities Lord Mahadeva gave Amba the boon that she would be born as the daughter of Drupadaraj and after being transformed into a male, she would be able to kill me. Blessed with the boon Amba gave up her life on the burning pyre to have a new life.

"In due course the Drupada Queen gave birth to a female child on the blessings of Lord Mahadeva. She, however, announced that a male child had been born and named her Shikhandi. Shikhandi who was being brought up as a male child, was married, on her coming of age, to the daughter of King Hiranyavarma. The Queen had the belief Mahadeva's boon would not go in vain and Shikhandi would actually transform into a man. King Hiranyavarma soon understood he had been deceived and declared he would attack and destroy Drupada's kingdom. Shikhandi holding herself responsible for her father's predicament, left his house and went to the forest. There on her request a Yaksha (demi-god) exchanged his gender with her whereupon she returned home transformed as a young man, while the Yaksha remained as a female. Shikhandi on having weapons training under Dronacharya, is now a celebrated warrior. Shikhandi is actually Amba, the daughter of the King of Kashi. It is my vow I shall not strike any woman or anyone who has transformed into a man from woman and even a person bearing a female name or in the guise of a woman."

Bhishma's description of the power and strength of the rival warriors and the story of Amba-Shikhandi are significant in many respects. We know Bhishma's deep antipathy to Duryodhana. That he is a well-wisher of the Pandavas is also a known fact. Yet, the same Bhishma is now the commander-in-chief of the Kaurava army in the war against the Pandava army. Duryodhana, we are aware, decided to proceed in the war mainly depending on Bhishma and Karna. The success in the war to a large extent thus depended on the united efforts of these two principal warriors. It is very surprising that a wise and experienced person like Bhishma completely forgot this vital truth and that too just one day before the war. He unhesitatingly made disparaging remarks about the power and strength of Karna in his very presence. He even predicted that Karna would be killed by Arjuna in the battlefield. Such statements of Bhishma were definitely demoralising and liable to create dissensions among the Kaurava warrariors. Karna was the main adversary of the Pandavas. If he was demoralised and the Kaurava warriors divided, it were the Pandavas who to gain. Karna rightly suspected Bhishma's real intention and denounced him as an agent of the Pandavas. His advice to Duryodhana to forsake Bhishma was also justified. Duryodhana himself was unhappy at Bhishma's denunciation of Karna. It was not, however, possible for him to take action against Bhishma. Karna did join the war only after Bhishma was severely injured in the war and rendered ineffective. This only helped the Pandavas. The pro-Pandava role played by Bhishma in the war completely justified Karna's assessment about him. Before his death Bhishma, we shall see later, confessed before Karna that he had wrongly classified him as an *ardharatha.*

The secret agents had a role in collecting details of the efforts of Amba to take revenge on Bhishma. This was disclosed by Bhishma himself. He told Duryodhana that he deputed his reliable agents in the disguise of old, infirm, deaf and dumb people to the Panchal kingdom to obtain first-hand information about the activities of Amba following King Shalva's refusal to marry her. These agents used to send him regular reports which revealed that Shikhandi was no other than Amba herself in her rebirth and she was born on the blessings of Lord Mahadeva to kill Bhishma in the war. Despite knowing this fact beforehand, we shall see later, that the Kauravas could not checkmate Shikhandi's advance towards Bhishma in the battlefield resulting in his fall thereby fulfilling the vow of revenge on Bhishma by Amba.

On the Pandava side, the five Pandava brothers particularly Bhimasena and Arjuna were the principal warriors. Victory or defeat mainly depended on them. Bhishma despite being the commander-in-chief of the Kaurava army, we know, would not fight with them. This indeed was an act of betrayal to the Kauravas on the part of Bhishma. Yet on the Kaurava side, Bhishma other than Dronacharya is the only person who can face Arjuna in the battle. That there is no place in the war for personal love and affection was forgotten by Bhishma. Arjuna, we shall find later, did not hesitate to strike grandfather Bhishma and Dronacharya, the traditional teacher of the Kuru clan to whom his gratitude knew no bounds, in the discharge of his responsibility as a warrior of the opposite side. He did not allow his previous personal relationship with them to interfere with his duty in the midst of war. It was Duryodhana's misfortune that he had to install Bhishma as the commander-in-chief of his army. In the world history there is no instance where a known sympathiser of the enemy has been appointed in such a responsible post as the head of the army by the king or the head of the state for his army. It was apparent that the fate of Duryodhana in the war was sealed before the war actually began.

Here another question cannot but be raised. Bhishma was known to be a person of high morality and truthfulness. When he realised it would not be possible for him to fight with Pandavas, on moral grounds he could have easily refused to accept the responsibility of leading the Kaurava army. This he did not do. He remained as the commander-in-chief of the Kaurava army and in that capacity he fought in a casual manner killing innumerable ordinary soldiers while refraining from striking the Pandavas, the main adversaries of

Duryodhana. He thus virtually ensured the victory of the Pandavas and the destruction of the famous Kaurava army with its principal warriors including Duryodhana himself. Was this his sense of justice and fair-play? What happened to his vow of protecting the kingdom of Hastinapura? Bhishma's actions actually led to its downfall.

The next morning, in course of discussions in the Kaurava camp about the war strategy, Duryodhana asked Bhishma and the other warriors to know how much time they would take to destroy the Pandava army. On this, Bhishma said he would take about a month to complete the task. Dronacharya said he would also take one month. Kripacharya said he would take two months. Ashvatthama said he was capable of destroying the Pandava army within ten days. Karna said he would require only five days to finish the job.

At the words of Karna, Bhishma burst into a loud laugh and told Karna that he was speaking wildly as he had never faced Arjuna in the battlefield accompanied by Krishna in the chariot.

In the rival camps, secret agents were stationed by the two sides. Yudhisthira's agents immediately informed him the details of all discussions in the Kaurava camp. On hearing everything, Arjuna told Yudhisthira, 'What has been spoken by the Kaurava warriors about their power and strength is all true. But you need not worry at all. I am alone capable of destroying the three worlds with the help of Krishna. All the divine weapons are under my possession. It would be, however, improper to kill human lives with the divine weapons and as such we shall take recourse to simple strategies with the help of our allies to defeat the enemy."

Thereafter, the representatives of the two sides, after discussions, agreed on a set of rules in the conduct of the war. Some of the important rules were:

1. Warriors of equal strength will fight with one another without resorting to any deception.
2. The two sides will establish cordial relationship at the end of fighting.
3. Verbal contest must be kept confined to the use of words.
4. The retreating soldiers must not be attacked.
5. Warriors on chariot, mounted on elephant or horse as also the foot soldiers will fight with their counter-parts only with due regard to their capability, enthusiasm, strength and desire.
6. The rival can be struck only after due warning; in no case those who are fatigued or bewildered can be attacked.
7. Those engaged in fighting with others, seeking mercy, unwilling to fight or having no weapons or armour cannot be attacked.

8. The charioteer, carrier of loads, reciter of hymns or the drummers must not be attacked.

One day before the start of the war, King Dhritarashtra was thinking with a heavy heart about the fate of his sons in the coming war. At that time sage Vyasa appeared there and told him, "My son, your sons as also many kings will perish in the war. Such catastrophes happen under the influence of time. Therefore do no grieve for the deaths of your sons. If you want to see the war, I can give you divine eyes." In reply Dhritarashtra said, "O great sage, I do not wish to see the destruction of my kinsmen. I am only willing to listen to the account of the war." Sage Vyasa then bestowed divine eyes to Sanjaya and told Dhritarashtra, "Sanjaya will give you a narrative of the war on seeing it with his divine eyes. No weapons will strike Sanjaya. At the end of the war, I shall narrate to the world the glorious acts of valour of the Kauravas and the Pandavas. Dhritarashtra, you can even now stop this war. You cannot allow this despicable fratricidal war to be fought. Let the Pandavas get back their kingdom and the Kauravas be pacified." In reply Dhritarashtra said, 'O father, kindly pardon me. I am helpless. My sons are not obedient to me."

Sage Vyasa left Hastinapura after explaining the different tenets of *dharma* to Dhritarashtra. At the end he said, "Victory is not possible with army alone. It depends on divine grace. Those who have won today, may be defeated tomorrow."

41.

The next morning the Kaurava and the Pandava armies equipped with various weapons faced each other in the vast land of Kurukshetra. On seeing the great Kaurava army arranged in the battle order, Yudhisthira told Arjuna, "Vrihaspati, the preceptor of gods has said if one's own army is small, it should be used in a firm compact body while the large army should be used in an expanded formation. As our army is smaller than the Kauravas', you may arrange it in a needle-like formation as advised by Vrihaspati." In reply Arjuna said, "*Maharaj*, in the present context I have followed the principles laid down by Indra. I have deployed our army in impregnable *achal* and *varya* – simultaneously as a narrow compact body and also in expanded formation so that our army appears large before the enemy – formations. "Assured at the words of Arjuna, Yudhisthira asked him," Dhananjaya, how shall we fight against the formidable well-trained Kaurava army led by grandfather Bhishma? I am worried at the sight of the impregnable Kaurava army arranged in battle-formation by Bhishma." On this Arjuna said, "*Maharaj*, the victory is obtained by truth, mercy, *dharma* and enterprise; it cannot be achieved by strength alone. You please give up all evil and greed and engage yourself in the war with enthusiasm without having any pride. We know victory follows *Dharma*. Vasuva who is the incarnation of *dharma*, is on our side. Our victory is certain." Yudhisthira's worries subsided at the assuring words of Arjuna.

Thereafter, Yudhisthira invoked the blessings of Goddess Durga by reciting Her hymn for the defeat of the enemy. Satisfied at his prayer, Goddess Durga said from behind the space, "O' hero, you shall soon be able to achieve victory over the enemy as Narayana (Supreme God i.e. Krishna) is with you."

42.

At this moment Bhishma announced the start of the war by loudly blowing his conch. Simultaneously the war drums were struck with its sound vibrating throughout the battle-field. Vasudeva then blew his *panchajanya* conch and following him other Pandava warriors blew their respective conches. Arjuna then requested Krishna, his charioteer to place the chariot in between the two armies to get a full view of the two armies. When the chariot was moved to the proper position, Arjuna looked around and saw his own elders, preceptors, teachers, kinsmen, relatives, friends and allies standing divided on the two sides. He immediately realised the terrible consequences of the war and became sad. He told Krishna, "O' Krishna, I do not consider it proper to kill my near relations. I am giving up my desire for victory. I do not want any kingdom. O' Madhava, how shall we be happy by killing our own kinsmen?"

In this way Arjuna cited many reasons for not fighting the venerable elders and other kinsmen. At the end he in a sorrowful mind put off his bow and sat down on the chariot. Krishna then asked Arjuna, "How have you been overwhelmed with this disgraceful mental delusion at this critical moment? Such unmanliness does not befit you. Give up your mental weakness and get ready for the war." Arjuna said, "Madhusudana, how shall I strike venerable grandfather Bhishma and Dronacharya with arrows? It is better to earn one's living by begging than killing the venerable elders. I am bewildered to understand the true significance of *dharma.* I am your disciple seeking your protection. You may kindly give me the correct advice."

In reply Krishna said with a smile, "Partha, you are speaking like a wise man, but I see no sign of wisdom in you. You are mourning for those whom you should not mourn for. A person with true spiritual knowledge does not mourn for anybody dead or alive. All persons after attaining boyhood, youth and infirmity are transformed in course of time into new bodies after death. No wise man gets deluded by this reality. He who pervades the entire universe is indestructible. None can destroy this Absolute Being (*Atman*). He is self-born, eternal, imperishable, and without any beginning. This Atman does not perish with the destruction of the body. As man wears new clothes discarding the torn ones, so *Atman* gets new bodies when the old ones perish. No weapon can cut Him, no fire can destroy Him and even water cannot make Him wet. He who is born is bound to die and rebirth of the dead is also certain. Thus none should mourn for this inevitable reality. And if you look at your own *dharma,* you should not be cowered with fear. There is nothing more beneficial for a *Kshtriya* than to fight for a *dharmayudha* (war for the establishment of a just and righteous society). If you withdraw from this *dharmayudha,* you shall be committing a great sin by losing your own *dharma* and fame. Remember, the performance of a disreputable act by a respectable person is more despicable than even death. All wise persons will think you have withdrawn from the war only out of fear. Your enemies shall make derisive comments about your power and strength. What can be more unfortunate for you than this? Partha, if you die in the war, you shall enjoy a blissful life in the heavens and if you win, you shall enjoy the entire world. Therefore treat happiness and sorrow, victory and defeat, and honour and dishonour as equal and proceed for the war."

Thereafter Krishna explained the tenets of *nishkam karma yoga* and said, "Partha, observance of this *dharma* even in a limited degree removes mind's great fear. Take refuge under pure virtue and goodness. Remember you have claim only to work and not to its result. Do not thus expect any returns from your work. At the same time never remain without work. Therefore, devote yourself to your prescribed duty without any selfish motive. O' Dhananjaya, perform your duty treating success and failure as equal. In this world I have no prescribed duty to perform, but even then I am engaged in work for the education of the people. One's own religion even without having any merits, you should know, is superior to others' however better it might be performed. It is better to die fighting for one's own religion. The religion of the other people must always be rejected as dreadful. Despite being the all pervading Supreme God I am born by dint of my own *maya* (illusion). I descend on this world in human form whenever there is any disgrace to the *dharma* and rise of the *adharma* (unrighteousness). I am born in every age for the deliverance of the virtuous, the destruction of the wicked and for the establishment of justice and righteousness."

Krishna after advising Arjuna on the various aspects of religion assumed *Vishwarupa* on his request. On seeing the *Vishwarupa*, Arjuna became overwhelmed with awe and said with folded hands, "O' *Deva*, (God) I am witnessing in your body all the gods, various moveable and immovable created objects, Creator Brahma on His lotus-seat, Narada and other godly sages and the serpent king Takshaka and other snakes. I am seeing all around your endless forms with many arms, bellies and eyes, but I am not seeing your beginning, the middle or the end anywhere. I am, however, seeing on all sides your strange scarcely visible appearance with crown, mace and *chakra* which is immeasurable, radiant, powerful and resplendent with the glow of *agni* (fire) and sun. You are the Supreme and Absolute Being. You are the only Person to be known. You are the only refuge of the entire world. You are the protector of *sanatana dharma*. You are the imperishable Eternal Being. I have absolutely no doubt about your true identity. *O' Mahabahu*, I am terribly afraid to see your fearsome huge appearance. I have developed an optical illusion. I am finding no peace. The Kauravas with many kings and warriors as also Bhishma, Karna, Drona and our own principal warriors are all entering into the terrible-looking cavity of your mouth with dreadful teeth. As insects enter into the fire for extinction so everybody is entering your mouth for death. O' Vishnu, the entire world has been afflicted with your glow. O' The Terrible, kindly tell me for what purpose you have appeared in this world."

Krishna said, "I am the terrible Kaala for causing death and destruction to human lives. I am now engaged in annihilating all these wicked people. Your rival warriors will all die even if you do not fight. Therefore, rise up for the fight. Earn fame by destroying the enemy and enjoy the kingdom free from danger. O' Arjuna, I have already destroyed them; be only a mere agent."

Overwhelmed with emotions Arjuna said, "O' the *Anantarupa* you are Adideva. Your existence pervades the entire universe. I salute you thousand times. Without knowing your divine glory, I have addressed you as O' Krishna, O' Yadava, *O' sakha*. On different occasions in course of poking funs and cutting jokes I have insulted you in the presence of the friends. I am asking for your pardon for all this. I am deeply perturbed to see your terrible appearance. Kindly reassume your well-known previous serene appearance."

Krishna then reassumed his normal appearance and advised Arjuna on various other matters. At the end he said, "O' Arjuna, you out of pride thought you would not fight, but your *Kshatriya* character itself would impel you to fight. Arjuna, by residing in the hearts of all people, the God by dint of *maya* directs them just as the machine operates a doll. You are my dearest friend. This is why I am telling you all these beneficial matters. You completely surrender to me. I assure you, you shall attain me. Remember me giving up all other religions. I shall liberate you from all sins."

Arjuna said, "O' Achyuta, due to your grace I am now free from all delusions. I have now understood what is my duty and what is not. There is absolutely no doubt in my mind. I assure you I shall perform everything as commanded by you." Saying this Arjuna holding his *gandivadhanush* stood up in the chariot to the great elation of the Pandava army.

The famous Geeta is a part of the Mahabharata epitomising these teachings of Krishna. What strikes most for the ordinary people like us is the *karma yoga*. Every man is engaged in some work or the other. As explained in the Geeta, this work which is different for every person, is the most significant. The sweeper is considered superior to the king if the former performs his duty more sincerely and honestly than the latter. The performance of the work and not the work by itself, underlines the character of the person. The Geeta enjoins upon every person to perform his allotted duty without any selfish motive and expectation of any return and to dedicate the result, if any, to the god as it is the god's work that we all perform. Success for the work comes only by following this path. Our work will be distracted if there is constant desire for returns with the required concentration being disturbed. Arjuna by scrupulously following the *karma yoga* was able to defeat the mighty Kauravas.

This *karma yoga* was evident even amongst the lower formations of the Pandava administrative apparatus. All their subordinate staff performed their allotted duties honestly and diligently on the instructions of the higher authorities. This was possible as they were imbued with the spirit of *karma yoga* following the example set by the virtuous Pandavas. In the conduct of the war, collection of prior information is a must. In innumerable incidents, we have come across how intelligently the secret agents of the Panadavas accomplished their tasks. Here also we see the same spirit of *karma yoga*. We may refer to a typical example of the high moral principle shown by an agent of Yudhisthira. During the stay of the Pandavas in Dvaita forest, Yudhisthira sent one of his agents to Hastinapura to secretly collect information about Duryodhana's administration and the extent of discontent, if any, amongst his subjects against him. The agent, after due enquiries, brought the information that the general people were happy under the rule of Durryodhana. Giving this information to Yudhisthira, the agent said, "*Maharaj*, it is the secret agents who are the eyes and the ears of the king. To furnish false or distorted information to the king is an unpardonable offence on the part of a secret agent. They must always give the king correct information pleasant or unpleasant. As an agent it is my *dharma* to get to the truth and I am giving you a correct picture of the situation at Hastinapura." Yudhisthira calmly received the information about his arch enemy Duryodhana's praise. This was possible as both Yudhisthira and his secret agent were wedded *to* the truth and the *karma yoga*. They both were equally great in their respective roles – one as the king and the other as his mere information gatherer.

43.

As soon as Arjuna stood up on the chariot, Yudhisthira performed a strange deed. He left his armour and the weapons on the chariot and proceeded on foot towards Bhishma in the midst of the Kaurava army. Arjuna and others asked him where he was going, but he remained silent. Krishna then told the Pandavas with a smile, "I am aware of the intention of Yudhisthira. He is going to Bhishma, Drona and other respectable elders to seek their blessings before the start of the war."

The Kaurava warriors denounced the conduct of Yudhisthira as cowardly. Appearing before Bhishma, Yudhisthira sought his blessings and the permission for the war. On this Bhishma said, "O king, I would have cursed you, had you not come to me for the permission. Now I am happy. I bless you, victory be yours. You may now pray for a boon from me." Yudhisthira said, "Grandfather, you are invincible. Kindly tell me how we shall defeat you in the war." Bhishma said in reply, "My son. there is nobody who can defeat me. My time of death has not yet come. See me later."

Yudhisthira then came to Dronacharya and said, "I am taking the vow, I shall conduct the war according to the principles of justice and righteousness. I seek your blessings for the defeat of the enemy." Dronacharya said, "O' king, carry on the fight without any fear. My blessings are with you. You shall come out victorious. Do you want to pray for anything from me?" On this Yudhisthira said, 'O' Brahmin, you are invincible in the war. Kindly let me know the means to defeat you so that we may feel assured." Dronacharya disclosed, "You may kill me only when I shall become unconscious in the battle-field after giving up my weapons." Yudhisthira thereafter appeared before Madraraj Shalya and said, "Uncle, you may kindly ensure reduction of the strength of Karna in the battlefield." Shalya said, "Yudhisthira, your wish will be fulfilled. Proceed to war without any fear."

After the return of Yudhisthira, Krishna went to Karna and said, "O Karna, you are against Bhishma. I have heard you would not join the war till Bhishma is killed. During this period you may fight along with us. After Bhishma is killed you may rejoin the Kaurava side." Rejecting Krishna's suggestion, Karna said, "O Keshava, I shall never commit treachery on Duryodhana. I can even sacrifice my life for the sake of Duryodhana." Krishna then rejoined the Pandava army.

Immediately, thereafter a fierce battle started between the Kaurava and the Pandava armies. The son of Virata king was killed by Madraraj Shalya. Another son of Virata king attacked Shalya to avenge the death of his brother when he was killed by Bhishma. Having failed to withstand the shower of arrows of Bhishma, the Pandava army began to retreat. The first day's battle was won by the Kauravas.

At the end of the fighting, Yudhisthira told Krishna, "O' Vasudeva, the way Bhishma has created a havoc in the battlefield, it appears he alone would destroy the entire Pandava army. In the circumstances you advise us on our course of action." Assuring Yudhisthira, Krishna said, "O *Maharaj*, ' You need not worry at all. Your brothers are all great warriors. Many kings as also myself are your well-wishers. The great warrior Dhristadyumna, is the commander–in-chief of the Pandava army. He will certainly destroy Bhishma." Thereafter Dhristaduyumna arranged the Pandava army in *krouncharan* (means heron – army formation on the pattern of herons flying side by side in a row) method and gave Arjuna the responsibility of guarding the front. In this way the Pandava army remained prepared for the second day's battle.

On the second day, Arjuna killed innumerable enemy soldiers. He also fiercely fought with Bhishma. The king of Kalinga and his sons lost their lives at the hands of Bhimasena. At this Bhishma became angry and destroyed the horses of Bhimasena's chariot. Bhimasena then took shelter in the chariot of Dhristadyumna. Satyaki immediately killed Bhishma's charioteer when the horses took Bhishma on the chariot to a safe place. The Kaurava army could not withstand the shower of arrows of Arjuna and his son Abhimanyu and began to flee. The Pandavas came out victorious in the second day's battle.

For the third day's battle both sides remained prepared for the fight arranging their armies in new formations. The Kauravas arranged their army in eagle formation i.e. army would appear narrow in the front and in the rear, and very wide in the middle like the eagle bird. On the other hand the Pandavas arranged their army in the formation of the crescent moon. Bhimasena and Arjuna guarded the right and the left flanks respectively. In the terrible fight of that day, Duryodhana became unconscious on being struck by Bhimasena and he left the battlefield with the help of his charioteer. The Kaurava soldiers in large numbers lost their lives at the hands of Bhimasena and other Pandava warriors. Despite vigorous efforts of Bhishma and Dronacharya they could not be protected. Later Duryodhana after having recovered appeared before Bhishma and said, "Grandfather, the Kaurava army is on the flight. What else can be more disgraceful than this when Dronacharya and you are still alive? At this indifference of yours to our soldiers I am constrained to feel your main aim is to help the Pandavas. Karna and myself have proceeded on this war only depending on Dronacharya and you. If I am not forsaken by you, it is my request that you carry on the fight according to your respective strength and valour." Bhishma angrily replied, "O' king, I have already told you that the Pandavas cannot be defeated even by Indra and other gods. Even then I am giving the word I shall leave no stone unturned in resisting the Pandavas."

Thereafter, Bhishma by showing his highest excellence in valour and strength, started destroying the Pandava soldiers- indiscriminately. The Pandava warriors could not resist him. On seeing the inevitable destruction of the entire Pandava army, Krishna got down from the chariot and rushed towards Bhishma with his famous disc in hand. Chastising Bhishma for his inaction during the dice game, Krishna said, "O Bhishma, you are alone at the root of this terrible destruction. It is the bounden duty of all righteous ministers to resist the king who is addicted to gambling. The ministers should abandon the king if he does not listen to their honest advice. Yet you have decided to fight on his behalf." Bhishma said in reply, "O' Janardana, I have many times given this advice to Dhritarashtra, He, however, did not listen to me because of his weakness for the sons. It appears it is the fate which is stronger and none can escape it." Arjuna then appeared before Krishna and said, "O' Keshava, kindly restrain your disc. I am giving the word in compliance of my earlier vow, I shall destroy the entire Kuru clan." Krishna then calmed down and mounted the chariot along with Arjuna. Thereafter, Arjuna fought with extreme valour and defeated the Kaurava army. This day's war ultimately ended in the victory of the Pandavas.

On the fourth day, Bhimasena started wholesale massacre and destruction in the battlefield. Many sons of Dhritarashtra lost their lives at the blow of Bhimasena's weapons. The remaining sons fled from the battlefield out of panic. Then a fierce battle started between Bhimasena and Pragjyotoshpuraraj Bhagadatta who was great warrior. Bhimasena was wounded by an arrow of Bhagadatta when Ghatotkacha, Bhimasena's son attacked him. The Kaurava warriors on seeing his valour did not dare to face him. They thought it prudent to flee from the battle-field. In the battle innumerable Kaurava warriors and soldiers lost their lives. The Pandavas came out victorious.

For the fifth day's battle, the Kauravas arranged their army in shark formation – in this formation the front and the rear of the army will look wide and the middle narrow like a shark. Such a shark-like formation becomes necessary when there is the apprehension of enemy attack from the front and the rear. Bhishma himself guarded all the sides of the new formation. The Pandavas arranged their army in hawk formation i.e., the front of the army looks narrow and the rear somewhat wide and the two flanks very wide. Bhimasena, Arjuna and the other Pandava warriors guarded the different flanks. In the fierce battle that ensued, the Pandava army had to retreat in the face of attack of Bhishma. The Kauravas became victorious in this day's war.

In the sixth day's battle, the Kaurava army suffered enormous losses at the fierce attack launched by Bhimasena and the other Pandava warriors. The flag-staff of the chariot of Duryodhana got broken. Many Kaurava warriors along with a few more sons of Dhritarashtra lost heir lives. At the end of the battle which went in favour of the Pandavas, Duryodhana became very much worried. He went to Bhishma and said, "Grandfather, I am bewildered at the dreadful sight of Bhimasena. I am depending on you for the destruction of the Pandavas. Kindly take adequate steps to annihilate the enemy." Bhishma said in reply, "My boy, for your sake I shall burn into ashes the gods, demons and all others not to speak of the Pandavas. You need not worry at all." Greatly satisfied at the assurance of Bhishma, Duryodhana ordered the Kaurava army to proceed to the war.

On the seventh day, Dronacharya killed Shankha, son of Virataraja. The Pandavas, however, maintained their supremacy in the battle-field. Bhimasena, Arjuna and the other Pandava warriors destroyed a large part of the Kaurava army.

In the mean time, Duryodhana became restless at the continuous losses of the Kaurava army. On his insistence, Bhishma prepared five arrows specially sanctified by incantation for the purpose of killing the five Pandava brothers on the eighth day of the war. This information immediately reached the Pandavas through their secret agents. On Krishna's advice, Arjuna went to Duryodhana in his camp in the night and asked for his crown reminding him of his promise given to him at Ghoshpalli. Duryodhana without any hesitation handed over the crown to Arjuna in fulfillment of his promise. He in the disguise of Duryodhana with his crown on his head met Bhishma in his camp and said, 'Grandfather, kindly give me the five arrows you prepared for the death of the five Pandava brothers. I shall myself accomplish this unpleasant task. You need not do it." Bhishma mistook Arjuna in disguise as Duryodhana and handed over the arrows to him. Bhishma's plan of killing the Pandavas thus ended in a fiasco.

The situation in the battle-field did not improve on the eighth day of the war. Many other sons of Dhritarashtra lost their lives at the attack of Bhimasena. Stricken with grief at the deaths of his brothers, Duryodhana again went to Bhishma and said, "Grandfather, Bhimasena is killing our brothers with impunity. Our army though fighting gallantly is not able to resist the Pandavas. Countless warriors and soldiers of ours are being killed every day and all this is happening when you are present in the battle-field. It is evident that you have forsaken us. Now I understand I have made a mistake in proceeding for the war on your assurance." Bhishma said, "O Duryodhana, I repeatedly asked you not to go in for this war. You have not listened to my good counsel. However, I assure you I shall not leave the battle-field under any circumstances. Dronacharya also will not stop fighting. I shall kill anyone I see on my front. You continue fighting with all determination.' In this day's fighting seven sons of Dhritarashtra, the brothers of Shakuni and Arjun's son Iravana (born of Nagaraj daughter Ulupi) were killed, among others. Ghatotkacha showed extra-ordinary valour in the fighting.

Duryodhana held a meeting with Shakuni, Karna and Duhshasana in his camp to discuss the war situation and to find out ways to defeat the Pandavas. Initiating discussions he observed, "It is a great surprise we are getting defeated though Bhishma, and Dronacharya as also other Kaurava warriors were fighting on our behalf. It appears that the Pandavas are invincible; they cannot be killed even by the gods." Karna said, "*Maharaj*, everybody knows Bhihma holds deep sympathy for the Pandavas. About his war tactics he is extremely proud. In fact his power is very limited. In the circumstances how would it be possible for Bhishma to defeat the Pandavas? I would advise you to ask Bhishma to withdraw from the war. He is actually a hindrance to our victory. I shall myself destroy the Pandavas if he withdraws from the war."

Agreeing with Karna, Duryodhana went to Bhishma and told him, "Grandfather, if you are unable to kill the Pandavas out of sympathy for them and hatred for me or for my misfortune, you may give up arms and invite Karna to join the war. He will be able to defeat the Pandavas."

At the suggestion of Duryodhana, Bhishma controlling his anger calmly told him, "O' Duryodhana, we have in the past got enough proof of Karna's cowardice. His boastful claim to power and strength has no meaning. Who is there to defeat Arjuna when Krishna, the preserver of the universe is his main stay? However, barring Shikhandi I shall destroy the Panchal and other Pandava warriors. Tomorrow I shall appear in the great battle."

On the ninth day of the battle, Bhishma himself prepared *sarbotabhadra* formation for the Kaurava army and went on a rampage of death and destruction in the battle-field. The Pandava warriors failed to resist Bhishma's attack. When the situation turned desperate, Krishna for the second time got down from the chariot and proceeded towards Bhishma to kill him with his disc. Arjuna immediately dissuaded Krishna saying, "O Vasudeva, you are promise-bound not to participate in this war. If you now join the war, you shall be proved to be untruthful. The responsibility of killing Bhishma rests on me. I shall accomplish the task myself." At the words of Arjuna, Krishna returned to the chariot. After a temporary cessation of fighting, Bhishma began destroying the Pandava army through a continuous shower of arrows. The fighting ultimately ended with the advent of the evening.

In the camp, the Pandavas held a meeting to discuss the means to kill Bhishma. Yudhisthira said, "O' Vasudeva, grandfather Bhishma is daily killing innumerable soldiers of ours. We have failed to resist him. At the sight of terrible death and destruction all around I have lost all desire for war. I think it is better for me to go to the forest. Devise some ways so that we can come out of the ordeal." Then on Krishna's advice Yudhisthira on the same night met Bhishma in the Kaurava camp. Krishna also accompanied him. Yudhisthira told Bhishma, "Grandfather, our army is faced with terrible losses from your arrows. Tell me how we shall come out victorious in the circumstances." Bhishma explaining the means of killing him said, "It is my vow I shall not attack any person who was woman before, but has now turned into a man. Drupada's son Shikhandi is that person. If I see Shikhandi in the battle-field, I shall give up arms. Arjuna can then strike me and cause my fall. Thus let Arjuna proceed against me in the battle keeping Shikhandi in the front. In this way your purpose will be fulfilled." After knowing the means to kill Bhishma, Yudhisthira and Krishna returned to their camp with a happy mind.

On the tenth day, a terrible fight began between Bhishma and the Pandava warriors. Keeping Shikhandi in the front, Arjuna while continuously shooting arrows proceeded towards Bhishma. Shikhandi's arrows also struck Bhishma's charioteer and destroyed his flag-staff. In compliance of his vow, Bhishma stopped shooting his arrows at the sight of Shikhandi. Arjuna's arrows pierced Bhishma's body in such a way that even a two-finger space did not remain imperforated. Wounded at the strike of the arrows Bhishma fell down from the chariot. It was some time before the sunset. Being covered with shower of arrows, Bhishma's body even after the fall did not touch the earth: the body remained lying on the bed of arrows. Bhishma got from his father the boon of voluntary death. He thus held his life even on the bed of showers waiting for the advent of the Tropic of Cancer. The Kauravas were submerged into a deep sorrow at the fall of Bhishma. On the other hand the Pandavas burst into loud rejoicings.

Thereafter, the Kauravas and the Pandavas appeared before Bhishma and stood around him with tearful eyes. Pleased to see them, Bhishma said, "O' kings, my head is hanging towards the earth. Immediately arrange some pillows underneath my head." The kings in no time brought some best pillows only to be rejected by Bhishma on the ground these were not suitable for a hero lying on the bed of arrows. Then on being directed by Bhishma, Arjuna struck the earth below his head with three arrows which acted as his pillow. Feeling somewhat comfortable, Bhishma said, "I shall give up my life when the sun will move to the Tropic of Cancer. Till then I shall remain lying on this bed of arrows. Now, O' Yudhisthira and Duryodhana, put an end to your enmity and come to a peaceful settlement."

The next day the women-folk of the city came to Bhishma and paid him their obeisance. They also adorned him with garlands and sandal-paste. Soon after Bhishma asked for drinking water. The kings immediately arranged pitchers filled with water along with various food stuff. Rejecting all these offers Bhishma said, "I have left this world. I cannot accept anything offered by the humans." He asked Arjuna to arrange drinking water for him. Arjuna then pieced the earth with a *parjanya* arrow (capable of extracting water) on the right side of Bhishma's head. Immediately nectar-like divine-scented cold water gushed out of that place and quenched his thirst. The kings present were thunder-struck to witness this wonderful act of Arjuna.

Feeling satiated Bhishma told Arjuna, "O mighty hero, all these acts are only possible for you. Sage Narada has pronounced you to be a former sage. The work which cannot be accomplished by Indra with the help of the gods, can easily be accomplished by you with the help of Vaasudeva. You are the greatest archer. I have told all this to Duryodhana many times before; but he did not listen to me. Soon he will be killed by Bhimasena."

Bhishma's words deeply hurt Duryodhana. Addressing Duryodhana, Bhishma then said, "My son, give up your anger. Arjuna, you must not forget, cannot be defeated even by the gods. Let this war come to an end with my death. You immediately come to a settlement with Yudhisthira by returning him his kingdom.Let friendship be established amongst all. You all shall be destroyed if you disregard my advice."

Bhishma's advice was not to the liking of Duryodhana. He remained silent.

After the departure of all others, Karna came to Bhishma alone and after touching his feet said with tearful eyes, "Grandfather, I am that Radheya (son of Radha) against whom you have always borne a deep hatred." On hearing these words, Bhishma after dismissing the guards embraced Karna as his own son. He then said, "O' Karna, you have always opposed me; but if you did not come to me now some misfortune would have befallen you. I have heard from Narada and other sages that you are the *kanin* (born of unmarried mother) son of Kunti. You are not the son of Radha. Adhiratha also is not your father. You always spoke ill of the Pandavas. For this I used to use harsh words against you in order to weaken you. I have no hatred against you. I am aware of your power and strength, charity and devotion. In the use of weapons you are equal to Vaasudeva and Arjuna. The great warrior Jarasandha is not even equal to you. O' the son of the Sun-god, it is not possible to overcome fate by manliness. If you want to do any good work for me, you may join the Pandavas."

Karna said in reply. "O' great hero, your words are true. There is no doubt that Kunti is my mother. I was, however, brought up in the house of Adhiratha on being abandoned by Kunti. Later I enjoyed the wealth and property of Duryodhana. I have dedicated everything to Duryodhana as Vaasudeva has abandoned everything for the Pandavas. Despite the fact the Pandavas and Vaasudeva are invincible, I am determined to carry on the fight for the victory of Duryodhana. Kindly allow me to go to the battle. You may kindly pardon me for using harsh words against you out of anger or fickleness."

Bhishma said, 'O' Karna, if you cannot forget the enmity, then join the war without having any pride and with all power and strength. For a *Kshatriya* to fight for a *dharmayudha* is the most beneficial work. I tried for a settlement but failed."

Karna then returned to his camp satisfied after paying obeisance to Bhishma.

After the fall of Bhishma, Dronacharya was installed as the commander-in-chief of the Kaurava army. Karna also joined the battle. Assuming the charge, Dronacharya asked Duryodhana to seek any boon from him. On this Duryodhana said, "Acharya, you may kindly capture Yudhisthira and bring him to me." On being asked why he was not praying for Yudhisthira's death, Duryodhana said, "If Yudhisthira is killed, Arjuna will destroy all of us. Now I understand even gods cannot defeat the Pandavas. If we can capture Yudhisthira who is wedded to truth, he can be induced to play the dice-game and on his defeat the Pandavas will be sent to the exile once again." Understanding the evil intention of Duryodhana, Dronacharya said, "O Duryodhana, if Arjuna fails to protect Yudhisthira in the battle-field, you may be certain that he has come under my control. I shall not be able to defeat Arjuna. Therefore every effort should be made to keep Arjuna engaged in battle away from Yudhisthira. In that opportunity I shall make Yudhisthira a prisoner and hand him over to you to serve your purpose." Duryodhana thought his prayer had been granted by Dronacharya and the Kaurava warriors and soldiers burst into cheers when the information was announced to them.

The details of conversation between Dronacharya and Duryodhana immediately reached the Pandava camp through their agents. Yudhisthra asked Arjuna to remain always near him so that Duryodhana's intention was not fulfilled. Assuring Yudhisthira, Arjuna said Dronacharya would not be able to cause any harm to him so long he was alive.

For the battle on the eleventh day, Dronacharya arranged the Kaurava army in *shakata* (cart) formation. (In this formation the front will be narrow and the rear wide. The *shakata* formation is suitable for attack from the rear.) Yudhisthira arranged the Pandava army in *krouncha* (heron) formation. Vaasudeva and Arjuna guarded the front. Abhimanyu, Arjuna's son with exemplary valour defeated Koushalaraj Vrihatavala and Souviraraj Jayadratha and mounted an attack on Madraraj Shalya. Bhimasena dissuading Abhimanyu, himself engaged Shalya in a mace combat. Both of them fell down on the ground being wounded. At the approach of the evening the battle for the day came to an end.

In the camp, Dronacharya feeling ashamed for having failed to capture Yudhisthira, told Duryodhana, "*Maharaj*, I have already stated that it is impossible even for the gods to capture Yudhisthira without defeating Arjuna. If Arjuna can be kept away from Yudhisthira by some other means, it will not be difficult to capture him. It is advisable to depute some other warriors to fight with Arjuna. A warrior of Arjuna's stature will never return without defeating them. In that opportunity I shall abduct Yudhisthira."

On hearing this, Trigartaraj Susharma and his brothers assured Duryodhana they would take Arjuna outside the battle-field and kill him. They accordingly, accompanied by a large army, challenged Arjuna to the fight. Arjuna told Yudhisthira, "*Maharaj*, I do never ignore any challenge for fight. This is my vow. Kindly, therefore, allow me to join the fight with the *sangsaptakas* (those who are determined to fight till death). I shall return immediately after destroying them. During my temporary absence the Panchal warrior Satyajit will protect you. You need not worry. In case Satyajit gets killed, you should leave the battle-field."

On the twelfth day of the battle, Arjuna had a fierce fight with the *sangsaptakas*. At the arrows of Arjuna many of them lost their lives. Finding Arjuna away fighting with the *sangsaptakas*, Dronacharya proceeded towards Yudhisthira. Dhristadyumna with his army tried to stop his advance. In the fierce fight that ensued Dhristadyumna's army was routed and it was difficult for him to maintain discipline among the ranks. Satyajit who was protecting Yudhisthira, was killed. Yudhisthira as instructed by Arjuna immediately left the battle-field thereby frustrating Dronacharya's plan to capture him. In the meantime, Arjuna after destroying a large number of the *sangsaptakas,* including their king Susharma, killed Pragjyotishpura king Bhagadatta, two brothers of Shakuni and many other Kaurava warriors. Many Kaurava warriors also lost their lives at the hands of Bhimasena and Dhristadyumna. At the advent of the evening the two armies departed to their respective camps.

In the camp accusing Dronacharya, Duryodhana said, "Acharya, you have broken your promise. You have allowed Yudhisthira to leave the battle-field though you got the opportunity to capture him. This is unbecoming of a righteous person like you." Dronacharya with a feeling of shame said, "None other than Mahadeva can defeat Vaasudeva and Arjuna. I am, however, giving the word I shall kill one of the important warriors of the Pandava side in tomorrow's battle. Keep Arjuna engaged away from Yudhisthira."

Dronacharya remained ready for the thirteenth day's battle by preparing *chakravyuha* (A kind of circular military array) for the Kaurava army with only one path of entry. In the morning as Arjuna remained engaged in destroying the remnants of the *sangsaptakas,* Dronacharya advanced towards Yudhisthira with a large army. Considering none of the Pandava warriors could resist Dronacharya, Yudhisthira gave this responsibility to Abhimanyu. He told Abhimanyu, "My son, none of us is capable of penetrating the *chakravyuha.* You are the only person who is capable of accomplishing this impossible task." Abhimanyu on this said, "For your victory I shall enter into the *chakravyuha;* but in case of any danger I shall not be able to come out of it. Father has taught me only the method of entry." Assuring Abhimanyu, Yudhisthira said, "You open the entry path for us. We shall enter into the *chakravyuha* along with you and ensure your protection." Bhimasena also assured Abhimanyu and said, "Once the entry path is opened, Dhristadyumna, Satyaki and myself, besides other principal Pandava warriors, will follow you inside and destroy the enemy."

Thereafter Abhimanyu by showing the highest excellence of valour, entered the *chakravyuha* by repulsing all enemy resistance. Dronacharya, Karna, Ashvatthama and other Kaurava warriors failed to stop his advance. Jayadratha, however, fighting with great valour, successfully resisted the Pandava warriors who were following Abhimanyu. Abhimanyu getting thus isolated from the Pandava warriors found himself in the midst of the Kaurava army. Inside alone Abhimanyu continued to fight with great courage and determination and killed many Kaurava warriors including Laxmana, Duryodhana's son. On hearing his son's death, Duryodhana got infuriated and instigated the Kaurava army to kill Abhimanyu. Then Dronacharya, Kripacharya, Karna, Ashvatthama, Kosalaraj Vrihadvala and Kritavarma surrounded Abhimanyu from all sides. Abhimanyu continued to fight valiantly and killed Vrihadvala and many other Kaurava warriors. Karna was seriously wounded. On the direction of Dronacharya, Karna attacked Abhimanyu from behind and broke his bow and later killed his horses and the charioteer. Thereafter, Dronacharya, Kripacharya, Karna, Ashvatthama, Shakuni and other Kaurava warriors began to strike Abhimanyu with showers of arrows. Abhimanyu then fell upon the enemy violently with sword and shield. At the arrow of Dronacharya, Abhimanyu's sword was broken into two. Abhimanyu still remained undeterred and rushed towards the enemy with only shield in hand. When his shield was also broken from the enemy arrows, he started fighting with his mace. On his mace being broken, his head was struck by Duhshasana's son with his mace. This blow proved fatal and Abhimanyu fell dead on the ground. Terrified at the death of Abhimanyu, the Pandava army began to flee. Yudhisthira unsuccessfully tried to regroup the army. In the evening the battle came to an end.

In the mean time, Arjuna after destroying the *sangsaptakas* returned to the camp and immediately fell into a swoon on getting the news of Abhimanyu's death. After regaining consciousness, he in a trembling body said, "I am taking the vow I shall kill Jayadratha tomorrow if he does not go into hiding. I am also taking another vow that I will give up my life by entering into the burning fire if I fail to kill him before sunset tomorrow."

The information about Arjuna's vow reached the Kaurava camp immediately through their agents. Jayadratha told Duryodhana and the other Kaurava warriors, "I am deadly stricken with fear. Allow me to go into hiding." Duryodhana assured Jayadratha, the Kaurava warriors would protect him. He should have no fear. In the night Jayadratha met Dronacharya and apprised him of his danger. Dronacharya told him, "Arjuna no doubt is more powerful than you. Even then you need not be panicky. I shall protect you. Carry on the fight in accordance with your own *dharma*." Being assured at the words of Dronacharya, Jayadratha gave up the fear and remained prepared for the fight.

Meanwhile, Krishna's agents brought information that Jayadratha would be protected by six Kaurava warriors namely Karna, Bhurishrava, Ashvatthama, Kripacharya, Shalya and Vrishasena. Giving the information to Arjuna he said, "You should not have taken this difficult vow without consulting me. It will be now your duty to save our prestige. Without defeating the Kaurava warriors you shall not be able to kill Jayadratha." Arjuna assured Krishna that he would kill Jayadratha in the very presence of Dronacharya.

On the fourteenth day of war, Arjuna after defeating the Kaurava army, appeared before Jayadratha some time before sunset. He first killed his charioteer and then broke his flag staff. Seeing the sun about to set Krishna said, "Arjuna, without first conquering the six Kaurava warriors who are protecting Jayadratha or alternatively without taking recourse to some deceit, you shall not be able to kill him. By dint of my *yogic* (spiritual) power I shall cover the sun. Thinking the sun has set, Jayadratha will come out of hiding. At that moment you shall kill him."

Accordingly Krishna by invoking his spiritual power, covered the sun with darkness. The Kaurava warriors burst into cheers thinking the sun having set Arjuna would now give up his life in burning fire in fulfillment of his vow. Jayadratha looking upwards, did not see the sun. Krishna then told Arjuna, "Look, Jayadratha is trying to see the sun without any fear in his mind. This is the most opportune moment to kill him. Without losing any time severe his head immediately; but listen carefully what I am saying about Jayadratha's birth history. At the time of his birth, father Vridhakshatra heard a divine voice that his son would be beheaded in the battle-field by his enemy. Vridhakshetra then uttered a curse that the head of the enemy who would severe his son's head would be torn into hundred pieces. Arjuna, you should severe Jayadratha's head in such a way that his head does not fall on the ground. Your own head will be torn into pieces if his head touches the ground. Vridhakshetra is now engaged in religious austerities in a forest."

As instructed, Arjuna severed Jayadratha's head with an arrow sanctified by *mantra*. Simultaneously, he struck several other arrows which carried the severed head of Jayadratha through the sky and threw it on the lap of Vridhakshatra who was then singing his evening prayers. Vridhakshatra, stricken with fear immediately stood up and saw his son's head adorned with black hair and earrings falling down on the ground. As a result of his curse his own head was split as the severed head first fell on his lap causing his instantaneous death.

Thereafter, the sun rose in the sky again. The Kauravas could understand all these miracles had happened because of Krishna's divine powers. At the death of Jayadratha, Duryodhana and other Kaurava leaders were overwhelmed with grief.

In this day's war, there were some significant incidents. Bhimasena followed Krishna and Arjuna when they advanced towards Jayadratha. Karna happened to meet Bhimasena on the way and immediately a serious combat ensued between the two. In the beginning, Karna struck Bhimasena mildly. Bhimasena, however, on remembering his previous enmity, severely struck Karna with arrows. When Duryodhana's brothers came to the help of Karna, thirty-one of them lost their lives at the hands of Bhimasena. Then the combat between Karna and Bhimasena took a serious turn. At last Bhimasena almost became unconscious being hit by Karna's arrows. Remembering mother Kunti's words, he did not kill Bhimasena. By touching his body with the end of his bow, Karna with a smile only said, "O' *makunde, (makunda* is a grown-up man whose beard has not grown. Bhimasena was actually a *makuṇda.*) you are simply a voracious eater. You know nothing of the art of warfare. You are unfit for the battlefield. The store-house stocked with food is the right place for you." Bhimasena said in reply, "What is that you are boasting for? In the past I defeated you many times. Even Indra, the king of gods had to accept defeat. I invite you to wrestling. I shall kill you like Kichaka."

Bhimasena on being released by Karna, got into the chariot of Satyaki and proceeded towards Arjuna. The Kaurava warrior, Bhurishrava intercepted Satyaki when a fierce fight ensued between the two. On Krishna's direction, Arjuna with a sharp arrow severed Bhurishrava's right arm. Bhurishrava told Arjuna, "O Kounteya, (Kunti's son) I am now engaged in fighting with another person. By severing my arm you have done a contemptible deed. This is against the principle of war. You should not have accepted the advice of Krishna who is deviated from the right path." Saying this Bhurishrava sat in meditation for departure to the *brahmaloka* (abode of the Supreme Being). Arjuna told Bhurishrava, "You are considering my act as wrong. But how is the killing of boy Abhimanyu without chariot, shield and weapons justified on moral ground? Bhurishrava remained silent. Soon after Satyaki severed with his sword the head of Bhurishrava.

In this day's battle, many other Kaurava warriors also lost their lives. Worried at these losses, Duryodhana appeared before Dronacharya and told him, "Acharya, I am certainly a great sinner. For my sake so many kings and warriors have sacrificed their lives. In the situation what is the necessity of my remaining alive? I am taking the vow either I shall destroy the Pandavas and the Panchals or I shall get myself killed at their hands. My present condition is entirely due to your apathy towards me. Kindly permit me to proceed to the war front."

Dronacharya said, "Duryodhana, why are you oppressing me with such harsh words? I am always telling you none can defeat Arjuna. He has brought about the fall of Bhishma after ensuring Shikhandi's protection. Why was Jayadratha killed when Karna, Kripa, Shalya and you were still alive? O' Duryodhana, the fall of Bhishma, a great hero who is true to his vow and invincible even to Indra, indicates that the entire earth has abandoned you. I am taking the vow I shall not give up my shield till I destroy the Pandava army. You take steps to protect the Kaurava army. Today battle will continue for the whole night." Saying this Dronacharya rushed towards the Pandava army.

Duryodhana then told Karna, "O' Radheya, Arjuna killed Jayadratha only with Krishna's help by successfully penetrating the impregnable *chakravyuha* prepared by Dronacharya himself. It is the greatest regret our principal warriors were killed in the very presence of the Acharya. It is my belief that had the Acharya resisted Arjuna more vigorously, Jayadratha's life would have been saved. Arjuna is the dearest disciple of the Acharya. I think for this reason he, without fighting, made it easy for Arjuna to enter the *chakravyuha.* Surprisingly he himself promised to protect Jayadratha. All this is apparently my own misfortune."

Karna said, "*Maharaj*, kindly do not speak ill of the Acharya. I do not find even the slightest deviation on his part. He is old and infirm, and incapable of moving fast. Even then he tried his best to resist Arjuna. On the other hand, Arjuna is young and well-versed in the use of all weapons. There is no point in blaming only the Acharya. We all also failed to resist Arjuna. It is clearly evident that none can transgress his fate. In the past also the Pandavas had been saved by the grace of god. Despite our all-out efforts, we could cause them no harm."

That evening, Dronacharya with Ashvatthama and other Kaurava warriors were engaged in a serous fight with the Pandava army. Though some very prominent warriors of both sides died in the fighting, losses of the Kaurava army were greater. Perturbed at the power shown by the Pandava warriors, Duryodhana requested Karna to protect Kaurava army. Karna told Yudhisthira that he will kill Arjuna that day itself.

On hearing Karna's words, Kripacharya said, "*Sutaputra*, without boasting unnecessarily, you may better proceed to the battlefield and fight. In the past you were always defeated by the Pandavas." Then an altercation ensued between Kripacharya and Karna. At the end Karna disclosed, "I shall kill Arjuna with the *shakti* weapon (spear-shaped infallible missile) given to me by Indra (in exchange for Karna's natural impregnable shield and the earrings). You are disregarding me because of your devotion to the Pandavas. If you dare to insult me again, I shall severe your tongue. I have understood your evil intention; you want to frighten the Kaurava army in order to protect the interest of the Pandavas."

On the use of such derogatory words against his uncle Kripacharya, Ashvatthama became furious. He immediately raised his sword and rushed towards Karna. Kripachaya and Duryodhana prevented him. After being pacified, Ashvatthama told Karna, "*Sutaputra*, I have pardoned you. But Arjuna will destroy your pride." Intervening Duryodhana said, "This is not the time for quarrel. All of you now shall have to carry out heavy responsibilities. Look, the Pandava army is advancing towards us."

Thereafter, a sanguinary battle started between the two armies. Both the sides suffered heavy casualties. In the face of the shower of arrows from Arjuna, the Kaurava army was on the retreat. On being goaded by Duryodhana, Dronacharya and Karna began to fight with renewed vigour. The sky was overcast with the shower of arrows from Karna. Out of fear, the Pandava army began to flee. Yudhisthira asked Arjuna to resist Karna. As Krishna brought the chariot near Karna, Krishna told Arjuna, "None other than Ghatotkocha and you have the ability to challenge Karna. It will not, however, be desirable for you to face Karna now. Only for your death Karna is preserving the *shakti* weapon gifted by Indra. Bhimasena's son Ghatotkocha is a great warrior. Besides he is an expert in the use of divine, *asura* (capable of killing demons) and *rakhashas* (capable of killing man-eating demons) weapons. He will certainly be able to kill Karna."

On Krishna's direction, Ghatotkacha then, by using his power of delusion, assumed various forms and began to fight with Karna. One of the horses of Karna's chariot was killed by him. As the situation turned desperate, on the request of the Kaurava warriors, Karna with his *shakti* weapon, which he kept preserved for Arjuna, pierced the chest of Ghatotkocha. His lifeless body rose up to the sky and then fell on the ground with a loud sound. Under the weight of his huge body a part of the Kaurava army was destroyed.

At the death of Ghatotkocha, the Pandavas were deeply stricken with grief. Krishna, however, began to dance with delight embracing Arjuna. Hurt at the behaviour of Krishna, Arjuna said, "Madhusudana, I am very much surprised to find you happy at the death of Ghatotkocha. There must be some reason behind it. Unless secret, please give out everything."

Krishna said, "If Ghatotkocha did not die today, you would have been killed with the *shakti* weapon gifted to Karna by Indra. In fact, Karna kept this infallible weapon only to be used against you. On being charmed by me,

Karna forgot his earlier decision and used the weapon on Ghatotkocha causing his death. Karna's plan to kill you with this weapon thus ended in failure. Earlier Indra had carried off Karna's imprenetrable natural shield covering his chest along with the earrings. With Ghatotkocha's death, this infallible *shakti* weapon is also gone. Now you have no danger. There is another reason for Ghatotkocha's death. He was sinful and bore hatred against the *Brahmins*. I myself would have killed him had he not died at the hands of Karna. O Arjuna, you need not worry about the death of Karna. There will not be any difficulty for you to kill Karna if you follow my advice. At the proper moment I shall tell Bhimasena about the means to kill Duryodhana."

That night, the two armies were taking rest on being tired after inflicting heavy casualties on each other. During the later part of the night battle resumed with all fury. King Virata and the three sons of Drupada were killed by Dronacharya. Slowly the sun rose in the eastern sky. Dronacharya's shower of arrows caused devastation on the Pandava army. Krishna then told Arjuna, "Dronacharya is invincible so long he holds his weapons in his hands. The situation has come to such a pass the we are to devise some means for our victory disregarding the principles of *dharma*. Dronacharya will give up his weapons on being overwhelmed with sorrow if he hears the news of the death of his son Ashvatthama. Now some one should tell him that Ashvatthama has been killed in the battle. Arjuna refused to say such untruthful words. At last, Yudhisthira, very reluctantly agreed to speak out this untruth. At this moment an elephant by name Ashvatthama of the Malavaraj was killed by Bhimasena. Bhimasena appeared before Dronacharya and timidly said Ashvatthama had been killed. Thinking his own son Ashvatthama had been killed, Dronacharya felt dejected; but without getting perturbed he attacked the Pandava army with renewed vigour. Innumerable Pandava warriors, soldiers, horses, elephants and chariots were destroyed. At this moment, as described in the Mahabharata, Viswaamitra, Jamadagni and other sages appeared before Dronacharya in astral bodies and told him, "Drona, your time of death has come. You have committed a great sin by misusing your divine weapons in killing innumerable innocent and inexperienced people in this war. Now you better give up your weapons."

Dronacharya then stopped fighting and asked Yudhisthira whether his son Ashvatthama had actually been killed. He had the belief Yudhisthira under no temptation would speak falsehood. Finding Yudhisthira hesitant, Krishna warned him, "Dronacharya will destroy your entire army just within half a day. For our protection, it will be advisable to take recourse to falsehood now. To speak falsehood for the protection of life, is not a sinful act." Bhimasena also requested Yudhisthira to act according to the advice of Krishna. Yudhisthira then in a loud voice said, "Ashvatthama has been killed." In the same breadth he said in low voice, "He is not a man but an elephant."

Afflicted with grief at the news of his son's death, Dronacharya threw away all the weapons from his hands. Dhristadyumna at that moment struck him with a long arrow. Severely wounded, Dronacharya loudly shouted for Ashvatthama who, however, did not turn up as he was away. Dronacharya then sat on the chariot in meditation for Vishnu, the Supreme God and departed for *brahmaloka.* A divine light came out of Dronacharya's dead body and immediately vanished to the sky. Dhristadyumna then severed the head of lifeless Dronacharya and threw it towards the Kaurava army.

Terrified at the death of Dronacharya, the Kaurava army fled from the battlefield. Bhimasena in joy embraced Dhristadyumna saying that he would embrace him again after the death of Karna and Duryodhana. The fourteen days war thus ended in the victory of the Pandavas.

At the time of the death of Dronacharya, Ashvatthama was engaged in fighting elsewhere. Seeing the Kaurava army fleeing in different directions, Ashvatthama hurriedly went to Duryodhana and came to know of his father's death. Wiping out the tears from his eyes, Ashvatthama heaving a deep sigh in anger said, "There is no word to condemn this killing of the unarmed father by the mean-minded Pandavas and the act of hypocrite Yudhisthira befitting only a non-Aryan. There is no sorrow if one dies in a righteous war. But my heart is bleeding to know father's hair has been being pulled in presence of the army. The wicked Dhristadyumna and Yudhisthira will not escape from my hands. I am taking the vow I shall not give up my weapons till I destroy all the Panchals. I have in my possession an infallible weapon which father got from God Narayana after worshipping Him. Duryodhana, I shall destroy the enemy with this weapon gifted by Narayana." Saying this Ashvatthama raised a menacing roar trembling the entire battlefield.

The Kaurava army being assured and regrouped marched towards the Pandava army under the command of Ashvatthama with the blowing of conch-shells and the beating of the war drums. Hearing the sound, Yudhisthira asked Arjuna, "Who did bring back the retreating Kaurava army? And yet who raised this terrible roar?" Arjuna said, "This roar is of Ashvatthama. Immediately on birth, Ashvatthama raised the neigh of the horse. For this he has been named Ashvatthama. Preceptor Dronacharya's hair has been pulled by Dhristidyumna. Ashvatthama will never pardon him. Despite being a virtuous person you have committed a great sin by taking recourse to falsehood simply to regain your kingdom. As Rama had earned defame by killing the monkey king Vaali in an unjust war, you have also earned the infamy in the three worlds, by taking recourse to falsehood, for the death of Dronacharya, our highly venerable preceptor. I am also a great sinner. Preceptor Dronacharya had the belief that I can even give up my life for his welfare. But at the time of his unjust killing I remained silent. I have absolutely no right to remain alive. It is better that I give up my life."

On hearing Arjuna's words, Bhimasena angrily said, 'O' Partha, you seem to be talking religion like a self-restrained *Brahmin* living in the forest as a hermit forgetting your *Kshatriya dharma*. Have you forgotten the irreligious acts of the Kauravas? They have deprived Dharmaraj Yudhisthira of his kingdom by deceitful means; they forcibly brought Draupadi to the open court by dragging her by the hair and tried to disrobe her in the presence of the king and other courtiers: they have subjected us to terrible sufferings in exile for thirteen long years. Now we are only taking revenge of their misdeeds. I shall kill Ashvatthama myself even if my four other brothers do not join the fight."

Dhristadyumna told Arjuna, "Dronacharya gave up his own *dharma* as a *Brahmin* and took up the duties and functions of a *Kshatriya*. This is derogatory for a Brahmin. He had killed our innumerable soldiers with his divine weapons. What was wrong if we have killed him by deceit? I am born out of the sacrificial fire as the son of Drupada only to kill Dronacharya. I have no regret about his death. You threw away Jayadratha's severed head to the land of the non-Aryans. I feel sorry for not having done that. As you have killed your father's friend Bhagadatta, so I killed Dronacharya. If the killing of grandfather Bhishma is not irreligious, why will the destruction of Dronacharya be irreligious? Dronacharya bore hostility to his disciples. Besides, he was a person of sinful mind. This is why I have killed him. O' Arjuna, Yudhisthira is not untruthful and I am also not irreligious. Proceed to the war now. You shall come out victorious."

On hearing his words, Arjuna severely reprimanded Dhristadyumna. Yudhisthira, Krishna, Bhimasena, Nakul, Sahadeva and other Pandava warriors remained silent with their heads down. Only Satyaki spoke his mind. He angrily said, "Is there no body here who can kill this boastful mean Panchal, (meaning Dhristadyumna) who is a disgrace to his family? O' Dhristadyumna, you have killed the venerable Acharya in the most disgraceful manner and yet you are speaking ill of him boastfully. Grandfather Bhishma disclosed on his own the means of his death and your brother Shikhandi had killed him. There cannot be any comparison between his death and the unjust killing of the Acharya. I shall cut your head into pieces if you dare to speak ill of the Acharya again."

Thereafter, Dhristadyumna and Satyaki started an altercation vilifying each other. At one time, Satyaki maddened with anger rushed towards Dhristadyumna with his mace in hand. On the direction of Krishna, Bhimasena prevented him. They were later pacified at the intervention of Krishna and Yudhisthira.

With the use of the Narayana weapon by Ashvatthama, the fifteenth day of war started in full fury. Innumerable burning arrows, iron balls, *shataghni* missiles, (each arrow capable of killing hundred persons at a time) maces and sharp-edged chakras (discs) coming out of this weapon covered the sky and began to destroy the Pandava army. Finding it impossible to resist this offensive, Yudhisthira asked Dhristadyumna and Satyaki to leave the battle-field with their respective army contingents. He said, "Vaasudeva can only deliver us from this catastrophe. I am directing the army to stop fighting. I shall give up my life along with my brothers by entering into the fire. We have killed our venerable Acharya by unfair means. We have no right to remain alive."

Krishna then raised his two hands and asked the army commanders to immediately get down from their chariots and stop fighting. This, he said, was the only means to thwart the impact of the Narayana weapon. Bhimasena disregarding Krishna's direction rushed to Ashvatthama on his chariot. Ashvatthama covered him with the shower of arrows belching fire. Krishna and Arjuna then forcibly disarmed Bhimasena and brought him down. Gradually, the Narayana weapon came under control. The Pandava army, thereupon, advanced towards Duryodhana. When Duryodhana asked Ashvatthama to apply the Narayana weapon the second time, the latter heaved a big sigh and said, "He himself will be killed if the Narayana weapon is applied twice. Due to Vaasudeva's machination, the Narayana weapon has lost its effectiveness. It was not possible to destroy the Pandava army as planned.' Thereafter in a fierce battle, Ashvatthama defeated the Pandava army. In the evening the battle came to an end.

That night on the suggestion of Ashvatthama, Karna was installed as the commander-in chief of the Kaurava army. On the sixteenth day of war, innumerable warriors and soldiers were destroyed on both sides. At one time, the Kauravas on being defeated at the shower of arrows of Arjuna retreated to their camp. Karna told Duryodhana, "*Maharaj*, Arjuna is an expert archer. Moreover, he has the patience. Besides, Krishna is constantly helping him with advice. Though our principal warriors have died and I have exhausted the *shakti* weapon gifted by Indra, I am superior to Arjuna in the art of warfare and valour. The bow gifted to me by Parshurama is stronger than the *gandiva* bow of Arjuna. There is no doubt in some respects that I am inferior to Arjuna. The strings of Arjuna's bow are of divine powers. He is also in possession of two inexhaustible quivers. Above all, Krishna is his charioteer. His divine chariot gifted by god Agni is impenetrable. His horses are as fast as the mind and the monkey on his flag staff is terrible. Despite all these, I am determined to fight with Arjuna. Madraraj Shalya is equal to Krishna in power and strength. There is none who is equal to him in the knowledge of the horses. If he becomes my charioteer, even the gods will have to accept defeat at my hands."

Duryodhana then went to Shalya and said, "O' king of Madra, you are aware of the war situation. All our principal warriors are dead. Only you and Karna, the two great warriors are there. I have great reliance on Karna. But Karna does not have a competent charioteer. There is none other than you who is capable enough to act as the charioteer of Karna. Kindly agree to become Karna's charioteer."

On hearing Duryodhana's suggestion, Shalya angrily said, "*Maharaj*, I am the king belonging to the clan of royal sage and a *maharatha*. I cannot be expected to accept the charioteering of *sutaputra* Karna. You are actually insulting me by making such a suggestion. You are considering Karna superior to me. In power and strength, Karna is not even one-tenth of me. On being insulted like this, I cannot join the war. Allow me to return to my own kingdom." Saying this Shalya rose from his seat.

Duryodhana in an attempt to pacify Shalya touched his body and spoke sweetly, "Madraraj, your words are true. Karna or any other king cannot be compared with you. Even Krishna will not be ale to withstand your valour. Considering all aspects I have chosen you with great pleasure as the charioteer of Karna. I think Karna is more powerful than Arjuna. The people also consider you to be superior to Vaasudeva. Your knowledge about horses is twice that of Vaasudeva."

Shalya said, "Duryodhana, I am very happy to hear I am superior to Krishna. I am agreeable to become the charioteer of Karna. I have, however, one condition. I shall have the right to speak out freely to Karna." Both Duryodhana and Karna agreed to this condition.

Thereafter, Duryodhana took Shalya aside and told him, "The great sage Parshurama, son of sage Jamadagni of the Vrigu clan obtained an infallible weapon from God Mahadeva after satisfying Him with his religious austerities. This weapon he gave to his disciple Karna. Had Karna been born in a *suta* clan, it would not have been possible for him to hold it. It is my firm conviction Karna has been born in a *Kshatriya* clan. He has been abandoned in order to keep his identity undisclosed. No *suta* woman can become the mother of this great warrior having long arms with natural armour and the earrings."

Shalya said in reply, "I have also heard this story. Yet even if Karna kills Arjuna, there is no escaping of your army. Vaasudeva himself will destroy everybody. There is none who can resist Krishna when he is enraged." Describing the power and strength of Karna, Duryodhana said, "When enraged, Karna can even kill Indra who holds the *vajra* (thunder) as his weapon. In physical power, however, none, can be compared with you. In the event of death of Karna, you shall command the Kaurava army." Shalya said, 'Duryodhana, you have stated I am superior to Krishna. I am happy at that. I shall act as the charioteer of Karna as desired by you. But Karna and you will have to tolerate whatever pleasant and unpleasant words I shall speak to Karna." Duryodhana concurred.

The next morning Karna proceeded to the war with Madraraj Shalya as his charioteer. At that time many bad omens were sighted all around. Disregarding all these, the Kaurava army raised a cry of joy for Karna. At the chariot, Karna declared that he would kill Arjuna today with the divine weapon he received from his preceptor Parshurama. On this, Shalya reminded Karna that he had in the past saved his life by fleeing from the battle-field on being defeated by Arjuna. This time, he said, Arjuna would certainly kill Karna. Shalya advised Karna to return to his camp if he wanted to save his life. Enraged at his words, Karna accused Shalya of acting like an enemy while posing as friend and expressed his determination to carry on the fight, Then Shalya further provoked Karna and belittled his strength and power compared to Arjuna. Shalya and Karna, thereafter, got engaged in a sharp exchange of words vilifying each other and it continued for quite some time. The quarrel ended at last at the intervention of Duryodhana. Karna with a smile then asked Shalya to drive the chariot to the battlefield.

The seventeenth day's war started in full fury causing heavy losses to both the sides. At one time Karna fainted at the attack of Yudhisthira. On regaining consciousness, Karna in a fierce-counter attack first killed Yudhisthira's personal guards and then destroyed his chariot after piercing his armour. Yudhisthira was left alone standing on the ground unprotected. Karna came down from his chariot and after touching his shoulder told him, "O' *Kuntiputra*, you do not know anything about the art of warfare. You better stop fighting and leave the battlefield." Yudhisthira then with a feeling of shame left the place. Immediately the Kaurava army was attacked and Bhimasena made Karna unconscious by the stroke of the arrows. Shalya took him to safety. Fighting valiantly on recovery, Karna broke the bow and the mace of Bhimasena. In the mean time Arjuna routed the *sangsaptakas* and made Ashvatthama unconscious.

As Arjuna was busy elsewhere, the Kauravas took this opportunity to abduct Yudhisthira. Advancing towards Yudhisthira, Karna severely wounded Nakula and Sahadeva. Then Shalya told Karna, "Why are you unnecessarily squandering away your weapons in fighting with Yudhisthira? Do not forget your main rival is Arjuna. Duryodhana holds you in great esteem only because you are the only person capable of killing Arjuna." Karna then left Yudhisthira and other Pandava warriors and came to the rescue of Duryodhana who had been attacked by Bhimasena. Yudhisthira who was wounded in the battle returned to his camp. Arjuna and Krishna on hearing this news hurried to the camp to enquire about his welfare. In the battlefield Karna with his shower of arrows continued to destroy the Pandava army.

Yudhisthira thought Arjuna had killed Karna and he had come to his camp to give him this information. But on being informed that Karna was still alive, he rebuked Arjuna and angrily said, "Arjuna, I did not know that you are so much afraid of Karna. How could you flee out of fear of Karna when you are mounted on the soundless chariot with the wise Krishna as the chrioteer and when you yourself are holding the golden sword and the famous *gandivadhanush*? You may hand over your *gandivadhanush* to any other king who is more competent than you in the science and art of using arms. Your death was preferable to your fleeing from the battle-field. Fie on your *gandivadhanush,* fie on your physical strength, fie on divine weapons. And fie on your chariot gifted by Agni (the fire-god)."

Enraged at his piercing words, Arjuna lifted his sword to kill Yudhisthira. Stopping him, Krishna said, "O' Partha, I find here nobody who deserves to be killed by you. Certainly you have been afflicted with mental delusion." Arjuna said in reply, 'O' Janardana, it is my vow that any body who will ask me to hand over the *gandivadhanush* to another person, shall be killed by me. Yudhisthira has asked me to do this in your presence. I proceeded to kill him in fulfillment of my vow. Tell me what shall I do now?"

Explaining the tenets of religion Krishna told Arjuna, "Dhananjaya, it appears that you have never received any advice from the wise men. You are god-fearing; but you are not aware of the true significance of religion. Only a mean person performs an act which should not be performed or does not perform an act which should be performed. I consider non-violence to be the noblest religion. Rather take resort to falsehood; but do not kill anyone.You are foolishly proceeding to kill your eldest brother who is like your preceptor and not engaged in fighting. It is sometimes difficult to distinguish between truth and untruth. When it is beneficial to speak falsehood, it is desirable not to speak the truth. There is no sin in speaking falsehood during marriage negotiations, love acts, risks of life, great dangers and for the good of the *Brahmins*. It is better to give false promise in order to gain freedom from the captivity of the wicked people. Here falsehood is really truth."

Krishna's advice helped Arjuna to understand things in correct perspective. He told Krishna, "I now understand my attempt on the life of the Dharmaraj had been a great sinful act. Now you may devise some means so that my vow does not go in vain and at the same time my life and that of the Dharmaraj is saved."

Krishna said, "Friend, Dharmaraj Yudhisthira has taken shelter at the camp on being severely wounded and humiliated at the hands of Karna. In this abnormal condition of his mind he used such harsh words against you. The intention of the Dharmaraj was to provoke you against Karna. Because you are the only person who is capable of killing Karna, and with the death of Karna, your victory will be certain. Now I am telling the means by which the Dharmaraj though living, can be considered as dead. By this your vow will be fulfilled and at the same time Dharmaraj's life will also be saved. Partha, it is an established fact in this world if a venerable person is disgraced, while living he is considered as dead. Now, you insult Dharmaraj with various invectives by addressing him as *tumi*."

As instructed, Arjuna addressing Yudhisthira as *tumi* said, "O' King, you always stayed away from the battlefield and as such you had no idea about the war situation. Bhimasena was engaged in a fierce battle with the Kauravas. He could have himself taken me to task had there been any dereliction of duty on my part. You always remain protected by a group of loyal warriors. Practically you have no contribution towards the war. You have absolutely no right to rebuke me."

In this way Arjuna, by hurling many harsh words towards Yudhisthira in the presence of Krishna and many others, insulted him severely. He then told Krishna, "I have committed a great sin by insulting our venerable eldest brother. I intend to expiate my sin by committing suicide." Krishna said in reply, "Partha, if you commit suicide, you shall be committing a greater sin than even as a slayer of your own brother. Now, praise yourself in the presence of others. This self-praise will be tantamount to your death." Accordingly Arjuna while indulging in self-praise said, "O' King, there is no archer other than Lord Mahadeva who is as expert as I am. I alone can destroy the entire world. As a result of my valour the beautiful assembly hall was built at Indraprastha. The performance of the *rajsuyayajna* was possible only because of me. In this war alone I have destroyed half the Kaurava army. Now Krishna and myself are proceeding to destroy Karna. I am taking the vow I shall not remove my armour without killing Karna today itself." Immediately Arjuna left his weapons and with folded hands appeared before Yudhisthira. Respectfully addressing him he said, "O' *Maharaj*, I am saluting you. Be gracious and pardon me. I am alive only to kill Karna."

In reply Yudhisthira said, "Arjuna, I have myself created all these problems for you. I am responsible for the destruction of our clan. I have no right to remain alive. You immediately severe my head; otherwise I shall leave everything behind and go to the forest. Let Bhimasena take over the royal duties. I am unable to bear your cruel words." Saying this, Yudhisthira rose from his seat to immediately proceed to the forest

Krishna after paying obeisance to Dharmaraj said, "*Maharaj*, you are not unaware of Arjuna's vow regarding the *gandivadhanush.* You have asked Arjuna to hand over the *dhanush* to another person. For this in order to fulfill his vow, he has insulted you on my advice. Insult to an honourable person is equal to his death. Myself and Arjuna are now seeking your mercy. Kindly pardon me for the crime I have committed in advising Arjuna to insult you. I am giving the word that Arjuna will kill Karna today itself." Yudhisthira said, "Krishna, your words are true. I have done a wrong thing by asking Arjuna to hand over the *gandivadhanush* to another person. Today you have saved us from a terrible catastrophe."

Thereafter on Krishna's direction, Arjuna fell at the feet of Yudhisthira and sought his pardon for the crime he had committed by insulting him. Yudhisthira embraced him dearly after raising him from the ground and began to weep. The temporary discord between the two brothers was thus settled at the intervention of Krishna. After some time Krishna and Arjuna after taking leave of Yudhisthira, left for the battlefield with the determination to kill Karna.

In the chariot Krishna told Arjuna, 'Though none is equal to you in power and strength, you should not belittle Karna. Till now Duryodhana has lost a large part of his army. On the Kaurava side Ashvatthama, Kritavarma, Karna, Shalya and Kripacharya are still alive. They are all great warriors. Ashvatthama is the son of your weapons teacher Drona, Kripa is the preceptor of your clan and your *acharya*, Kritavarma is the relative from your mother's side, while Shalya is the brother of your step-mother. For this reason you may have some weakness for them. But do not hesitate to kill Karna who is a great sinner. Therefore proceed immediately to kill him."

At the sight of Arjuna in the battlefield, he was attacked on Karna's direction, by Duryodhana, Kritavarma and other Kaurava warriors. Karna's plan was to tire out Arjuna in this way and kill him at the opportune moment. But his plan failed miserably.The Kaurava warriors began to flee being afflicted by Arjuna's shower of arrows. Thereafter Bhimasena and Duhshasana were engaged in a fierce battle with maces. At the blow of Bhimasena, Duhshasana on being severely wounded fell down on the ground. At that moment Bhimasena, after getting down from his chariot, pierced Duhshasana's chest with his sword and drank his blood in fulfillment of his vow to avenge the humiliation of Draupadi during the dice-game. At this grotesque sight, the Kaurava army was terrified and began to flee in different directions.

Thereafter, Bhimasena killed Karna's son Vrishasena along with ten sons of Dhritarshtra. Moved by the news of his son's death, Karna angrily challenged Arjuna to the battle. Brahma, Shankar, Indra and other gods in astral bodies, as described in the Mahabharata, appeared there to witness the great battle between Karna and Arjuna. The Sun-god and Indra started quarrelling wishing victory to their respective sons. Karna and Arjuna stirred the entire battle-field by hurling powerful divine weapons against each other. As a result innumerable horses, chariots and foot soldiers were destroyed on both sides. Perturbed at the wide-spread death and destruction all around, Ashvatthama held the hands of Duryodhana and said, "Duryodhana, immediately stop this war. Give up your hostility towards the Pandavas. Arjuna will certainly stop fighting on my request. Krishna himself does not want war. If you agree to any settlement, the Pandavas will remain subservient to you." Agreeing with Ashvatthama, Duryodhana said, "What you have said is certainly justified. But how will peace be possible now after the dastardly killing of Duhshasana? Moreover, the Pandavas will not trust me in view of the past enmity. Karna also cannot be restrained. Today Arjuna while fighting, has become very much tired. I think it will not be difficult for Karna to kill him."

In the fierce fighting the strings of Arjuna's bow once got snapped at the arrows of Karna. At this opportunity Karna, while covering Arjuna with a shower of arrows, struck Krishna with a long arrow. It appeared Krishna and Arjuna had been defeated. The Kaurava army raised a cry of joy. Soon after Arjuna put new strings to his bow, struck Karna, Shalya and other Kaurava warriors and then destroyed Karna's guards. At this, the remnants of the Karauva army began to flee out of panic disregarding Duryodhana's orders.

During the burning of the Khandava forest, the mother of Ashwasena, son of Takshaka, was killed by Arjuna. To avenge his mother's death Ashwasena assumed the form of an arrow and entered into the the quiver of Karna. Without knowing it, Karna put this very powerful arrow to his bow. Charioteer Shalya asked Karna to replace this arrow as, according to him, Karna would not be able to severe Arjuna's head with it. Disregarding Shalya's advice, Karna discharged the arrow. All burst into a loud lamentation. The terrible-looking arrow went to the sky with a piercing sound and started emitting a shower of fire. Sensing danger to Arjuna, Krishna immediately downed his chariot into the ground by one cubit. All the four horses of the chariot simultaneously kneeled down touching the ground. Karna's arrow only destroyed the golden crown of Arjuna and his life was saved. Ashwasena then introduced himself to Karna and requested him to use his arrow for the second time keeping his eyes very carefully on the target. He explained in this way– Arjuna who happened to be common enemy of both of them, would be killed. Karna refused saying he did never accomplish his task with the help of others.Then, Ashwasena himself proceeded to kill Arjuna. On Krishna's direction, Arjuna shot him down. After Arjuna came out of danger, Krishna raised the chariot on the ground with his two hands. All plans to kill Arjuna thus ended in failure due to Krishna's help.

Thereafter, Karna and Arjuna were again locked in a fierce battle. At one time Karna's golden crown, earrings and armour were destroyed at the arrows of Arjuna. At this condition his chest unprotected by armour, was pierced by Arjuna's arrows. As a result Karna left his bow and the arrows and fell down in a swoon on the chariot. As Karna was then unarmed the virtuous Arjuna refrained from discharging further arrows on him. Understanding his mind Krishna said, "O' Arjuna, you are getting confused unnecessarily. The wise men obtain both *dharma* and fame by killing the enemy in distress. You should thus immediately kill Karna without showing him any mercy. Otherwise Karna after regaining his senses will attack you." On Krishna's advice, Arjuna began to strike Karna repeatedly with arrows. Karna who in the mean time had regained senses, was seriously wounded and despite being afflicted by severe pain started shooting at Arjuna.

As the time of his death had come, *Kaala* appeared there unseen by others and telling him about the curse he got from the *Brahmin* said, "*Sutaputra*, the earth is swallowing your chariot." Immediately Karna forgot the *mantra* he learned from his preceptor Parshuram about the use of his weapons. (Karna learned this *mantra* from Parshurama by introducing him as a Brahmin. When it was found out that Karna was was actually a *Kshatriya*, Parshurama uttered the curse that he would forget this *mantra* in times of his ultimate danger making it impossible for him to use the weapons). In this terrible crisis Karna sad and bewildered uttered with regret, "According to the wise men the virtuous are always protectd by Dharma. Though I followed the path of virtue, Dharma did not come forward to help me. It appears Dharma without protecting the virtuous, only destroys them." Even in this desperate situation, Karna continued to oppress Arjuna with continuous shower of arrows. On Krishna's direction, Arjuna then placed a powerful divine arrow to his bow. Meanwhile, Karna's chariot went down further into the earth. Without finding any other way, Karna himself came down from his chariot and tried to retrieve wheels; but all his efforts went in vain.In anger with tears in his eyes, Karna asked Arjuna who was about to strike him, "O' son of Pandu, please stop fighting for a few moments. The wheels of my chariot are grounded. I am trying to retrieve them. Do not behave like a coward. All warriors with noble mind do not strike his rival who is in the midst of extreme distress without having arms and armour. You are mounted on your chariot. It will not be proper for you to kill me till the wheels of my chariot are retrieved. I am not at all afraid of you or Vaasudeva. I am born in the *Kshatriya* clan. Remembering the *dharma* of your clan, please excuse me for a few moments."

This time Krishna gave the reply. He said, "O' Radheya, you are now telling us the story of *dharma*. Where was your *dharma*, when you all humiliated Draupadi in the open court at Hastinapura? Where was your *dharma*, when with your approval Duryodhana with the help of Shakuni captured Yudhisthira's kingdom in the deceitful dice-game? And yet where was your *dharma*, when you along with other Kaurava warriors mercilessly killed Abhimanyu? Now you cannot escape by referring to the principles of *dharma."*

Karna remained silent. With trembling lips in anger, he struck Arjuna with a terrible arrow. Arjuna lost his conscious-ness and his *gandivadhanush* fell from his hands.At this opportunity, Karna again tried to retrieve the wheels of his chariot, but failed. Arjuna regaining his composure, first destroyed the flag-staff of Karna's chariot with a sharp-edged arrow and then beheaded him with another very powerful arrow. A glow emanating from the lifeless body of Karna rose towards the sky and gradually entered the disc of the sun. The Pandava army raised a huge cry of joy at the death of Karna. Shalya then returned to the camp in the chariot bereft of the flag-staff. The blood-soaken dead body of Karna remained lying on the ground.

On Karna's death, Duryodhana with a large force rushed to the enemy army. But his men, being unable to withstand the attack of the Pandava army, began to flee in different directions. He failed to maintain discipline amongst them. At the request of Shalya, Ashvatthama and other Kaurava warriors, Duryodhana in despair with tears in his eyes constantly uttering, "O' Karna, O' Karna" returned to the camp with the men still alive.

Yudhisthira was brought to the battlefield to witness the battle between Karna and Arjuna. But he returned to the camp on being wounded again by one of Karna's arrows. Arjuna came to his camp and gave him the good news of Karna's death. Later he accompanied Krishna and Arjuna in their chariot to the battle-field and saw the lifeless body of Karna lying on the ground. He profusely praised both Krishna and Arjuna for the victory and told Krishna, "O' Govinda, after a long time I shall today have sleep with comfort due to your grace."

At the Kaurava camp, Kripacharya told Duryodhana, 'All our principal warriors have been killed in the war. With the few men who are still alive, your life is also in danger. As the situation stands at present, I think the best course for you would be to agree to any settlement with the Pandavas. I trust at the request of Dhritarashtra and Krishna, Yudhisthira who is a man of compassion, will give you the entire kingdom."

Duryodhana said in reply, "O' Acharya, as a dying man has no inclination for medicine, I too am unable to accept your beneficial advice. We have banished Yudhisthira from his kingdom; we have defeated him in the deceitful dice-game. Why will he listen to us now? We have cheated Krishna during his peace mission. Why will he too trust us now? How will the Pandavas forget the death of Abhimanyu? Bhimasen is determined to destroy us. Nakula and Sahadeva are ready to join the war. Dhristadyumna and Shikhandi are our old enemies. On being humiliated during the dice-game, Draupadi took to severe religious austerities wishing our destruction. She will never pardon us. Specially the fire of enmity which has been ignited after the death of Abhimanyu can never be extinguished. After enjoying the entire world, how shall I enjoy my kingdom at the mercy of the Pandavas? Now it is not the time to show any weakness. We shall have to carry on the fight at all costs. I am not agreeable to accept any kingdom because of my indebtedness to the innumerable brave warriors who have sacrificed their lives for my sake. I shall be condemned by the people if I accept the kingdom and save my life on having a settlement with the Pandavas after the death of our venerable grandfather and other elders. Departure to heaven after sacrificing my life in the battle is now more beneficial for me. I have no desire for kingdom." Duryodhana's statement drew wide applause from the assembled kings and princes.

After the death of Karna, Madraraj Shalya was installed as the commander-in-chief of the Kaurava army. Yudhisthira became worried on getting the information and sought Krishna's advice regarding the plan of action of the Pandavas. Krishna said, "*Maharaj*, none except you will be able to kill Shalya. You should not, however, show any mercy to him as your maternal uncle. Observe the *dharma* of the *Kshatriya* and kill the Madraraj."

On the last eighteenth day's terrible battle, three sons of Karna were killed by Nakula while Shalya's son died at the hands of Sahadeva. In the battle between Bhimasena and Shalya, both were wounded. Victory or defeat remained uncertain. Thereafter while directing Bhimasena, Arjuna and other warriors, to protect the different flanks of the Pandava army, Yudhisthira himself attacked Shalya and destroyed the four horses of his chariot and killed his two charioteers. Ashvatthama then took Shalya to his chariot. After some time Shalya returned to the battle-field in another chariot and started fighting with Yudhisthira. At the arrows of Yudhisthira all the four horses of Shalya's new chariot were killed. Shalya then got down from his chariot and rushed towards Yudhisthira with his sword and shield. Bhimasena promptly intervened and destroyed both his sword and the shield with arrows. At this moment, Yudhisthira remembering Krishna's advice, killed unarmed Shalya with a powerful weapon sanctified by incantation. Shalya's brother while advancing towards Yudhisthira was also killed by him.

In this day of battle, King Shalva, (who refused to marry Amba, princess of Kashi on being released by Bhishma) Shakuni, his son Uluka, the remaining sons of Dhritarashtra and many other Kaurava warriors lost their lives.The few Kaurava soldiers who were still alive, while fighting bravely on being encouraged by Duryodhana, also got killed. In this way, Duryodhana's eleven *akshouhini*-strong army was destroyed at the hands of the Pandavas.The losses on the Pandava side were also heavy. Out of their seven *akshouhini* strong-army, ten thousand foot soldirs, five thousand horses, seven hundred elephants and ten thousand chariots were only saved.Realising it was fruitless to carry on the fight any longer, Duryodhana wounded and exhausted, left his dead horse in the battle-field and proceeded towards the east with his mace in hand.

In the mean time Sanjaya, while proceeding to Hastinapura, was attacked by Satyaki; but his life was saved by sage Vyasa. After some time he met Duryodhana on the way and gave him the latest news about the war. Duryodhana asked Sanjaya to inform Dhritarashtra that he was going to take shelter inside the Dvaipayana lake.

Inside the lake, Duryodhana created a cylinder by dint of his *maya* (magic) power and took shelter there. Kripacharya, Ashvatthama and Kritavarma who were moving together after leaving the battle-field, came to meet Duryodhana at the Dvaipayana lake on getting the information of his hiding-place from Sanjaya. They asked Duryodhana to come out of the water and join them in their fight against the Pandavas. Ashvatthama expressed his determination to kill the Panchals and their allies that night itself. This conversation between Duryodhana and Ashvatthama was overheard by a group of hunters who came to the lake to drink water. These hunters used to supply meat to the Pandava camp during the war. Understanding Duryodhana was hiding in the water of the lake, they immediately gave the information to Bhimasena. The Pandavas then hurried to the lake only to find that Kripacharya and others had already departed from the place. Yudhisthira told Krishna, "Vaasudeva, Duryodhana by dint of *maya* power has taken shelter in a cylinder inside the water of the lake. He has thus no fear from any humans. But Duryodhana will not be allowed to go scott-free." Krishna said, "*Maharaj*, by dint of your superior *maya* power, you may destroy the *Maya* power of Duryodhana.You may destroy Duryodhana by devising some novel means. In this way only the Danava king Bali, Ravana,Tarakasura and others were killed."

Understanding the meaning of Krishna's words, Yudhisthira with a smile told Duryodhana hiding inside the water, "Kururaj, why have you entered into the water after destroying so many *Kshatriya* warriors and your near and dear ones only for saving your own life? You are born in the proud *Kshatriya* clan. It is not proper for you to remain hiding in the water out of fear for war. It appears you were boasting in vain before others that you are a great hero.

The real heroes do not flee out of fear of the enemy. You may immediately come out of the water and after defeating us, enjoy the entire world or otherwise get killed in our hands and accept the bare ground as your bed." Duryodhana said in reply, "I have no inclination for war after the death of grandfather Bhishma, Dronacharya and Karna. I have decided to go to the forest having lost all desire to enjoy the kingdom." On this Yudhisthira said, "Kururaj, the people will be in doubt about our victoy and defeat if both of us remain alive. For the decisive result of the war one of us must get killed. Your life is now under my control. Come out of the water immeditely and join the fight."

On coming out of the water, Duryodhana said, "O' son of Kunti, all of you have surrounded me. Besides, you are all mounted on chariot and armed. On the other hand I am without any chariot and tired. You may fight with me one by one." Yudhisthira said, "All right. It will be done that way. The entire kingdom will be yours if you can kill even one of us." As Duryodhana challenged the Pandavas to the fight, Krishna angrily told Yudhisthira, "*Maharaj*, why have you given this promise if one of you is killed by Duryodhana, he will get the entire kingdom? Do you understand what would be the consequences if now Duryodhana choses you, Arjuna or Nakuala or Sahadeva to the mace-fight? Amongst you there is none except Bhimasena who is equal to Duryodhana in the mace-fight. Even Bhimasena has not practised mace-fight for so long as Duryodhana has done. It seems the Pandavas are destined not to regain their kingdom." On hearing Krishna's words, Bhimasena came forward and challenged Duryodhana to the mace-fight saying he would extinguish the fire of enmity by killing Duryodhana.

At this moment Balarama appeared there and heard about the imminent mace-fight between his two disciples, Duryodhana and Bhimasena. At his suggestion the fight was held at Kurukshetra. This terrible mace-fight continued for a long time. None of them, despite being wounded, admitted defeat. On a question of Arjuna – who was superior between the two warriors – Krishna said, "Bhimasena is no doubt physically stronger; but in skill and endeavour Duryodhana is superior. In the just fight it will not be possible for Bhimasena to kill Duryodhana. He will have to take recourse to deceitful means for this purpose. Let him fulfill his vow of breaking the thighs of Duryodhana he took during the dice-game. If Bhimasena continues to fight depending on his strength, he will only bring in disaster to Yudhisthira.' Arjuna understood the significance of Krishna's words and hinted to Bhimasena by striking his own thigh. Bhimasena then at the opportune moment struck Duryodhana at his thighs with the mace. With the broken thighs Duryodhana immediately fell down on the ground. Appearing before Duryodhana, lying on the ground, Bhimasena said, "O' villain, now you suffer the consequences of your derisive comments against us and the humiliation inflicted on Draupadi in the open court at Hastinapura." After saying this, Bhimasena began to kick Duryodhana's head repeatedly with his left foot.

Yudhisthira then told Bhimasena, 'You have fulfilled your vow whether the means adopted by you was just or unjust. Now be pacified. Duryodhana is our kinsman. He was the Kaurava king having under his command eleven *akshouhini* strong army. It has not been proper for you to insult him in this way by kicking his head taking advantage of his helplessness." Saying this, he went to Duryodhana and said, "O' the jewel of the Kurus, so many of our friends and relatives have lost their lives for your fault. At last you have also been killed. Whatever that may be, now you should not have any grief. Death will end all your sorrow and grief. And we shall live with the grief due to the destruction of our near and dear ones.We shall also remain deeply stricken with curse from the widowed daughters-in-law of Dhritarashtra as also from his grandsons' widowed wives.' Saying this Yudhisthira burst into wailings.

Meanwhile, Baldeva chastised Bhimasena for striking Duryodhana at the thighs. He angrily said that in the *dharmayudha* Bhimasena had committed a contemptible deed by taking resort to unrighteousness in striking Bhimasena below the navel. Never before, he pointed out, such a sinful act was seen committed. Saying this, he raised his plough (Balarama always carried a plough as his weapon) and rushed towards Bhimasena to kill him. Krishna immediately stopped him by holding his arms. Requesting him to control his anger, Krishna said, "O' great soul, in the scriptures six kinds of gains are mentioned. These are – personal gain, gain of own friends, gain of own allies, harm of the enemy, harm of the friends of the enemy and harm of the allies of the enemy. According to the wise men, one should always remain careful in protecting his own interests and those of his friends. The Pandavas are the sons of our paternal aunt.They are our natural allies. It is our bounden duty to extend all help to them in their danger. Bhimasena earlier took the vow that he would break the thighs of Duryodhana in the battle-field. There was even a curse from the sages on Duryodhana that he would die after his thighs are broken. In the circumstances, I find no fault on the part of Bhimasena. Kindly control your anger. There is no doubt we shall also gain from the Pandavas' victory."

Balarama remained unconvinced. He said, "It is not easy to comprehend the essence of *dharma*. Only the virtuous people observe *dharma* understanding its true spirit. Desire for wealth and attachment make man devoid of *dharma*. He who treats *dharma*, wealth and attachment equally, is only happy. Whatever might be your explanation, I harbour no doubt whatsoever that Bhimasena has committed an irreligious act." Despite all efforts, Krishna failed to pacify Balarama, who asserted, "Bhimasena has killed the virtuous Duryodhana by sinful means. For this shameful act,

Bhimasena would be known in the world as a *kutayodha* (crooked-minded warrior). As Duryodhana has sacrificed his life in *dharmayudha,* he will attain heavenly bliss in the other world, while he will gain fame and glory in this world." Saying this Balarama left for Dwaraka in his chariot leaving the Pandavas, the Yadavas and the Panchals immersed in deep sorrow.

After the departure of Balarama, Krishna asked Yudhisthira how being a virtuous person he could condone such an inhuman conduct of Bhimasena towards the Kaurava chief Duryodhana lying almost dead on the ground. Yudhisthira said in reply, "I did not want Bhimasena to kick the head of Duryodhana by his foot. But we shall have to consider the condition of his mind which was vitiated by deceitful actions and invectives of the sons of Dhritarashtra. Considering all aspects, I have ignored Bhimasena's conduct towards Duryodhana." Krishna despite having reservations, approved Yudhisthira's explanation.

Thereafter, the Pandava warriors began to abuse Duryodhana and praise Bhimasena. Krishna then told the assembled kings, "You should not hurl abuses towards Duryodhana in this manner. When Duryodhana deprived the Pandavas of their rightful claim to their kingdom disregarding the advice of the elders, I could undersand this was all fated by destiny. Now Duryodhana has neither any enemy nor friends. He has turned into an inert object like a piece of wood."

At the words of Krishna, Duryodhana slightly raised his body from the ground and angrily said, "O' Vaasudeva, on your hints Bhimasena has broken my thighs in an irreligious war. I am surprised that you are not ashamed even after that. It is you who have killed our grandfather by placing Shikhandi in front of him. When an elephant by name Ashvatthama was killed, by resorting to deceit you craftily disarmed our venerable Acharya and in this state Dhristadyumna advanced towards him to kill him, you did not prevent him. Because of your trick, Karna's arrow killed Ghatotkocha instead of Arjuna. Your trick also aborted Karna's serpent arrow directed against Arjuna. When Karna was engaged in retrieving the wheels of his chariot, Arjuna on your direction unjustly killed Karna. Who is the greater sinner, heartless and shameless than you? It is the irony of fate we got killed along with the virtuous kings in an unjust war."

Krishna, without replying to his charges, told Duryodhana that he was only reaping the consequences of his misdeeds.Without being subdued, Duryodhana said, "O Krishna, I have throughout my life performed various religious deeds. At last I have embraced death in the battle-field which every *Kshatriya* prays for. I am now departing to the heaven with my brothers. Now you all live in this world like the dead losing your near and dear ones."

Immediately scented shower of flowers began to descend from the sky. Simultaneously, the Gandharvas played melodious tunes on their musical instruments, while the celestial damsels started singing in praise of Duryodhana. The divine saints too applauded Duryodhana. Vaasudeva and the Pandavas were ashamed to witness such wonderful scenes and began to express their grief for killing Bhishma, Drona, Karna, Bhurishrava and Duryodhana in an unjust war.

Seeing the worried Pandavas, Krishna said, "O Pandavas, you could never be able to kill Bhishma and the other Kaurava warriors in just war. I myself for your good have killed them by devising various means and by using my divine power.There is no necessity to discuss the fact that Bhimasena has killed Duryodhana by deceitful means. It is well-known that if the enemy is stronger, various deceitful means are to be adopted to destroy him. The gods killed the Asuras by following this strategy. Let us now return to our respective camps." Saying this, Vaasudeva along with others raised a cry of joy on the death of Duryodhana with the blowing of the conch–hells.

The next day, on the request of Yudhisthira, Krishna came to Hastinapura to console Dhritarashtra and Gandhari. He told Dhritarashtra, "*Maharaj*, desite all our efforts this war could not be prevented because of your non-cooperation. You are alone responsible for the destruction of the Kuru clan.There is no doubt all this has happened due to the influence of time. Queen Gandhari and you may now kindly restrain your grief and renounce the anger against the Pandavas. Look after them with assurance of safety. Yudhisthira, even after destroying all his enemies, is immersed in deep sorrow. Out of shame he could not appear before you."

Later Krishna appeared before grief-stricken Gandhari and told her, "O' Subalanandini, (daughter of Subala) you advised your sons many times to give up their erroneous path; but they did not listen to you. You have even told them that victory will be there where the *dharma* lies. Now your utterance has come true. Kindly give up your grief. You are a virtuous lady. Your flame of anger can destroy the entire world. Kindly do not destroy the Pandavas." Gandhari said in reply, "Vaasudeva, I have regained my peace of mind at your words. Now you look after King Dhritarashtra who is blind having no sons." At this moment suddenly the evil design of Ashvatthama struck his mind. He informed Gandhari that Ashvatthama had contrived to kill the Pandavas. On Gandhari's direction, Krishna immediately rushed to the camp to protect the Pandavas.

In the mean time, on getting the information that Duryodhana was lying on the ground in a dying condition with broken thighs, at Kurukshetra, Ashvatthama, Kripacharya and Kritavarma came to the battle-field. On seeing

Duryodhana in that condition, they were overwhelemed with grief. Ashvatthama with tearful eyes said. "O King of the world, you despite being honourable to all people and posessing immense wealth like Indra, are now lying in dust on the ground. Seeing your distress, it appears Goddess Lakshmi does not stay permanently with anybody." Addressing Kripacharya, Ashvatthama and Kritavarma, Duryodhana said, "O heroes, according to the wise men all created beings and things perish one day under the influence of time. My death proved this inevitable truth once again. I have never turned away from any open fight. The sinful Pandavas have defeated me by deceitful means. Fortunately your lives have been saved in this terrible war. Do not grieve for me. If the teachings of the Vedas are true, I shall certainly get my abode in the heavens. Despite all your efforts, victory eluded us. Evidently none can transgress the fate."

Ashvatthama said, "*Maharaj*, the mean-minded Padavas have mercilessly killed my father. But my feeling of grief for you is deeper. I am taking the vow in this night itself I shall kill all the Panchals in the very presence of Vaasudeva. I am awaiting your order." Duryodhana then installed Ashvatthama as the commander of the Kaurava army in a make-shift ceremony. Ashvatthama thereafter raised the roar of a lion which created a terrible trembling all around and left the place with Kripacharya and Kritavarma on his daring mission.

In the forest, during the night Ashvatthama disclosing his plan of action to Kripacharya and Kritavarma said, "It will not be possible to defeat the victorious Pandavas in face to face fight. We shall have to adopt a different method to achieve our objective. We shall by a sudden attack destroy the wounded and tired enemies in their deep sleep." Disapproving Ashvatthama's plan, Kripacharya said, "My boy, it will be irreligious to kill anyone while asleep. You may attack the enemies after the sunrise."

Disregarding Kripacharya's advice, Ashvatthama proceeded towards the Pandava camp with Kripacharya and Kritavarma following him. At the entrance of the camp Ashvatthama saw a terrible-looking great man having a huge body. An accumulation of glow from his mouth, nostrils, ears and eyes was emitting innumerable Hrishikeshs holding conch, *chakra* and mace. Ashvatthama without any fear began to hurl divine weapons towards him; but all went in vain.The terrible-looking person remained unharmed blocking the entrance. Ashvatthama understood without being armed with divine power, there was no possibility of achieving his purpose. He then got down from the chariot and sought the protection of Mahadeva.After paying obeisance to Mahadeva, he recounted His great glory and said, "O' Devesha, (King of gods) you are greater than the greatest. With earnest devotion I am seeking your protection. I shall worship you by sacrificing my body made of the five elements if I can come out of this danger." As the prayer ended, there appeared before him a burning golden platform. Many queer-looking ghosts - all disciples of Mahadeva – coming out of the fire, rushed towards him in a body. Without being afraid, Ashvatthama with folded hands uttered the name of Mahadeva, "O God, today I shall sacrifice myself in the burning fire for your pleasure. Kindly accept my humble present." Saying this, Ashvatthama entered into the fire-pit. At this moment, Mahadeva appeared there and said, "O' hero, there is none who is dearer to me than Krishna. For this I protected the Panchals with my power of delusion in order to safeguard the honour of Krishna and to test your power and strength. But the Panchals under the influence of time will die today itself." Saying this Mahadeva handed over His own sword to Ashvatthama and Himself entered into his body.

Ashvatthama thus armed with divine power went inside the camp alone holding the sword with great delight. Kripacharya and Kritavarma remained at the gate. Inside the camp, Ashvatthama, after destroying all resistance of the guards, mercilessly killed with the divine sword Dhristadyumna and Shikhandi, both sons of Drupada, Panchal heroes Uttamauja and Yudhamanyu and all the five sons of Draupadi in their deep sleep. Many other Pandava soldiers lost their lives at his hands. Kripacharya and Kritavarma also destroyed a large number of fleeing solders.

On successful completion of the mission, Ashvattthama along with Kripacharya and Kritavarma hurriedly came to Duryodhana to give him the good news. Duryodhana was then vomitting blood being stricken with unbearable pain.A group of terrible-looking jackals were waiting around him to devour his flesh on his death. Ashvattthama, Kripacharya and Kritavama began to weep to see Duryodhana in that condition. Ashvatthama told Duryodhana, "*Maharaj*, Bhimasena by killing you in the unrighteous war will remain ever condemned in the world. On departing to the heaven you may tell my father Dronacharya that I have killed the wicked Dhristadyumna."

On hearing the details of the happenings in the Pandava camp, Duryodhana told Ashvattthama, "O' hero, you have successfully completed the work which could not be done even by grandfather Bhishma, Karna and your father Dronacharya. On the death of the mean-minded Pandava commander Dhristadyumna, I am considering myself as Indra, the king of the gods. Be blessed with prosperity. We shall meet again in the heavens." Saying this, Duryodhana embraced the three heroes and breathed his last.

Meanwhile, on hearing the news of the massacre and the death of their sons in the camp, Yudhisthira stricken with grief fell down on the ground in a swoon. Regaining his composure soon after he said in the words of lamentation, "How strange it is! We ourselves have been defeated by the enemies who have been defeated by us. The passage of time is even unknown to the wise men. Now it appears we have been defeated even after victory, while the enemies have become victorious on being defeated. The victory which causes repentance is actually a defeat. I am unable to control myself thinking of the condition of Draupadi's mind. How will she bear this terrible grief?"

After some time, Draupadi came to the camp, and on hearing about her sons'death lost her consciousness in grief. On regaining consciousness, she told Yudhisthira, "I have heard Ashvatthama has got a natural jewel on his forehead. If this jewel is placed on your forehead, I shall get some peace." Saying this Draupadi asked Bhimasena to procure the jewel after killing Ashvatthama.As it would be impossible for Bhimasena to kill Ashvatthama alone, Krishna along with Yudhisthira and Arjuna followed him in fast-moving chariots. Seeing them coming, Ashvatthama discharged the terrible *brahmashira* weapon which he learned from his father and was capable of destroying the entire world saying, let the Pandava clan be destroyed. On the direction of Vaasudeva, Arjuna discharged his own *brahmastra* saying, let the weapon of Ashvatthama be destroyed. At the discharge of the two terrible divine weapons fire broke out all around bringing the entire world to the brink of destruction.

At this time Sages Narada and Vyasa, after placing them-selves in between the two divine weapons, asked Ashvatthama and Arjuna to immediately retrieve their respective weapons saying no archer had ever used such weapons in the past. Arjuna, in compliance retrieved his divine weapon by dint of his own power. But Ashvatthama could not as he failed to recollect the retrieval *mantra.* He admitted he had done a wrong thing in discharging this weapon out of anger to destroy the Pandavas. As the weapon could not be retrieved, it would no doubt, he said, destroy the Pandavas. Krishna then told Ashvatthama, "Arjuna has not discharged his weapon to kill you. He was compelled to do it only to neutralise your weapon. On our direction Arjuna has already retrieved his weapon. Now, you immediately retrieve your weapon. Let the Pandavas be safe. *Dharmaraj* Yudhisthira does not want to win the war by any irreligious means.You immediately hand over the jewel on your forehead to the Pandavas." While agreeing to hand over the jewel, Ashvatthama said, as it was not possible for him to retrieve his weapon, it instead of killing the Pandavas would now strike the unborn children in the wombs of the Pandavas' wives.

As predicted by Ashvatthama, his weapon flying without any interupption fell on the womb of Uttara, Abhimanyu's wife and killed her unborn child.Vaasudeva immediately revived the child by his own divine power. The name of this child is Parikhshita. Vaasudeva cursed Ashvatthama for his crime of killing the child of Uttara saying he (Ashvatthama) would move about in a deserted place for three thousand years being afflicted with various diseases. Ashvatthama then handed over his jewel to the Pandavas and with a sad heart entered into the forest. After bidding farewell to Sages Narada and Vyasa, Krishna along with Yudhisthira and Krishna returned to their camp. Draupadi was somewhat consoled when Yudhisthira put on Ashvatthama's jewel on his own forehead. Thus ended the great war of Mahabharata with the defeat of the Kauravas. Yudhisthira on getting back the entire kingdom, ascended the throne of Hastinapura.

44.

An analysis of the pre-war and war-time events will reveal the factors behind the victory and defeat of the two sides.The victory of the Pandavas was mainly due to:

1. Collection of adequate information about the war preparations of the enemy and its intelligent assessment and application.
2. Collection of timely day-to-day information as also counter intelligence through secret agents about the enemy's plans and programmes during the war.
3. Creation of dissensions in the enemy ranks and the gain of support of the principal warriors of the enemy side during the actual fighting, and
4. Krishna's deceitfulness and *maya* power.

On the other hand the defeat of the Kauravas was mainly due to:

1. Belittling the power and strength of the Pandavas and their failure to collect adequate information about the enemy and the superficial assessment of the collected information.
2. Dissensions among their principal warriors and their betrayal.
3. Disinclination to use the *maya* power and too much dependence on their own power and skill in warfare and
4. Absence of any person versed in the art of deceit like Krishna on the other side.

We have already noticed how the Pandavas successfully collected information about enemy's war preparations through their emissaries and the secret agents. They did not remain contended only with collection of intelligence. They minutely scrutinised and assessed the collected information and took timely and adequate steps to use the same in furtherance of their own interest. Krishna's intellect, knowledge of war strategy, political wisdom and far–sightedness along with his guidance immensely helped the Pandavas in this regard. Krishna's political experience was much greater than that of the Pandavas. He had personal contact with many kings, princes and senior state functionaries of different kingdoms. He used to get useful information from them about the enemy. He knew the importance of advance information in the conduct of war.This work, he performed with extreme deftness for the benefit of the Pandavas.We are aware how Krishna's collection of advance information facilitated Jarasandha's destruction in his own capital. We also know of his collection of Duryodhana's war strategy from Vidura during his peace mission to Hastinapura. He had under him many reliable agents and contacts through whom he maintained an independent channel of information. On a study of his entire activities we may, without any hesitation, describe Krishna as the greatest intelligence operator of all times.

As an intelligence operator, we have seen, the contribution of Vidura was also immense. His intelligence inputs furnished to Yudhisthira helped the Pandavas to escape safely from the *jatugriha* at Varanavat. Even though he was indebted to Duryodhana for his livelihood he did not join the war against the Pandavas like Bhishma, Dronacharya and Kripacharya. Duryodhana also did not seek his direct participation in the war. It appears during this opportunity of his stay at Hastinapura, Vidura with the help of his faithful agents collected information about the plans and programmes of the Kauravas. This work was easier for him as he was the prime minister of the Hastinapura kingdom having control on the inlelligence services. As prime minister, he himself was privy to many secrets including deliberations in the royal court. It is reasonable to believe that Vidura and Krishna worked in concert in the matter of intelligence collection and maintained secret contact with each other through some reliable conduits.

The intelligence operations undertaken by the Pandavas before and during the war were fully reflected in the conduct of the entire war. Besides collection of intelligence, Krishna and the Pandavas, we have seen, successfully created dissensions among the principal Kaurava warriors. Bhishma, himself the commander-in-chief of the Kaurava army and Dronacharya, known for his versatility in the art and science of using arms, on both of whom Duryodhana depended so much, fought the war in a ding–dong fashion destroying mainly the ordinary soldiers. Their disclosure of the means of their own death to the enemy Pandavas was an act of gross betrayal deserving utmost condemnation. In the world history, such betrayals are rare particularly that of Bhishma who happened to be the commander-in-chief. Madraraj Shalya's betrayal is no less blatant. We are aware how openly he tried to weaken the morale of Karna and misled him in the war as his charioteer. This is in sharp contrast to Krishna's charioteering of Arjuna. Of course, all this indicates the success of the Pandavas in winning over such formidable enemy warriors to their side. Arjuna's collection of the death-arrows of the Pandavas prerepared by Bhishma on entering his camp in the guise of Duryodhana under the cover of darkness, was also a daring and successful intelligence operation.

Both sides engaged agents in the rival camps to collect information regarding army formation, mobilisation of troops, war strategy, names of the participating warriors and many other related matters. From the nature of collected information, it appears many of the agents had direct contact with the leading personalities. Such under-cover intelligence operations, involving a large number of trained personnel, are difficult and time-consuming. Naturally both sides took up these delicate intelligence operations much before the commencement of the war. There were also reliable arrangements of quickly reaching the collected information to the designated persons of the other side. For this, the supervising staff had under them a group of reliable persons who had easy access to the other camp.The hunters who used to supply meat and other food stuff to the rival armies had the required permission to visit the two camps for their job. It seems many of these hunters were used as carriers of information.They first passed the information to their designated handling officials who in turn sent it to the proper authorities. Some of these agents even directly passed on the information to the authorities mostly under cover of darkness.

In some of the writings based on the Mahabharata, it has been mentioned that the hunter who lost his wife and the five sons in the *jatugriha daha* at Varanavat, was one of the principal intelligence agents of Krishna. Suspecting that the Pandavas had a hand in the death of his wife and the sons, he was engaged in conspiracies to take revenge on them. Krishna who was keeping a close watch on the situation after the incident at Varanavat, came to know from his other agents, about the sinister motive of the hunter. He met the hunter at the Khandava forest and patiently explained to him that the sufferings and even death of the innocent people were unavoidable in any big incident. Though distressing, this was normal and inevitable in human society. During the walking of a person, it was pointed out, many worms and insects get destroyed being trampled under feet. For this, he said, it would be wrong to blame the person.

In the context of the coming terrible war between the Kauravas and the Pandavas, the death of his wife and the sons, though painful was not unnatural and for this, Krishna explained to the hunter that the Pandavas should not be blamed. He assured the hunter he would be able to satisfy his revenge if he helped the same Pandavas against whom he was conspiring. He told the hunter that in the war, the entire Kuru clan as also the sons and many other near and dear ones of the Pandavas would be destroyed and the distress of the Pandavas would be as deep as his. None, he pointed out, could cause any harm to the Pandavas as they were under his protection. He advised the hunter to follow his advice shunning all animosity. At the end the hunter understood the truth of Krishna's arguments and agreed to act according to his direction. Then after careful briefing and debriefing, Krishna engaged him in the collection of intelligence about the Kauravas.

This hunter and his large retinue of supporters were later engaged as official suppliers of meat and other food stuff to the rival camps in the Kurukshetra battlefield. For this they had free access to both the camps. Many of these hunters were also utilised by the Kauravas to act as their agents for the collection of information. These double-agents had their first loyalty to Krishna and were working efficiently under his able guidance. It was said that every evening Krishna used to leave the camp without the knowledge of others. This was not known even to his dearest friend Arjuna. Everybody thought Krishna had departed to the unknown place for meditation and performance of the religious rites. It seems, Krishna in fact, under the cover of darkness, went to meet the hunter and his men to obtain the latest information about the Kaurava's plans and programmes. It appears, Krishna managed to obtain from the hunter the password for entry to the Kaurava camp facilitating collection by Arjuna of their death-arrows from Bhishma. Though all these details are not mentioned in the Mahabharata, they are conjectural in nature, the circumstances seem to indicate the events took place along similar lines. There is no mention in the Mahabharata about any role, if any, of the hunter who lost his wife and the sons at Varanavat. It is, however, mentioned that the hunters used to supply meat for the two armies during the war. That the hunters were also informants, was known when a group of them promptly passed on the hiding place of Duryodhana inside the Dvaipayana lake to the Pandava camp. It is quite possible that the hunter who suffered the loss of his wife and the sons, had a role in these developments under Krishna's guidance.

We have noticed that all vital operational intelligence reached the opposite camp in no time. How was this possible? The Mahabharata is silent in the matter. No courier could do the job so quickly. The question may arise as to the methods used for such instant communication of intelligence. We are aware that very powerful divine weapons were used in the war by the two sides. It appears the same divine power was also utilised in the matter of communication of such vital intelligence.

We are aware that the Pandavas on the advice of Krishna resorted to various deceitful means to win the war disregarding the code of conduct mutually agreed upon. Krishna's *maya* power was also a contributing factor. The Kauravas, on the other hand, generally fought by observing the principles of war. The killing of boy Abhimanyu was said to be their only deviation. He, however, was killed in actual fighting. The Kaurava-supremo, Duryodhana was in possession of *maya* power; but he abhorred its use in the conduct of war as a *Kshatriya*. The Kauravas under his leadership mainly fought the war depending on their power and strength. Krishna, we know, himself admitted that without deceit and falsehood and his *maya* power, it was not possible for the Pandavas to win the war. One of the arguments of Krishna was that the gods also resorted to similar deceitful means in order to defeat the *Asuras*. This argument is apparently untenable. If the gods had resorted to unfair means to serve their purpose, there was no justification that Krishna would also follow similar methods particularly in a *dharmayudha*. Indra, king of the gods and well-known for his lascivious character, was the perpetrator of many evil deeds. None is expected to emulate his example. Each action has to be judged on its own merit. Obviously, the victory of the Pandavas would not have been that easy had the Kauravas resorted to unjust means and *maya* power as those of Krishna. It is no doubt a fact even in the use of such means one must be armed with prior information and proper assessment of the prevailing situation, which the Kauravas did not have. The Pandavas, under Krishna's guidance and help, were much ahead of the Kauravas in this regard.

The breaking of the thighs of Duryodhana by Bhimasena in the mace-battle at the instance of Krishna is perhaps the most despicable incident. As Duryodhana's thighs were broken by Bhimasena by striking him below the navel in violation of the principles of war. Balarama, we know, being enraged proceeded to kill him with his plough. When Krishna prevented him justifying Bhimasena's action on the ground of his vow to break Duryodhana's thighs in the battle and of the curse of the sage on Duryodhana, Balarama explained the tenets of religion to which Krishna could not give any reply. Yet we know how Krishna saved the lives of Yudhisthira and Arjuna nullifying the latter's vow in respect of the *gandivadhanush.* This incident indicates that there was provision by which such vows and curses could easily be nullified with no sin accruing to anyone. Krishna cannot be expected to show similar favour to Duryodhana, though justified on the grounds of *dharma.* Krishna's justification of Bhimasena's action is obviously an example of his double standard. The kicking of Duryodhana's head by Bhimasena, when he was lying on the ground in excruciating pain with broken thighs, was cruel and utterly despicable and its justification by *Dharmaraj* Yudhisthira and later by Krishna, deserves strongest condemnation. Be magnanimous in victory – this noble dictum was completely forgotten by Yudhisthira and Krishna – one the son of Yama Dharma and the other the incarnate of the Supreme God – both being the embodiments of truth, justice and fair-play. Our enigma persists and we are at a loss to get to the truth. From the role of Krishna in the war, it appears that he completely ignored the question of justice or injustice and unhesitatingly, without any qualm of conscience, resorted to all sorts of unfair means to achieve his objective. Yet the war at Kurukhshertra was a *dharmayudha* and the warring sides were supposed to adhere to just methods in their fight.

Krishna's role in the killing of the Panchals and the sons of Draupadi by Ashvatthama in the Pandava camp is also a big enigma to us. Despite the fact, that the evil design of Ashvatthama came to his mind, he took no effective steps to save their lives. Ashvatthama, we know, after satisfying Lord Mahadeva with his prayer attained divine power and carried on his carnage indiscriminately with the sword gifted by Him. Was it not possible for Krishna to intervene in the matter and pacify Ashvatthama with the help of Mahadeva? We are dumbfounded with astonishment at the dastardly killings caused, as mentioned in the Mahabharata, due to divine reasons. About the impending danger, Krishna did not even give any warning to the Pandavas. Yet on the instruction of queen Gandhari he hastened to the Pandava camp from Hastinapura to stop any further blood-shed. If they were alerted in time, the Pandavas, particularly Arjuna who possessed all divine weapons, could have certainly put up a strong resistance to Ashvatthama. In that case, such a one-sided carnage on the part of Ashvatthama would not have been possible. Krishna suppressed everything. Was this carnage yet another manifestation of Krishna's new role as the Great Destroyer as mentioned in the *Geeta.*? Or is this the easy fulfilment of Mahadeva's desire and an acknowledgement of His supremacy by Krishna? We are unable to find any answer to these apparent contradictions with our common sense. Yet Krishna had earlier proved his superiority over Mahadeva. This would be evident from the following incident mentioned in the *Haribamsha Purana.*

The great demon Bana, son of Bali was then the king of Shonitpura kingdom. Being satisfied with Bana's prayer and devotion, Lord Mahadeva recognised him as his own son and assured him, he and his son Kartikeya would defend his kingdom. The gods were defeated again and again when they attacked Bana's kingdom. Meanwhile, Usha, daughter of Bana on the boon of Goddess Parvati had union during the sleep with Anirudhva, grand-son of Krishna and wanted to get him as her husband. Anirudhva too during the dream became attracted to Usha. One of the female attendants of Usha then, by dint of the magic power obtained from sage Narada, brought Anirudhva secretly on her direction from Dvaravati to Shonitpura where they were married as per the *gandhvarva* principles. All this happened without the knowledge of Bana. When he came to know of the incident, he sent a large army to kill Anirudhva. As the army got defeated at the hands of Anirudhva, Bana then on the advice of his minister accepted him as his son-in-law.

In the mean time, Krishna on learning the whereabouts of Anirudhva attacked Shonitpura kingdom and defeated Bana's army. Mahadeva then along with his followers started fighting with Krishna. In view of the devastation caused by the fighting, God Brahma restrained Mahadeva, explaining Krishna and Mahadeva were parts of the same soul and there was no reason for them to fight. Krishna thereafter attacked Bana who had thousand arms. Krishna began to severe his arms one by one with his disc. When only two arms of Bana were left, Mahadeva appeared before Krishna and admitted that he was invincible. None in the three worlds could defeat him. Mahadeva requested Krishna to spare the life of Bana whom he had promised protection. Krishna then retrieved his disc and Bana escaped from certain death. Anirudhva was rescued unharmed.

This battle proved the superiority of Krishna though he and Mahadeva were parts of the same soul. Judged from this point of view, it was not at all difficult for Krishna to save the lives of the Panchals and the sons of Draupadi from the hands of Ashvatthama despite the fact he had acquired the divine power and the sword from Mahadeva, particularly when he had the premonition of the impending danger. If it was not possible for Krishna to get himself directly involved in any battle, he could have easily directed the Pandavas to do the fighting. He did nothing. It appears for divine reasons Krishna for the fulfillment of some greater purpose, preferred to remain indifferent in the matter in order to cause only death and destruction.

Krishna's indifference in protecting the lives of his own warriors and kinsmen, is apparently inexcusable. This carnage while destroying Pandavas' joy of victory, threw them into a sea of sorrow. By hurling the last successful strike, it is the vanquished Kauravas who had the real joy of victory. Duryodhana breathed his last, somewhat relieved at the good news of successful completion of Ashvatthama's mission. With the befitting reply to the Pandavas' unjust war, the Kauravas had actually the last laugh.

45.

On an analysis of the events in the Mahabharata, we find serious differences between the theoretical postulations in the Geeta on truth and religion and their practical application. Krishna whom we see in the Geeta as the symbol of righteousness and fair-play, is apparently absent in the battle-field of Kurukshetra. We know theoretical postulations concerning human actions cannot be implemented in total in practical ever-changing situations. Some differences are bound to crop up. But here in the Mahabharata, such differences seem to be too deep indicating the practices have no bearing with the theories. We find no relation between the nectar-like immortal teachings of Krishna in the Geeta and his deceit and falsehood resorted to in the war. Was it necessary to resort to such immoral methods to kill Jarasandha in his own capital? Could he not be killed in some other normal means? Was it not possible to kill Dronacharya without recourse to such naked falsehood? What heroism was there in showing utter disrespect to the revered Acharya in throwing his severed head, pulling it by the hair towards the Kaurava army? Krishna's silence to this despicable act suggests his approval. The death of Jayadratha was also a revelation of Krishna's naked falsehood. How can we support Arjuna's attack on unarmed Karna on Krishna's instigation and the severing by Satyaki of the right arm of Bhurishrava when he was engaged in fighting with another person? We have already mentioned the condemnable role of Krishna in the mace-battle of Bhimasena with Duryodhana and the breaking of the latter's thighs and the disgraceful act of kicking the severely wounded Duryodhana's head by Bhimasena and its approval by Yudhisthira and Krishna. How could they forget the basic tenets of religion? All these actions of Krishna and the Pandavas are not worthy of emulation by the people.

There arises doubt as to the truth in Krishna's statement that the Kauravas could not be defeated without deceit and falsehood. In the Geeta, Krishna advised Arjuna to treat victory and defeat, and happiness and misery equally, offer the results of work to God and to perform the allotted duty with single-minded devotion. According to him, yoga is actually the attainment of mental equanimity, fair-mindedness and impartiality. But in the actual field of work, we find Krishna deviating from his own universally accepted principles of *dharma,* took the easy path of deceit and falsehood like the ordinary people in ensuring the victory of the Pandavas. He gave more importance to the results of work than work itself in contradiction of his own teachings in the Geeta. By his action he actually nullified his own teachings. On the other hand we find the 'wicked' Duryodhana disregarding the question of victory and defeat, gave up his life fighting to the last, and departed to the heavenly abode most coveted by a true *Kshatriya*, leaving behind for Yudhisthira a war-ravaged country and innumerable grief-stricken families of his kinsmen, friends and allies. Yudhisthira having lost his peace of mind at the wide-spread death and destruction, understood it was Duryodhana who actually won the war. It appears, as if, Duryodhana actually followed the teachings of the Geeta. The teachings in the Geeta emanated from Krishna as the Supreme God, while his actions in the battle-field of Kurukshetra were those of his human incarnation of the God with all imperfections. Perhaps this explains the differences between the two roles of Krishna.

We are enchanted at Krishna's wisdom, far-sightedness, worldly knowledge, uncanny knack for intelligence gathering and many other wonderful qualities unseen in others. Besides, he had the divine power. We are naturally pained to see such indiscriminate application of unrighteous means in the righteous war at Kurukshetra and that too at the behest of Krishna, the incarnation of God. We would have been happy if Krishna could conduct the war in strict conformity to the lofty principles as laid down in the

Geeta. We would have then been relieved to see the successful implementation of theoretical principles in actual worldly conditions. Perhaps the composer of the Geeta and the writers of the other portions of the Mahabharata were not one person. This has perhaps widened the inconsistencies in the innumerable events in the epic occurring at different times.

46.

The principles laid down in the Mahabharata on state-craft and other related subjects are worthy of emulation in the context of the present-day conditions of India. The law and order situation of the country is far from satisfactory. The activities of the foreign-aided militants are the main problem. The Kashmiri militants supported and aided by Pakistan are actively carrying on their armed depredations despite a number of confidence-building measures following an agreement to settle all outstanding problems between the two countries through peaceful negotiations. There is also no abatement of violence of the different separatist groups in north-eastern India. Many other parts of India too are afflicted with extremist violence resulting in loss of human lives and destruction of property on a large-scale. The general criminal activities in the form of murder, robbery, kidnapping, cheating, caste and communal clashes etc. continue to be a serious problem. Evidently there is serious degradation of the moral standard in all walks of our life. A large section of people are still deprived of education, health, work and other fundamental rights. With deterioration in the quality of the governance, the general people are in a despair. Virtually, a negative atmosphere has been created in the country.

Our political leadership has to be mainly blamed for the present unfortunate situation. A section of the leadership is gripped with corruption and various other malpractices. The leaders seem to be more concerned in furthering the interests of their own parties and groups. Almost all issues are sought to be exploited to derive political mileage over the rival parties. In the absence of consensus among the political parties, problems facing the nation and the people have in many cases remained unsolved. Internal bickering and personality clash in the leadership of the political parties are hampering their coherent functioning. Even the ruling coalition group is beset with serious policy differences delaying solution to some of the urgent national issues. The unscrupulous elements in the different echelons of the administration and among the people are exploiting the situation in their favour.

Though the current socio-political situation is different from that of the Mahabharata days, there cannot be any justification for such divergence in human conduct between the two periods. In the Mahabharata days, we have seen, the king and his council of ministers were all virtuous persons wedded to the welfare of the people. The administration was good with strict enforcement of the rule of law. All deviations in the society invited immediate retribution, while the good were assured of protection. The king was ever ready to help his subjects by removing their grievances as he understood the happy and the contented people were the main safeguards of his kingdom. In fact, such a benevolent administration was established by Yudhisthira at Indraprastha with the help of his virtuous brothers. Under the impact of the new situation marked by the establishment of peace, prosperity and happiness of the people under Yudhisthira's rule, the rebel kings and the princes, as also the robbers and the anti-social elements, came forward of their own accord to surrender before him. The dishonest elements in the royal administration also followed suit. We cannot, of course, expect such miracles in the present day conditions. There is, however, no gainsaying the fact with all-out efforts our political leaders can effect substantial changes in the situation. Yudhisthira, on ascendancy to the throne raised a band of faithful agents with advice from sage Narada, and collected all information good and bad regarding the happenings in the kingdom for taking suitable remedial action. Unfortunately, our leadership is bereft of the honesty of purpose as shown by Yudhisthira. We have seen how the information collected by the agents of the Pandavas contributed to their victory in the war over the Kauravas with a comparatively smaller army. He knew that the collection of information by itself was not enough. For the successful implementation of the collected information a strong force was an imperative. Arjuna, we are aware, was deputed to the kingdom of Indra to acquire divine weapons for the purpose of strengthening the Pandava army. In the war, we have seen Arjuna's wonderful heroism with the help of his divine weapons.

The strength of the country, of course, does not depend only on its armed forces. This strength primarily depends on the spontaneous support of the people marked by national unity, economic stability and social justice. In these respects, India is still to traverse a long path. That a large section of people stand alienated from the government is evident from their continuing violent defiance. Police and army operations attended with various pacification programmes, so far undertaken to win over the discontented elements, have produced only limited results. The operations by the security forces causing untold sufferings to the ordinary people are only deepening their alienation with all its harmful consequences. The ending of this increasing alienation remains an urgent task. We shall forget to our peril the teachings of history. In the past, large empires fell more due to internal decay than due to external assault.

The problems of corruption and other vices in our society are too deep-rooted to be removed by some institutional changes like reforms in the criminal justice system with provision for stricter enforcement of laws and stringent punishment for the offenders. What is needed is the fundamental changes in the old spurious attitude and beliefs of the people. This calls for an intellectual awakening of the people through a well-coordinated programme of social reforms. People require to be educated about the evils of uncontrolled mammoth-worship which help breed corruptions in the society. Material acquisition has to be insulated with moral and spiritual enlightenment. In the Mahabharata (and also in the Ramayana) this fact has been repeatedly emphasised. We may justifiably follow the teachings of our epics in establishing a cleaner society and administration.

A Message

India is a country with a great cultural heritage. The people are simple, god-fearing, intelligent and hard-working. Their requirements are few. With proper guidance they are capable of achieving miracles. For this we require a selfless responsive leadership with a high morality completely wedded to the welfare of the people, a well-organised intelligence service as its eyes and ears and a trained well-equipped army as a bulwark against internal and external threats as was prevelent in the days of the epics.

Glossary

1. *Achyuta* – Krishna's another name.
2. *Adharma* – Sin, unrighteous action, opposite of Dharma.
3. *Adideva* – Primeval Being.
4. *Akshowhiṇi* – consisted of 1,09,350 foot-soldiers, 65,610 horses, 21,870 chariots and 21,870 elephants.
5. *Amrit* – Nector.
6. *Anantarupa* – One having endless forms and shapes.
7. *Antardhyana Astra* — Invisible divine weapon gifted by Kuvera to Arjuna.
8. *Bana* – Also called Banasura having thousand hands, son of Bali, an ardent devotee of Lord Shiva, a powerful king, ruled present-day Central Assam with capital at Sonitpura.
9. *Bhajamana* – Those who are loyal.
10. *Brahmachari* – Person sworn to bachelorhood.
11. *Brahmaloka* – Abode of the Supreme Being or God.
12. *Brahmastra* – The most powerful among the *Astras. Astras* used in the Mahabharata war had miraculous effect having been discharged after chanting of specific *mantras* (incantation).
13. *Chakra* – A sharp-edged wheel-shaped infallible missile, Krishna's weapon.
14. *Chaturdashi* – Fourteenth day of the dark fortnight.
15. *Danda* – Long iron divine staff gifted by Yama to Arjuna.
16. *Devata, Daitya and Danava* – According to Hindu mythology the Devatas (gods), Daityas (demons) and Danavas (giants) belong to the same family. Prajapati (Procreator of all living creatures) Kashyapa married all the thirteen daughters of Prajapati Daksha. Among the thirteen daughters, Aditi's sons with attributes of virtue and goodness were known as Devatas, Diti's sons Daityas and Danu's sons Danavas for their evil and destructive qualities. Because of their similarity of nature Daityas and Danavas gradually united together against the Devatas and fought many battles against them; but they were ultimately vanquished. Daitya-Danavas are actually *totems* (an animal (superstitiously) regarded by a tribe as its emblem). They are all actually humans with excess of *tamaguna* (i.e. lowest element of human nature).
17. *Dharma* – Duty as laid down in religion or custom.
18. *Gandharvas* – Semi-divine powerful beings, Celestial musicians. The Kauravas were defeated by the Gandharvas at Ghoshpalli.
19. *Gandivadhanush* – Bow known as gandiva.
20. *Geeta* – Known as Bhagavad Geeta, it is a part of Mahabharata comprising 700 verses in 18 chapters. The teacher of Bhagsvad Geeta is Krishna, who is regarded as the supreme manifestation of the Lord Himself. The Geeta is described as a non-sectarian concise guide to Hindu Philosophy and also a practical, self-contained non-fear based guide to peaceful life and ever-lasting world peace. It is also described as a lighthouse of eternal

wisdom that is capable of inspiring any man or woman to supreme accomplishment and enlightenment.

21. *Indriya* – Five organs of senses namely eye, ear, nose, tongue and skin.
22. *Jugas* – see *Yuga*
23. *Kaal* – Time of Death/God of Death.
24. *Kabach* – Armour proof Body cover.
25. *Kangsa* – Son of Ugrasena, brother of Devaki, son-in-law of Yarashandha.
26. *Khanaka* – Digger.
27. *Kheer* – A sweet-dish - Rice boiled in milk with sugar.
28. *Krittim* – Those who have been won over with money.
29. *Kshatriya* – Warrior class – the second of the four castes in which the Hindu society is divided viz, (1) *Brahmin*, highest of the four castes devoted to religious austerities, (2) *Kshatriya*, the ruling and warrior class (30 *Vaishya*, the trading class and (4) *Sudra*, the serving class.
30. *Kshastriyadharma* – Duties and obligations of a *kshatriya*.
31. *Mahabahu* – Mighty.
32. *Maharaj* – Your Majesty.
33. *Mahamantri* – Prime Minister.
34. *Mantra* – incantation
35. *Martya* — The earth.
36. *Nagaraj* – The king of snakes.
37. *Nagaloka* – Continent of snakes.
38. *Nar* – A human being.
39. *Nara* – Revered sage possessing the holy traits of Sureme God Narayana.
40. *Nishkam karma yoga* – Self-dedication to the work of one's own life without any consideration of gain or loss.
41. *Pasha* – Divine rope (Bandanastra) to bind the enemy – gifted by Varuna to Arjuna.
42. *Patala* – Netherworld (hell). Dead sinners suffer punishment in hell.
43. *Putra* – son
44. *Puranas* – The Puranas explain India's ancient religious and social doctrines. They also give detailed account of the various Gods and Goddesses, their incarnations, teachings etc. There are 18 main Puranas such as Vishnu Puranas, Naradiya Purana etc. The Ramayana and Mahabharata are also considered important Puranas.
45. *Pashupat Astra* – Infallible divine weapon named Brahmashira gifted by Lord Shankara to Arjuna.
46. *Rajdharma* – Royal duties.
47. *Rajsuya Yajna* – Sacrifice performed by a king to establish his superiority over other kings.
48. *Rakshashi* – Female Demon.
49. *Sahaja* – King's own relatives.
50. *Sakha* – Friend.
51. *Samartha* – Those having same interest as that of the king.
52. *Sanatanadharma* – Religion eternal.
53. *Sarbotabhadra* – Well-protected and impenetrable with many entrances.
54. *Shakti* – Spear.
55. *Shataghni* – Iron missile emanating innumerable thorns of fire.
56. *Treta-Yuga* – One of the four epochs or eras.

57. *Tumi* – A less respectful form of addressing.
58. *Swarga* – *Devaloka* (abode of the gods). The pious people are said to depart to *Swarga* to enjoy blissful life.
59. *Vaanprastha* – Going to the forest, third stage of life in ancient Hindu society when one goes to the forest for practising austerity and spiritual meditation.
60. *Vedajna* – Versed in the Vedas.
61. *Vedas* – The oldest religious texts containing hymns, incantations and rituals of ancient India – said to be composed by Vyasadeva. These are in four books – *Rig-veda, Yajur Veda, Saama Veda* and *Atharva Veda.*
62. *Yama* – God of Death
63. *Yuga* – In Hindu philosophy Yuga refers to the name of an epoch or era within a cycle of four ages. The four basic ages comprise (1) the Satya Yuga, (2) the Treta Yuga, (3) the Dwapar Yuga and (4) the preset Kali Yuga. The Yugas are conceived to repeat in cyclical manner. The characteristic features of each Yuga are as follows: (1) Satya Yuga (Golden age), time span – 1,728,000 human years, average life span – 100,000 rears, method of self-realization – meditation on Lord Vishnu, (2) Treta Yuga (Silver age), time span – 1,296,000 human years, average life span – 10,000 years, method of self-realization – performance of *Yajnas* (The Ramayana was composed in this age), (3) Dwapar Yuga (Bronze age), time span – 864,000 human years, average life span – 1000 years, method of self-realization – worship of deities in houses and temples (The Mahabharata war was fought in this age) and (4) Kali Yuga (Iron age) – it is an age of hypocrisy and quarrel, time span – 432,000 human years, average life span – 100 years only, method of self-realization – *sankirtana* or chanting of Holy names of Lord God. It is believed, Satya Yuga will reappear at the end of Kali Yuga.

Who's Who

1. *Amba* – Eldest daughter of the king of Kashi — Shikhandi in the next birth.
2. Ambalika – Third daughter of the king of Kashi, wife of Vichitravirjya, mother of Pandu.
3. Ambika – Second daughter of the king of Kashi, wife of Vichitravirjya, mother of Dhritarashtra.
4. Arjuna – Third son of Pandu, fathered by Devaraj Indra on Kunti.
5. Ashwathama – Son of Dronacharyja and wife Kripi.
6. Balarama – Baldev, Krishna's elder step brother, brother of Kunti, son of Shura.
7. Bali – A virtuous king belonging to Daitya clan, occupied Swargarajya, but was dislodged by the Devatas by deceitful means.
8. Bhagadatta – King of Pragjyotishpura (Assam), said to be belonging to Mlechcha (non-Aryan) Asura (demon) clan.
9. Bharata – Son of Dushmanta and Shakuntala, forefather of Kurus and Pandavas.
10. Bhima – Second son of Pandu, born of union of Pabanadevata (Wind God) with Kunti.
11. Bhishma – Debabrata, son of Shantanu and Ganga, later came to be known as Vishma for his unswerving vow of celibacy to facilitate his father's marriage with Satyavati.
12. Bhurishraba – Son of Somadatta, fought on the Kaurava side.
13. Brahma – The Creator, one of the Hindu Trinity. The others are Lord Vishnu, the Preserver and Lord Shiva, the Destroyer.
14. Chitrangada – Daughter of Manipur king Chitrabahana, wife of Arjuna, mother of Babrubahana.
15. Chitrasena – King of the Gangharvas.
16. Daruka – Charioteer of Krishna.
17. Dhananjaya – Arjuna's another name.
18. Dharmarajya – Kingdom ruled with righteousness and justice.
19. Dhoumya – Priest of Drupda.
20. Dhristadyumna – Son of Drupada, brother of Draupadi.
21. Dhritarashtra – Eldest son of Vichitravirya, born of union with Vyasadeva.
22. Draupadi – Krishnaa, Panchali, daughter of Panchal king, wife of the Pandavas.
23. Dronacharya – Son of sage Bharadwaj, weapons instructor of the Pandavas, brother-in-law of Kripacharya.
24. Drupada – Panchal king, father of Dhrishtadyumna, Shikhandi and Draupadi.
25. Duhshala – Daughter of Dhritarashtra and Gandhari, wife of Yayadratha.
26. Duhshasana – Second son of Dhritarashtra and Gandhari
27. Duryodhana – Eeldest son of Dhritarashtra and Gand
28. Gandhari – Daughter of Subala, King of Gandhara, wife of Dhritarashtra, mother of hundred sons including Duryodhana.
29. Ghatotkocha – Son of Bhima and Rakshasi Hirimba.

30. Hanumana – Son of Vaayu (Wind God), a learned person, a great devotee of Ramachandra of Ramayana fame.
31. Hirimba – Rakshasi wife of Bhima, mother of Ghatotkocha
32. Indra – The chief and the king of the gods.
33. Indrasena – Charioteer of Yudhisthira.
34. Janardana – Krishna's another name.
35. Kangsa – Son of Ugrasena, brother of Devaki, son-in-law of Yarashandha.
36. Karna – Born of union of Suryadeva (Sun God) with Kunti before her marriage, brought up by Adhiratha of Suta (born of low-caste woman) clan and his wife Radha. Karna accordingly addressed as Radheya.
37. Kartikeya – Son of Lord Shiva and Parvati, commander-in-chief of Devasena (army of the Devatas). Kartikeya's birth history – Shiva had six faces with a central eye in each. Out of these eyes sprang sparks which fell into a lake where they turned into infants. Parvati grabbed the six infants and squeezed them into one – Kartikeya.
38. Kichaka – Commander-in–chief of king Virata, brother of his wife Sudeshna.
39. Kripacharya – Son of Sage Sharadwana, one of the weapons teachers of the Pandavas, brother-in-law of Dronacharya.
40. Krishna – Son of Vasudeva and Devaki, step brother of Balarama and Subhadra.
41. Kritavarma – Yadava hero, fought on the Kaurava side.
42. Kunti – Another name Pritha, daughter of Shura (father of Vaasudeva), sister of Vasudeva, foster daughter of Kuntibhoj, first wife of Pandu, mother of Bhima and Arjuna.
43. Kuvera (Kuber) – God of Wealth.
44. Kuntibhoj – Son of Shura's paternal aunt, foster father of Kunti..
45. Kuru – Son of King Sangbarana and Tapati, a great king. The Kuru dynasty is known by his name.
46. Madhava – Krishna's another name.
47. Madhusudana – Destroyer of demon Madhu— Krishna'a another name.
48. Madri – Sister of Madraraj Shalya's sister, second wife of Pandu, mother of Nakula and Sahadeva.
49. Matali – Charioteer of Devaraj Indra.
50. Moy Danava – Brother of Namuchi, builder of the Pandava rajsabha (royal court) at Indraprastha.
51. Nakula-Sahadev – Pandu's fourth and fifth twin sons, born of union of Madri with the twin Deva vaidyas (physician) by name Aswinikumara.
52. Narada – Divine saint said to have sprung from the forehead of the Creator Lord Brahma, constantly roams around the three worlds of Heaven, Earth and Hell chanting the name of Narayana (Lord Vishnu), depicted in Hindu mythology as witty and clever with an uncanny knack to cause quarrels among gods out of playfulness.
53. Narayana – Supreme God according to Hindu scriptures.
54. Pandu – Second son of Vichitravirya born of union of Vyasadeva (Satyavati's son before marriage) with Ambalika.
55. Parikshita – Son of Abhimanyu and Uttara, grandson of Krishna.
56. Partha – Son of Pritha (Kunti), Arjuna.
57. Sanjay – Charioteer of Dhritarashtra belonging to Suta clan, narrator of the events of Mahabharata war to Dhritarashtra
58. Satyaki – Yadava hero, son of Satyaka. Accompanied Krishna to Hastinapura in his peace mission with a large army.

59. Satyavati – Another name Matsyagangha, born of fish, mother of Vyasadeva, wife of Shantanu and mother of Chitraganda and Vichitrvirjya
60. Shakuni – Maternal uncle of Duryodhana and his brothers, son of Subala (king of Gandhar)
61. Shalva – Son of Krishna and Yambavati.
62. Shalya – King of Madra desha, brother of Madri.
63. Shankha – Eldest son of Virata.
64. Shantanu – Son of Pratipa, father of Bhishma, Chitrangada and Vichitravirjya.
65. Shikhandi – Son of Drupada, Amba (daughter of the king of Kashi in the previous birth).
66. Shishupala – King of Chedi, son of Damaghosha, Krishna's cousin brother from the father's side.
67. Somdatta – Belongs to Kuru clan, father of Bhurishrava.
68. Susharma – King of Trigarta.
69. Sutaputra – Son born of low-caste.
70. Swayambarasabha – A gathering of perspective brides and bridegrooms to choose the life partner.
71. Takshaka – Brother of serpent king Vasuki who killed King Parikshita.
72. Uluka – Son of Shakuni.
73. Ulupi – Daughter of Nagaraj (Serpent king), wife of Arjuna.
74. Uttar – Youngest son of Virata.
75. Uttara – Daughter of Virata, wife of Abhimanyu, mother of Parikshit.
76. Vaasudeva – another name of Krishna, son of Vasudeva.
77. Varuna – Sea God.
78. Vasudeva – Father of Krishna, Balarama and Shubhadra, brother of Kunti, son of Shura.or Shurasena.
79. Vichitravirya – Son of Shantanu and Satyavati, step-brother of Vishma.
80. Vidura – Born of union of Vyasadev with low-caste maid.
81. Vikarna – One of the brothers of Duryodhana.
82. Virata – King of Matsha kingdom, father of Uttar and Uttara.
83. Vishma – Devabrata, son Shantanu and Ganga, named Vishma for his unswerving vow of celibacy to facilitate father Shantanu's marriage with Satyavati.
84. Vishnu – One of the chief gods of Hindu Trinity.
85. Viswaamitra – Son of Gadhi, king of Kanyakubya, grand son of Kushika.
86. Vrihadkshatra – Nishadraj. Eldest Kekayraj.
87. Vswarupa – One in whom the universe is represented, Supreme God Lord Vishnu.
88. Vyasa – Krishnadyaipayana, son of sage Parasara and Satyavati, father of Dritarashtra, Pandu and Vidura. Composer of Mahabharata.
89. Yaksha – One of the mythological races of demi-gods or demons known for their greed for money and wealth.
90. Yayadratha – King of Souvir, husband Dhritarashtra's daughter Duhshala.

The Places: Then and Now

1. Andhradesh – Areas comprising the northern parts of modern Tamilnadu state and some parts of modern Andhra Pradesh.
2. Angadesh – Located in the present districts of Mungher and Bhagalpur, Bihar.
3. Bhoj – A country in Malava and Vidarva region of central India. Krishna's Yadu Dynasty.
4. Chedi – A country near Jabbalpur, Madhyapradesh between the rivers Godavari and Narmada.
5. Desl – region, state
6. Dwaita forst – Located on the bank of river Saraswati in Punjab.
7. Ekchakra Nagari (city) – Situated in the Ara area of Bihar; but this may not be correct
8. Gandhara – Located on the both sides of the Sindh and the Kabul rivers. Also said to located in Pakistan's North West Frontier Province.
9. Giribraja – Capital of Yarasandha, located near modern Rajgir, Bihar.
10. Hastinapura – Situated to the east of Delhi near Meerut on the southern bank of the Ganges.
11. Indraprastha – Situated near Delhi.
12. Kalinga – Country from the rivers Mahanadi and Godavari on the bank of the Bay of Bengal.
13. Kamyaka forest – Near the gulf of Kutch on the bank of river Saraswati..
14. Kurukshetra — Located in Haryana between Karnal and Ambala.
15. Madra desh – Located between the rivers Chandrabhaga and Iravati in Punjab.
16. Magadha desh – Near Patna and Gaya, Bihar.
17. Mahendra mountains – The eastern range of mountains of the Deccan known as the Eastern Ghats.
18. Manipur – Not modern Manipur, Actual location unknown.
19. Martsya desh – On the west of Dholpur, Rajasthan. According to another opinion it is modern Jaipur.
20. Panchal – The country lying between the rivers Ganga and Yamuna.
21. Shonitpura (Sonitpura) – Present-day Tezpur, Assam.
22. Trigarta desha – Located in Kangra valley of Punjab's Jalandhar district. According to another opinion located in *Marupradesh* on the coast of the river Shatadru.
23. Varanavat (Varanavata) – Located near Prayaga, confluence of the rivers Ganga, Yamuna and Saraswati, Uttar Pradesh.
24. Vidarva desh – Modern Berar, Maharashtra.
25. Videha desh – North Bihar or Mithila.